The Futures of the City Region

Does the 'city region' constitute a new departure in urbanisation? If so, what are the key elements of that departure? The realities of the urban in the 21st century are increasingly complex and polychromatic. The rise of global networks enabled by supranational administrations, both governmental and corporate, strongly influences and structures the management of urban life. How we conceive the city region has intellectual and practical consequences. First, in helping us grasp rapidly changing realities; and second in facilitating the flow of resources, ideas and learning to enhance the quality of life of citizens.

Two themes interweave through this collection, within this broad palette. First are the socio-spatial constructs and their relationship to the empirical evidence of change in the physical and functional aspects of urban form. Second is what they mean for the spatial scales of governance. This latter theme explores territorially based understandings of intervention and the changing set of political concerns in selected case studies. In efforts to address these issues and improve upon knowledge, this collection brings together international scholars building new data-driven, cross-disciplinary theories to create new images of the city region that may prove to supplement if not supplant old ones.

The book illustrates the dialectical interplay of theory and fact, time and space, and spatial and institutional which expands on our intellectual grasp of the theoretical debates on 'city-regions' through 'practical knowing', citing examples from Europe, the United States, Australasia, and beyond.

All the chapters in this book have been published within *Regional Studies*, and the majority formed a single special issue.

Michael Neuman is Associate Professor in the Department of Landscape Architecture and Urban Planning at Texas A&M University, USA. He directs the Sustainable Urbanism Research Consortium and was founding chair of the Sustainable Urbanism Certificate Program.

Angela Hull is Professor of Spatial Planning at Heriot Watt University, Edinburgh, UK. She directs the Masters in Research Programme and the Planning, Regeneration and Governance research centre.

Regions and Cities

Managing Editor of the Series:

Gillian Bristow, University of Cardiff, UK

Additional Series Editors:

Maryann Feldman, University of Georgia, USA;
Gernot Grabher, University of Bonn, Germany;
Ron Martin, University of Cambridge, UK

Regions and Cities is an international, interdisciplinary series that provides author-itative analyses of the new significance of regions and cities for economic, social and cultural development, and public policy experimentation. The series seeks to combine theoretical and empirical insights with constructive policy debate and critically engages with formative processes and policies in regional and urban studies.

1. Beyond Green Belts
Managing Urban Growth in
   the 21st Century
Edited by John Herrington

2. Retreat from the Regions
Corporate Change and the
   Closure of Factories
Stephen Fothergill and Nigel Guy

The Futures of the City Region

Edited by
Michael Neuman and Angela Hull

Routledge
Taylor & Francis Group

LONDON AND NEW YORK

First published 2011
by Routledge
2 Park Square, Milton Park, Abingdon, Oxon, OX14 4RN

Simultaneously published in the USA and Canada
by Routledge
711 Third Avenue, New York, NY 10016

Routledge is an imprint of the Taylor & Francis Group, an informa business

This book is a reproduction of the journal of *Regional Studies*, vol. 43.6. The Publisher requests to those authors who may be citing this book to state, also, the bibliographical details of the special issue on which the book was based.

Typeset in Times New Roman by Taylor & Francis Books

British Library Cataloguing in Publication Data
A catalogue record for this book is available from the British Library

ISBN13: 978-0-415-58803-4

Disclaimer
The publisher would like to make readers aware that the chapters in this book are referred to as articles as they had been in the special issue. The publisher accepts responsibility for any inconsistencies that may have arisen in the course of preparing this volume for print.

Contents

Introduction: The Futures of the City Region

Michael Neuman and Angela Hull

The Ascendance of the City Region

Urban space is so replete with descriptions that Pandora's jar could not contain them. Like the Greek myth Pandora, the plethora of urban spatial descriptions is almost a curse on those who attempt comprehensive understanding. Today, the debates surrounding regional questions are more complex than ever in many dimensions. They are multi-disciplinary and multi-scalar, and the phenomena under analysis are themselves more complex, as evidenced by an abundance of empirical and theoretical research in the last decades.

National planners are anticipating the growth of connected networks of metropolitan areas or 'megaregions' in America 2050 (Dewar and Epstein, 2007) and in Europe the reach of urban areas is conceived as spreading from city centres to the remote countryside across 'city-region' territories (Ravetz, 2000). Urbanization, in this sense, is both an empirical and an imagined/discursive question. The focus of this book is whether and how the 'city region' constitutes a new departure in urbanization, and if so what are the key elements of that difference. We have invited contributors to situate and debate these questions through the analysis of social and economic conditions and/or the governance narratives in the spatial contexts they are familiar with.

In this introduction we present a broad sweep of academic preoccupations with the city-region and then select a set of these debates, which link these to the socio-spatial interactions and the chapters that follow.[1] Within this broad palette, two themes interweave through the introduction. First, is the socio-spatial constructs and their relationship to empirical evidence of change in the physical and functional aspects of urban form. Second, is what they mean for the spatial scales of governance. This latter theme is more closely tied to territorially based understandings of intervention and the changing set of political concerns. The chapters in this book, therefore, reply to the critics of 'new regionalism', who claim that it reifies the region over other geographical scales and neglects the effects of power and politics and wider processes of uneven development (Lovering, 1999; Cumber et al, 2003; Jonas and Ward, 2007).

As rich and suggestive as contemporary formulations are, so were those of Park and the Chicago school, or Weber, Simmel, Christaller, and Losch in their day and beyond. Earlier generations limited their focus on "the city". Yet the city, and urbanism, the study of cities, have changed radically since.[2] Megacities, megalopolises, mega-city regions, mega-regions, megapolitan regions, and polycentric metropolises all represent fundamentally new constructs and sometimes conflicting understandings of the patterns of urbanity. (Unless specified, we adopt the general term "city region" to capture the broad sense of urban phenomena at metropolitan and larger scales). Following part of the specifications of Lang and Dhavale (2005), it contains two or more metropolises in relatively close geographic proximity and functional connectivity with a population of ten million or more. These terms are contested and subject to debate.

Our aim here is to step back and more deeply understand how we think about the debates themselves. The chapters in this book reflect a range of current debates regarding representations of the city region. This introduction reviews some of those debates, and offers frameworks for interpretation. These frameworks link the multiscalar and multi-temporal quality of city regions and their governance, and seeks to specify the mutually interactive bridge between them as "spatial-institutional isomorphism". This last term replaces a diffuse space and society combine by suggesting a mirroring that takes place between urban spatial constructs and the networked governance constructs that purport to manage them.

This book's authors synthesize several theoretical strands as well as examine the empirical evidence of physical transformations in the morphology of the city region in the 21st Century. This book, in this respect, expands on our intellectual grasp of the theoretical debates through "practical knowing", drawing on evidence from Europe, the United States, Australasia, and beyond.

What are the cognitive constructs that frame the debate? We embed the critical thinking of the contributors to this book in the 'spatiality' of city-regions, a concept just beginning to be explored by topographical geographers (Amin, 2002: 386). In this respect we have deliberately drawn on critical thinkers from other socio-spatial disciplines in addition to economic and relational geographers. So doing draws together various understandings of different kinds of processes, in order to examine how these 'play out' in various combinations of local and global contexts.

While space does not permit the unpacking of all of the debates, we will identify exemplary themes and point out the consequences that different ways of thinking have for theory and analysis. In this, we follow the meta-analytic method of "frame reflection" advanced by Schön and Rein (1994). There they applied a reflexive approach to understanding the bases ("frames") that underlie what they named "intractable policy problems".

We undertake this task in the following four sections. We first offer a brief overview of the spatial definitions of city regions and the empirically based theories of spatial form. Then the discussion marks out how the city-region has been imagined in the recent past in the form of linkages, gradients and cartographic and geographic representations. The third and fourth sections pose the question of whether the new constructs of mega-regions and city-regions will help to establish new institutional structures at these scales. We look at the possibilities and challenges and the consequences for institutional design before, finally, setting out an agenda for future research.

Spatial Definitions of City Regions

Notwithstanding the recent chapter by Etherington and Jones reproduced in this book, when city regions were last discussed in *Regional Studies*, the focus was on the spatial distribution of trade, commuting, and capital flows between the inner core and the surrounding hinterland (Parr, 2005). The impetus for this book's exploration responds in part to the opportunity identified by Sudjic (1992). He indicated that we lack the means to grasp the new complexities of the '100 mile city'. This book seeks to understand the various meanings attached to city region in the 21st century, all of which recognise the multidimensionality and interactional nature of the construction of space (Amin, 2002). As David Harvey indicates, "Human beings have typically produced a nested hierarchy of spatial scales within which to organize their activities and understand their world" (Harvey, 2000, 75). Our contributors attest to the fact that the city region occupies a prominent place in that hierarchy, even as it is linked intricately to other scales.

This book is timely in that the UK's Economic and Social Research Council Cities research programme, the European Commission's POLYNET programme, and the US-based America 2050 initiative renew long-standing arguments that policy-making ought to be organised around more expansively delimited city-regions (Marvin et al, 2006; Buck et al, 2005; Hall and Pain, 2006; Carbonell and Yaro, 2005). In the United States there is a renewed attempt to make "megaregions" matter (Dewar and Epstein, 2007), despite a half century elapsing since geographer Jean Gottmann's seminal analysis of megalopolis. In a significant contribution to the megalopolis debate, Vicino, Hanlon, and Short's (2007) analysis of the Northeastern Seaboard of the US shows that fifty years on, megalopolis indeed does matter. While being more suburbanized than before, their analysis suggests that the old contrasts of space (city-suburb) and race (black-white) do not represent the "five distinct clusters of urban places ... 'affluent, poverty, Black middle class, immigrant gateway, and middle America'" (Vicino, Hanlon, Short, 2007, 344).

According to other mega-region analysts, what is different now in North America are three things: scale, number of travel trips and resulting traffic congestion and pollution, and land per capita. For Teitz and Barbour, the "real difference" is this third item, land consumption per capita (2007). We can add a fourth, as shown by the contributors to this book, that the mega-region is a new spatial *and* temporal entity, a polycentric multi-metropolis of shifting and dynamic multi-scalar and multi-speed architecture whose developmental logics respond to a new set of conditions. Those city regions that can integrate service delivery for the greatest number of people via multi-modal transport links with widely available broadband and cellular connectivity are precisely those perceived to be enjoying social and economic prosperity. It would seem that the higher the velocities and bandwidths, and the greater the range of options, the greater the accessibility for global investors. This is supported by Eurolille, the proliferation of high speed rail, a world-wide wave of major airport expansions, and booming North American city regions centered on internet trunk lines, like Washington, DC and the Texas Urban Triangle.

The first two contributions in this book attempt to analyse and understand the spatial-temporal dynamics across the city region using the available statistical data on their case study areas. **Robert Lang** and **Paul Knox** focus their contribution on the spatiality of the changing city region morphology over time in the United States by using the US Census Bureau's metropolitan data and statistical categories to analyse the trends in metropolitan form, scale, and connectivity. Their analysis suggests that urban form has been "stretched and reshaped", with new commuting routes determining patterns of spatial-economic integration. They postulate the existence of 10 megapolitan areas containing nearly 70% of the US population. They use this spatial model to extrapolate existing trends to 2040 and to predict the emergence of an even larger trans-metropolitan urban structure—the "megapolitan region." They conclude "that the fragmented post-modern metropolis may be giving way to a neo-modern extended region where new forms of networks and spatial connectivity reintegrate urban space".

Contributor **Peter Hall** arrives at a similar conclusion, drawing on his experience and research. He employs a spatial-temporal analysis by couching his look forward by looking backward, à la Bellamy. He looks back at the accuracy of H.G Wells' predictions in 1901, concluding that history exhibits "long term steady state trends", in spite of punctual occurrences such as war, economic depression, and technological innovation. He then examines environmental, demographic, technological, and economic parameters at the beginning of the 21st century before tracing their spatial consequences forward to 2050. He foresees that cities will retain their unique role of organizing the economy on account of the historical weight of infrastructure and alliances embedded there. Yet new infrastructure in the form of high speed trains will drive the transformation of spatial-temporal relations in metropolitan areas and further the dispersal of urban form, creating dynamic edge city places to compete with the central city cores as business hubs. He advises spatial planners to use these infrastructure opportunities as a key structuring element in regional spatial strategies.

These two analysts are decidedly spatial in their take on the city region, distinct from our other contributors, whose analytical perspectives are relational and governance oriented, as we discuss further on. It is also worth noting that the metropolitan statistical data they rely on only gives "partial glimpses" of multi-scalar interactions (Taylor, 2004). The aforementioned chapters differ in important ways, in their scans backward and forward in time. Their empirical research focuses on trade, commuting and development/ investment patterns. As sensible in their prognostics as their internal logics allow, the key drivers of economic growth in the future may turn out to be scarcity of prime materials, food, and fibre, including those considered free and public today: water and air. Forty years on, in view of the UN's population projections and increasing consumption of countries currently "in development", economic and ecological conditions disquiet projections and cause questioning of fundamental assumptions taken for granted now. Yet they share the premise that the city region, whatever its composition and whatever future conditions portend, is and will continue to be the locus of societal activity of all kinds. City regions are the integrators of the spaces of flows.

The understanding of spatial-temporal analytics we wish to convey here extends the economic-based spatial models most often employed by regional and economic geographers (Jonas and Ward, 2007) and other disciplines, such as regional science and regional economics. Our contributors apply conceptual and analytical models and data that consider not just social, political, and governance phenomena, which Jonas and Ward call for to counterbalance the dominant economic regional approach (2007). They add technological, infrastructural, and ecological networks for a more complete portrait that can guide future analytical modeling. Taken together, our contributors illustrate the dialectical interplay of theory and fact, time and space, and spatial and institutional; all of which depend on frames of reference – the conceptual models and mental images employed by scholars.

Imagining the City Region: A Plethora of Interpretations

Throughout the twentieth century, urban theorists have conceptualised city development through their own *Weltanschauung*. Each variant is intended to make the city region more intelligible and to help us grasp rapidly changing realities: world cities, global cities, megacities, metropolises, megalopolises, megapolitan regions, metacities, gig@cities. Sometimes these analyses are unitary, with a focus on a single concept or phenomenon, such as the city or the region, or a single aspect of it (Weber, 1958; Park, 1925; Scott, 2001; Davis, 2006). Others employ dualisms to convey the nature of place / space relations, such as the dual city of rich and poor, or black and white (Mollenkopf and Castells, 1991; Goldsmith and Blakely, 1992).[3] Yet such constructs, whether unitary or duality, dialectic or dichotomy, can obscure more than clarify. The realities of the urban are complex and polychromatic. How to conceive the city region has intellectual and practical consequences: so we can investigate it effectively, inhabit it knowledgeably, and govern it sensibly.

Spatial analysts have been studying the internationalization of resource flows and their shaping of contemporary cities. Their findings persuasively suggest that, despite telecommuting and other real-time global interactions, the city survives as an important venue for business, social, and cultural transactions. Face-to-face interaction is still vital for securing joint collaboration for mutual benefit, particularly in high value-added situations and intimate personal settings (Hall, 2003; Graham and Healey, 1999; Madanipour et al, 2001). Consequently, no matter how it is dissected or represented, the city region is still is what it and the city before it have always been, a specialized and concentrated "transaction maximizing system" (Meier, 1968). The city as a system had a rich if short tradition (Berry, 1964: Bourne and Simmons, 1978) and is one example of a schema used to convey complex urban conditions.

To illustrate the variety of mental schema used to describe city region conceptions, a review article posits three categories of "[spatial] models of regional definition", each with its characteristic spatial flows and examples (Dewar and Epstein, 2007, 116).

Framework	Spatial flows	Typical example
Linkages	Connections between points	Freight flow analysis
Gradient	Fluctuation of a phenomenon	Air and water pollution analysis
Bounded	Contiguous extent	Political jurisdiction, watersheds

The linkages model reflects a network understanding, the gradient model a topological understanding, and the bounded model equates to cartographic approaches.

Lagendijk identified a three-fold framework as well, whose functional, structural, and voluntary categories reflecting geographical representations of the city region (2007). These and other analysts struggle to devise "spatial grammars" (Macleod and Jones, 2007). With so many approaches in circulation, the models seem as multiform as the regions themselves.

These differing conceptions, sometimes contrasting, sometimes complementary, have an underlying mental model or analytical frame. These models or "imagined spatialities" simplify and synthesize our knowledge of processes of change, and can be expressed using images and metaphors captured in theories and concepts. For example, in this book, Peter Hall tackles images of cities in the historical past and those projected well into the future, and finds that city regions fifty years hence may not look so different from today. Ananya Roy's piece dissects numerous mental models that shape and constrain our thinking about urban theory and consequently, policy intervention. Robert Lang and Dawn Dhavale posit a new image, the "megapolitan region" to replace not only megalopolis, but awkward bureaucratic terminology such as consolidated metropolitan statistical areas.

Some theorists construct their models in supra-urban economic and social terms. This is expressed in studies on the transition from Fordism to flexible accumulation (Scott, 2001; Harvey, 2003, 2001, 1989) and on the rise of a globalised network society (Castells, 2000, 2001; Sassen, 2001). Their analyses contrast images and metaphors of modern capitalism – hierarchy, linearity, rigidity – with those of postmodernism – networks, interactivity, flexibility. They follow a long tradition at the robust meeting point of the social and economic sciences, beginning with Marx and Engels and continuing through the German theorists Weber and Simmel, the Chicago School of Park, Burgess, McKenzie, and Wirth; through a wide range of German, French, Italian, British, and American theorizations which evince increasing degrees of contagion. Their common ground is built upon the metaphors and images they employ as their persuasive tools, such as concentric rings, mental illness, living bodies, and machines.

Political economy attempts to explain urban development as the interaction of micro and macro forces that manifest themselves as regimes or growth machines (Molotch, 1976; Stone, 1990; Simpson, 2004). Other political scientists have offered socio-cultural explanations of city-region development as either more networked or more hierarchical phenomena (Saxenian, 1994). The wealth of city regions' conceptualizations matches the fecundity of the researchers' analytical interpretations of their observations.

The relations between social (subsuming economic, political, cultural) processes and their built and virtual environments, formerly called space and society, are now increasingly conceptualised by economic and political geographers as the multi-scalar relations between institutions and environments (Cox, 1998). As Harvey notes, "spatial scales are never fixed, but perpetually redefined, contested, and restructured" (Harvey, 2000, 76). Networked infrastructures lower the transaction costs associated with multiscalar interactions to the extent that the power of flows may exceed the flows of power (Castells, 1989).

Yet as potent as the network metaphor has become, the latest complex modeling of urban environments reveals that networks are not the only form of representation. Fractals, cellular automata, space syntax, and others are compelling ways to comprehend them (Graham, 1998; Batty, 2005; Transportation Research Board, 2004; Massey et al, 1999). A challenge for empiricists and theorists is to resolve this plethora of interpretations, each conditioned by its own frame of analysis.

The theories reviewed above are among those that enrich our grasp of cities and urbanization. A strength of each of them is that each posits an image (in the mind's eye that represents its way of knowing. The image may represent a concept, metaphor, story, rational structure) to sediment complex realities in a simplified way in a mental model. This strength nonetheless leads to a general critique of these theories: they tend to ignore those parts of reality that the theoretical construct and conveying image cannot capture, and thereby gloss over the complexity of the contemporary city region. Their limitations are compounded by dogma packaged in disciplines and ideologies, which when properly understood are one and the same.

Furthermore, as contributor **Ananya Roy** points out as a limitation to broader and more accurate understandings, much theoretical work on city regions is "firmly" located in North America and Europe (Chicago, New York, Paris, Los Angeles). Her question becomes: can the experiences of the global South "reconfigure the theoretical heartland of urban and metropolitan analysis"? Some work has begun to explore this such as the work compiled by Klaus Seberg, whose collection looks at Johannesburg, Mumbai, São Paolo, and Shanghai in the context of urban region spatial formation (Seberg, 2007). Their findings show that the complexity and fragmentation of urban region space in the global south rivals if not exceeds that in the north, albeit in different forms.

Ananya Roy claims our one-dimensional preoccupation with the financial flows between certain "global" cities produces the familiar dichotomies of "overdeveloped versus underdeveloped" and "growth versus dependency". Experiencing the "spaces outside" urban theory in the fast growing cities of the global South (Shanghai, Cairo, Mumbai, Mexico City, Rio de Janeiro, Dakar, Manila) will not only widen out the sites from which urban theorists can theorise but also introduce them to the "heterogeneity and multiplicity of metropolitan modernities" that will dominate the 21st century. She sets a new agenda for the production of a variety of dynamic typologies and deep relations which she calls the "worlding of cities".

In efforts to address these issues and improve upon disciplinary knowledge, some scholars have been building new data-driven, cross-disciplinary theories, thus creating new images that may prove to supplement if not supplant old ones.[4] Yet the very number and variety of investigative methods and theoretical underpinnings suggests that we are in the midst of a paradigm shift, where old ones (plural) have clearly broken down, and a number of potential pretenders are fighting to become the dominant new paradigm (Kuhn, 1961). Just as there has not been a single dominant paradigm in the past for city regions - regional science competed with the descriptive approach of Patrick Geddes, for example - there is clearly not one paradigm that is emerging now as dominant.

Amidst all this good work, is something fundamental lost? Is there a perspective on city region space-society relations in all its manifestations that current scholarship is pointing toward but not yet hit the mark? From this point of view, is it surprising that metropolitan and regional governance debates are also scattered across the intellectual map, as vertical government paradigms based on the city (understood as a discrete municipal jurisdiction) and the nation-state weaken in the face of globalization, networks, and city regions?

The Regional Governance Imperative

The rise of global networks enabled by supranational administrations both governmental and corporate strongly influence and structure the management of urban life. The complex global transactions of finance and labour that both link and set cities apart (Allen et al, 1998) creates a "transnational hierarchy of cities" and division of labour between cities at different levels (global, supra-national, national) (Sassen, 2000: 104; see also Taylor, 2004). Underpinning this superstructure, the "geographical scaffolding" of capital accumulation includes physical connectivity via telecommunications and transport infrastructure, but also social networking connectivity (Coutard, et al., 2005; Brenner, 1999).

These new structures and interactions are thought to be eroding the "entrenched relationships of 'mutuality'" (Brenner, 1999: 432) between cities and the nation state and creating new 'geographies of power' with concepts of 'polycentricity', 'peripheral cities' and 'peripheralization' standing in contrast to the centrality of major cities in developed countries. Sassen differentiates between cities on the 'inside' and 'outside' of the "world market-oriented subsystem". Places that fall outside the new grid of digital highways are "peripheralized" (Sassen, 2000: 113). These peripheral-central forces and counter forces accentuate the various divides marking the 21st Century City. These forces are channeled through infrastructures, ever and again at the forefront of reshaping urban space, and space-society interplay. Accordingly, city region governance activities are increasingly focused on strategic infrastructure.

City region governance is complicated by many factors, not the least of which being "City regions share one characteristic: not one of them functions as a unitary actor" (Seberg, 2007, 1). While it is questionable that "mere" cities ever functioned as unitary actors, his more significant contribution refers to "decisive power currencies" that governance manages. They are not just military or economic currencies. In this regard he refers to power deriving from the "extreme asymmetries" between interacting actors in most if not all fora and arenas (Seberg, 2007, 6). These asymmetries lead to instability and unsustainability – potent governance challenges.

One concomitant result, egregious in developing city regions, is that collective notions of social and built spaces – civic, public, commons, community – wither as a consequence of increasing separation and isolation (Alexander 2006). Finding common ground, a prerequisite for effective governance, becomes increasingly challenging for at least two fundamental reasons. First, urbanites are becoming ever more diverse through massive migrations. Second, disparities among income, education, and other defining social indicators are growing. Yet the evidence of increasing urbanization worldwide, and the unrelenting growth in the size of cities, point to the imperative of regional governance to solve these and other problems.

"When we contemplate urban futures we must always do battle with a wide range of the emotive and symbolic meanings that both inform and muddle our sense of 'the nature of our task'. As we collectively produce our cities, so we collectively produced ourselves" (Harvey, 2000, 159). This claim suggests that the collective production and governance of the urban region owes to the collective production of its images, a finding of Christine Boyer's *The City of Collective Memory* (1994). Lewis Mumford's and Kevin Lynch's command of urban imagery reflects the same understanding of the importance of the image of a city and city region. Humans have always used images to construct their understanding of space, urban or otherwise, as a precursor to actually constructing settled place.

What has changed today is the complexity and scale of the mega city region, and its multiple intersections with virtual spaces and flows of globalization. This complexity and scale not only has clouded our image of the city (even as it has reinforced its centrality), it has clouded our very ability to construct an image of the city region. This of course has direct consequences for the ability to govern one. If we cannot imagine, then we cannot manage. Can we be surprised to encounter, in this light, contributor **Patsy Healey's** questioning of the very possibility of city region planning and governance? "What then is a 'city region' and what is its value as a planning and governance concept?" Only after we answer this question clearly will we become able to reply to her other challenge: the value of and justification for creating 'city region' institutional arenas. Can the city region claim, in her words, "some kind of 'integrated' policy attention?" Do we have a choice, as the city region becomes a sort of "region state", filling the gap between cities and nation states (Ohmae, 1993)?

Patsy Healey's focuses on the "imagined regions" of North West Europe. She asks "who is doing the summoning up of the idea of a city region" in what arenas and to what purpose? Taking two case studies of England and the Netherlands, she finds, as expected, that attempts to "bottle-up" the "relational webs" of the urban life of metropolitan regions that are dynamic and ambiguous into a coherent "concept of a relationally-integrated urban space" have not mobilized the imagination of residents of that space. The concept engaged policy and government actors in both case study areas, nevertheless. In England it has engendered new networking and collaboration on metropolitan strategy development to capture funding from central government. Whilst in the Netherlands, with a stronger tradition of collaboration among levels of government, she discerned a new discourse of economic competitiveness that has "opened up" the governmental alliance to focus on economic development and infrastructure priorities.

Ivan Turok picks up on emerging concerns raised by Healey about the neglected social and environmental dimensions of the contemporary city-region concept. He discusses the dominant economic arguments for large or 'mega' city-regions and draws attention to the conflict that can emerge between local needs and regional interests if a narrow policy agenda is pursued. He illustrates this argument with a case study from the UK's prominent Thames Gateway initiative. It seeks to concentrate the supply of new housing in response to regional growth pressures, at a time when local communities need jobs, skills and improved services, rather than more housing for incomers. The lesson for city-region theory and practice is not to constrain the role envisaged for secondary cities and towns in relation to the core city.

So, is mega-city region governance viable? Another perspective emerges when political issues are taken into account. According to Harvey "It is interesting to note how the figure of the city periodically re-emerges in political theory as the spatial scale at which ideas and ideals about democracy and belonging are best articulated" (Harvey, 2000, 239). Is it true, however, that the city is the best urban container of our every day lived experience, as Healey and Harvey attest? This assumption comes under increasing pressure, given globalization and attendant flows and movements at all scales. The metropolitan region, however, is still the locus of most daily experiences for most people: home, work, commuting, school, shopping, community and religious affiliations, recreation and pleasure, and so on.[5] This holds whether you are experiencing your own city region or when you happen to find yourself temporarily in another. This leads to the *networked politics of the metropolis.* Networked politics, a radical departure from the old dictum "all politics is local", reshapes the boundaries of governance by the very networking processes of public management (Agranoff, 2007).

Growth management and spatial planning, terms in use in the United States and Europe, respectively, are the networked metro politics of urban development. Recent studies of city region planning indicate that it is increasingly being attempted by using flow management (linkage capacities, switching capacities at nodes) instead of or in addition to spatial management (urban growth boundary lines and green belts, development zones) tools (Dewar and Esptein, 2007; Hall and Pain, 2006). This has led to new techniques of mapping of the spaces and conduits of city region flows and the production of descriptions of situations and places.

Taken further into the institutional sphere, it implies a relational approach to institutional design, and points to relational agency. Relational process mechanisms include coordination, collaboration, consensus building, and facilitation. Moreover they inspire the redesign of fora and arena that best accommodate relational mechanisms. But will the transaction costs of city region democracy gain the political support and commitment necessary to respond to their problems and opportunities? In this moment of transition what occurs is both modes simultaneously: relational governance and hierarchical government. As a result we see conflicting and / or hybrid languages and styles, which provide obstacles for common understanding, much less common governance.

This is evident in the final two contributions to this book that examine efforts to integrate sustainability into regional planning. **Etherington** and **Jones** expand on the earlier contributions by Healey and Turok in this book through examining the socio-economic sustainability of the re-constructed narratives on city-region competitiveness in England and Wales and posing the question: "Does this reinforce existing patterns of labour market inequality and social exclusion?" They focus on the contradictions of the supply side market and private sector approach to economic regeneration in the rust-belt city of Sheffield and the proliferation of government funded agencies tasked with enhancing labour market participation whilst the national state concentrates on underpinning the competitiveness of the global city of London. Their historical review of output data suggests that city-regions/ regions have limited capacity to act against the national state and market reproduction of socio-economic disparities.

The final contribution in this book from **Stephen Wheeler**, as do Roy and Healey, also draws attention to the production of authoritative knowledge in the theorizing on sustainability. He evaluates the success of regional planning initiatives across Europe and North America and finds an inordinate gap between regional visions of sustainability and current practice. In most places, he finds weak metropolitan and city region governance with a singular preoccupation with coordinating economic competitiveness of the territory in response to perceived global forces. Given the rapid growth and coalescence of city regions into mega regions in the foreseeable future, he identifies strategies to "nurture" more effective planning for sustainability. These include ecological systems thinking to integrate actions horizontally and vertically across different spatial scales with proactive support from higher-level governments and coalitions of interest.

We observe that shifting flow patterns, indeterminate boundaries, and the multi-scalar properties of spatial conditions and institutional actions do not bode well for the type of institutional fixity that attends to spatially based levels of government, and even governance at a single scale. Part of the problem, as Hall and Pain point out, is the "mismatch between functional and territorial logics (Hall and Pain, 2006, 178).

Seberg's skepticism goes beyond Healey's, Wheeler's, and ours. He claims that massive and globally circulating "capital and content flows are difficult to organize and cannot be regulated effectively, at least not by traditional instruments and strategies." He goes on to say that "regulation and control is [sic] in crisis" and furthermore that "the term *governance* is in crisis" (Seberg, 2007, 6-7, emphasis in original). The real issues attendant to Seberg's view are twofold. First, regulation belongs to the language of the past related to more rooted entities, and thus can conflict with the logic of flows. Second, it points to the notion that there may be better mechanisms of regional or larger scale governance than regulation. We note that the first is not necessarily so, as regulation depends on what is regulated, how, and by whom. These are questions of institutional design, that is, governance.

Yet the very fact that capital and content are flowing freely and massively indicates effectiveness of some sort. In fact, the flows are regulated strictly by a variety of organizations, national and international in scope. We believe that a significant part of the problem radiates from the fact that there is a disconnect between the regulation of capital and content flows and the governance of city region development.

One such better mechanism for regional relational governance and planning is a contract. A contract stipulates for a fixed period of time and a determinate set of actors a work programme to be accomplished and a specific set of relations among the actors. Contracts are relational by definition, and offer a definite option to overcome regional governance difficulties (Motte, 2007). City region governance "contracts" thus can alleviate the experimental nature of spatial strategy formulation at this scale, giving more certainty to what Balducci calls a "field of experimentation" (Balducci 2005). Experimental designers strive to hold parameters constant to gain credible results. In politics and policy making, this can be interpreted as risk management. Contracts are designed to manage risk. Contracts are relational means to establish obligations, rights, and responsibilities among the contracting parties. In the past, the spatial plan – especially the city general plan – coupled with institutionalized implementation instruments such as zoning, was this contract.[6] What does this mean for our current circumstances? A new type of contractual spatial plan? Many metropolitan governmental associations and non-governmental entities already use contractual plans.

Spatial-Institutional Isomorphism

Contemporary analytical approaches to comprehending the city region, briefly sketched above, highlight one characteristic over all others: the deep and complex interplay between urban space and the processes that produce that space. The relational geographies documenting this interplay underscore the multiple scales, sites, and speeds of city region phenomena. The patterns of interactions in and among city regions, and between individuals and institutions in attempts to govern city regions, occur through networks in built and virtual environments. Many times they occur through the same networks. This reveals how institutionally networked space mirrors urban networked space, a phenomenon we call spatial-institutional isomorphism. Institutional-spatial isomorphism, particularly when understood as the interplay of spatial, institutional, and virtual network phenomena, may well reconfigure analytical approaches and reconceptualise space-society relations.

This is possible because the networking of institutions is now superposed on the networking of space, one providing a mirror image of the other. This stands to reason, as both networked institutions and networked space are mediated by the same networked infrastructures.[7] This holds for all institutions, whether governance, corporate, non-governmental, or mixed; as it does for all urban space, whether local, regional, global, or "glocal". As much empirical evidence and theoretical research is showing, these are increasingly multi-scalar in nature (Neuman, 2007). Focusing on a single scale such as the city or the city region has less relevance, as the European Union experiment in continental governance of spatial planning and territorial cohesion is revealing, through both policy initiatives and ESPON, the European Spatial Planning Observation Network. One implication is that governance, through institutional networks, acts on infrastructural networks that are the eventual shapers (and shapes) of space at all scales. Another implication is for institutional design, outlined below.

A clear example of spatial-institutional isomorphism at a continental scale is identified in the fine study by Hein of the polycentric European Union headquarters' network. The institutional network of the headquarters and field offices of the numerous EU institutions are scattered yet well connected by intentional institutional design throughout the expanded Europe of 27 nations (Hein, 2004). The EU's polycentric institutional structure mirrors the polycentric spatial structure at the continental scale of the city regions of Europe. At the global scale a parallel observation can be made about the United Nations headquarters' network. While the UN's global headquarters is in New York, the International Court of Justice has its seat in the Hague, the World Bank in Washington, the ILO, UHCHR, and WHO in Geneva, the UNEP in Nairobi, UNESCO in Paris, the Food and Agricultural Organization in Rome, and so on. The UN, as the EU, spreads its institutional web by design across the global space it seeks to govern.

At the city region scale, institutional networks of governance are patterned by the polycentric space they occupy. In the US it is common for city region associations, called Associations of Governments, to be engaged in some form of metropolitan planning and governance. They are constituted of hundreds of local government entities in many cases. A European equivalent is the Mancomunitat de Municipis of the Barcelona metropolitan area. It is not identical in that it combines the functions of the Associations of Governments with what in the US is called a Metropolitan Planning Organization, responsible for metro transport planning. The San Diego Associations of Governments is one American example that combines both.

Governance entities in many city regions are comprised of hundreds of jurisdictions and organizations of all types spread throughout their area. Examples include Envision Utah, Blueprint Planning in California and Houston, the Regional Plan Association of New York, the Thames Gateway London Partnership, and the Pla Estratègic Metropolità de Barcelona (now called the Pacte Industrial de la Regió Metropolitana de Barcelona). In city region economic production systems, firms and economic actors are also networked across urban space in social patterns that mirror urban patterns. The better they are networked, the better they perform (Storper, 1993; Saxenian, 1994). These instances of spatial-institutional isomorphism open a window to view both institutional design for city region governance, and spatial design for planning and policy, as they grapple with the uncertainties and complexities of development in the future. Peter Hall's evocative chapter in this volume, while not explicitly about iso-morphism, is suggestive of the future forms it may take, and the future issues they'll have to contend with.

Challenges for the Future

Understanding the complexity of the contemporary city region and the forces that shape it has proven too much a challenge for a single mind or discipline – hence our collection of disparate and polyglot scholars and our focus on both city region spaces and their governance institutions. Examining space and governance at any scale in a serious way would employ a range of methods of network analysis that measure factors such as nodes, linkages, gateways, and switches. We believe this could form part of the agenda for future research.

The points that follow – sustainability, learning, and governance – are brought together in what we see as a new logic that should penetrate all aspects of studying and governing city regions. They build on the ideas in the prior two sections. They contrast with earlier approaches which were discipline- or sector-specific. Earlier approaches served regions poorly because they fragmented the whole into parts, among other reasons. Instead of analysis, many scholars and practitioners, cited by the authors in this book as well as in this introduction, are finding that evolutionary and emergent approaches that explicitly avoid a single hegemonic logic seem to be serving, or have the potential to serve, city regions better.

One way to integrate these understandings is via sustainability as a learning endeavor (Meppem and Gill 1998), and governance as a learning endeavor (Paquet 1999). These come together in sustainability as a governance learning effort (Johnson and Wilson 1999). This type of governance learning is emergent, evolving from the collaboration of a wide variety of interests (Innes, et al. 1994, Healey 2006). The brief remarks below illustrate this approach further.

A key governance concern imperative for the 21st century is sustainability. Stephen Wheeler indicates in this book that sustainability is a quiet concern, overshadowed by economic development and competitiveness at the regional scale. Without entering the debate, we can venture selected propositions that situate sustainability within the dis-courses about the city region. One proposition is an underlying concern about the long-term consequences of prevailing settlement patterns and the "lock-in" they signify in terms of unsustainable practices. "Lock-in" occurs because these patterns are instan-tiated in institutional patterns and practices, as we delineated above, following the philosophical underpinnings of Lefebvre (1991). As Wheeler suggests, city-regions lack a coherent framework and supportive metrics for promoting sustainability. Moreover, images and models of a truly sustainable city region have not yet begun to populate the collective consciousness.

Another general concern is the extent to which regions can "learn" to govern them-selves, to develop sustainably, to distribute equitably, and so on. The "learning region", with its direct implications for most of the issues addressed in this introduction as well as by the contributors, has been a conceptual frame for fifteen years (Storper, 1993; Florida, 1995; Rutten and Boekema, 2007). Storper found that dynamic production regions "which are leaders of international trade, [and] continually re-define the best practices" owing to their "intricate social division of labor" (Storper, 1993, 440). In other words, the regions learn, and thus innovate, to maintain their competitive advantage. Florida takes the concept further by applying it to all knowledge creation related activities, and situates it in the city region. "Learning regions provide a series of related infrastructures which can facilitate the flow of knowledge, ideas, and learning" (Florida, 1995, 528). For Florida, knowledge infrastructure networks are central, and as such serve as predecessors to necessary conditions for effective regional governance, a finding underscored by a study of 13 California regions (Innes, et al., 1994).

Just as asymmetric distributions of wealth, resources, impacts, etc. form the basis of social equity considerations as a part of sustainability; Phillip Cooke identifies a shortcoming in learning region schema. He identifies it as "asymmetric knowledge". Different actors in the region have different levels and different types of knowledge. Cooke sees it as an "epistemic" problem, which we pose as ripe for "frame reflection (Schön and Rein, 1994). He further cites a review of 200 studies on regional innovation systems whose conclusion was that regions improve their performance in innovation by "redesigning" their [knowledge] boundary-crossing mechanisms, or "bridging social capital", following Putnam (2000) (Cooke, 2007, 184-5). In this we can trace the influence of J. D. Thompson, who posited that organizations expand their boundaries to capture uncertainties or threats in their environment in order to bring them under their control (Thompson, 1967). Another point of Cooke's is that discovery, change, and in the end, learning; are not so much products of "learning" as of "unlearning" (187). In all instances, regional learning is essential to the prospects of regional governance, development, and evolution. Yet to portray learning as regional implies collective action, and so is linked to governance.

This book provides the opportunity to monitor, interpret, and reflect deeply on changes in socio-spatial relations in city regions. Is a new urban landscape really emerging? If so, are the terms urban and landscape even appropriate? Are the ways in which humans individually and their ever-different and ever-changing groupings inhabit place becoming untethered, or will our place-based and community-enriched genetic code still be appropriate for the 21st Century?

Whether looking forward or reflecting, most of our authors have questioned the very essence of city regions and how we construct and manage them. This invites radical reflection. If we are to be truly sustainable in the future, changing city region scale urbanism and governance practices invites radical rethinking. This is thus the challenge confronting those studying and managing city regions in the future.

Notes

1 Three special issues in 2007 of *Regional Studies* and the *International Journal of Urban and Regional Research* devoted to understanding the region and regional studies more generally are especially pertinent to gain a background on which our arguments – specific to the city region – are framed. See PIKE, A. (2007) Editorial: Whither Regional Studies? *Regional Studies* 41, 1143–1148; JONAS, A. and WARD, K. (2007) Introduction to a Debate on City-Regions: New Geographies of Governance, Democracy and Social Reproduction, *International Journal of Urban and Regional Research* 31, 169–78; and PIKE, A. *et al.* (2007) Editorial: Regional Studies: 40 Years and More … *Regional Studies* 41, supp.1:1-8.

2 Another, traditional meaning of urbanism refers to urban planning and design practices to shape the physical urban development of cities, a topic left unexplored in this book.

3 These dualities are well represented in urban conditions today: two and a half billion living on less than two dollars a day, scores making more than two and a half billion dollars a year.

Life expectancy around forty years in some African nations, life expectancy over eighty years in several Mediterranean nations. Slums and mansions side-by-side. Digital divides, North-South divides, East-West divides, First and Third Worlds, global cities on a planet of the slums – all coexisting in urban space. Extremes, and contrasts between them, are not only commonplace descriptors, they color our conceptual palette as well.

4 We have selected a number of authors for this book using this criterion.

5 Harvey makes the observation that most nation-state boundaries were drawn between 1870 and 1925 (2000 p. 60). This is coincident with the rise of the first true metropolitan regions, such as London, Paris, Berlin, New York.

6 The Local Area Agreements, negotiated between national government in England and the Local Strategic Partnerships (LSP), representing key public and private actors, are one example of a contract which has supplanted the traditional land use development plan. In return for funding, the LSP agrees to deliver national policy priorities at the local level to agreed standards.

7 The institutionalist perspective that has emerged in governance studies acknowledges the role of agency, rules, and norms that constitutionally structure interaction in social contexts. Institutions have become the media through which most human agency occurs. Institutions have the resources and means of interactivity that extend individual agency across social space and time. Moreover, they have the most wherewithal to create, extend, and use networked infrastructures to perpetuate themselves.

References

Agranoff R. (2007) *Managing within networks: adding value to public organizations.* Georgetown University Press, Washington, DC.

Alexander J.C. (2006) *The Civil Sphere,* Oxford University Press, Oxford.

Amin A. (2002) Spatialities of globalisation, *Environment and Planning A* **34**, 385-399.

Balducci A. (2005) Strategic planning for city regions: the search for innovative approaches, Paper to AESOP Congress, Vienna, July.

Barbour E. and Teitz M. (2006) *Blueprint Planning in California: Forging Consensus on Metropolitan Growth and Development*, Public Policy Institute of California, San Francisco.

Batty M. (2005) *Cities and complexity: understanding cities with cellular automata, agent-based models, and fractals,* MIT Press, Cambridge, MA.

Berry B.J.L (1964) Cities as Systems within Systems of Cities, *Papers of the Regional Science Association* **13**, 147-163.

Bourne L.S. and Simmons J. W. (Eds.) (1978) *Systems of Cities: Readings on Structure, Growth, and Policy,* Oxford University Press, Oxford.

Boyer M.C. (1994) *The City of Collective Memory: Its historical imagery and architectural entertainments,* MIT Press, Cambridge, MA.

Brenner N. (1999) Globalisation as Reterritorialisation: The Re-scaling of Urban Governance in the European Union, *Urban Studies* **36 (3)**, 431-451.

Buck N., Gordon I., Harding A. and Turok I. (2005) *Cities: Reimagining the Urban*, Polity Press, Cambridge.

Carbonell A. and Yaro R. (2005) American spatial development and the new megalopolis, *Land Lines* **17 (2)**.

Castells M. (2000) *The Information Age: Economy, Society and Culture I: The Rise of the Network Society*, 2nd edition, Blackwell, Oxford.

Castells M. (2001) *The Internet Galaxy: Reflections on the Internet, Business, and Society*, Oxford University Press, Oxford.

Cooke P. (2007) Regional Innovation Systems, Asymmetric Knowledge, and the Legacies of Learning, in Rutten R. and Boekema F. (Eds) *The Learning Region: Foundations, State of the Art, Future,* Edward Elgar, Cheltenham, UK, 184-205.

Coutard O., Hanley R. and Zimmerman R. (Eds) (2005) *Sustaining Urban Networks: The Social Diffusion of Large Technical Systems*, Routledge, London.

Cox K. (1998) Spaces of dependence, spaces of engagement and the polities of scale or: looking for local politics, *Political Geography* **17**, 1-24.

Cumbers A., Mackinnon D. and McMaster R. (2003) Institutions, Power and Space. Assessing the Limits to Institutionalism in Economic Geography, *European Urban and Regional Studies* **10**, 325-342.

Davis, M. (2006) *Planet of Slums*, London: Verso.

Dewar M. and Epstein D. (2007) Planning for "Megaregions" in the United States, *Journal of Planning Literature* **22**, 108-124.

Dickinson R E. (1947) *City, Region, and Regionalism*, Routledge and Kegan Paul, London.

Florida R. (1995) Towards the Learning Region, *Futures* **27**, 527-36.

Goldsmith, W. and E. Blakely. (1992) *Separate societies: Poverty and inequality in U.S. cities*, Philadelphia: Temple University Press.

Graham, S. (1998) The end of geography of the explosion of place? Conceptualising space and information technology, *Progress in Human Geography* **22**, 165-185.

Graham S. and Healey P. (1999) Relational Concepts of Space and Place: Issues for Planning Theory and Practice, *European Planning Studies*, **7**, 623-646.

Hall P. (2003) The end of the city? "The report on my death was an exaggeration", *City*, **7 (2)**, 145.

Hall P. and Pain K. (2006) *The Polycentric Metropolis: Learning from Mega-City Regions in Europe,* Earthscan, London.

Harvey D. (2003) *The new imperialism*, Oxford University Press, Oxford.

Harvey D. (2001) *Spaces of Capital: Towards a critical geography,* Edinburgh University Press, Edinburgh.

Harvey D. (2000) *Spaces of Hope,* University of California Press, Berkeley.

Harvey D. (1989) *The Condition of Postmodernity: An Enquiry into the Origins of Cultural Change*, Blackwell, Cambridge, Massachusetts.

Healey, P., (2006) *Collaborative Planning: Shaping Places in Fragmented Societies.* 2nd edition. New York: Palgrave McMillan.

Hein C. (2004) *The Capital of Europe: Architecture and Planning for the European Union*, Praeger, Greenwood, CT.

Innes J., Gruber J., Neuman M. and R Thompson (1994) *Coordinating Growth and Environmental Management Through Consensus Building*, California Policy Seminar, Berkeley, California.

Johnson, H. and Wilson, G. (1999) Institutional Sustainability as Learning *Development in Practice* 19,1-2, 43-55.

Jonas, E.G. and Ward, K. (2007) Introduction to a Debate on City-Regions: New Geographies of Governance, Democracy and Social Reproduction, *IJURR* **31(1)**, 169-178.

Kuhn, T. 1961. *The Structure of Scientific Revolutions.* Chicago: University of Chicago Press.

Lang, R. E. and Dhavale, D. (2005) Beyond Megalopolis: Exploring America's New "Megapolitan" Geography, *Metropolitan Institute Census Report Series* 05:01.

Lagendijk, A. (2007) The Accident of the Region: A Strategic Relational Perspective on the Construction of the Region's Significance *Regional Studies* **41**, 1193–1207.

Lefebvre H. (1991) *The Production of Space,* Blackwell, Oxford, UK.

Lovering J. (1999) Theory - led by policy? The in adequacies of the new regionalism in economic geography, *International Journal of Urban and Regional Research* **23**, 379-395.

Macleod, G., and Jones, M. (2007) Territorial, Scalar, Networked, Connected: In What Sense a Regional World? *Regional Studies* **41**, 1177-1191.

Madanipour A., Hull A.D. and Healey P. (2001) *The Governance of Place: Space and planning processes*, Aldershot, Ashgate.

Marvin S., Harding A. and Robson B. (2006) *A Framework for City Regions*, ODPM, London.

Massey D. Allen J. and Pile S. (1999) *City Worlds*, Routledge, London.

Meier R. (1968). The Metropolis as a Transaction-Maximizing System, In Meyerson, M. (Ed) The Conscience of the City, *The Journal of the American Academy of Sciences* 97 (Fall), 1292-1314.

Meppem, T., and Gill, R. (1998) Planning for sustainability as a learning concept. *Ecological Economics* **26**, 2, 121-137.

Mollenkopf, J. and M. Castells, eds. (1991) *Dual city: restructuring New York*, New York: Russell Sage.

Molotch H. (1976) The City as a Growth Machine, *The American Journal of Sociology*.

Motte A., (Ed) (2007) *Les agglomérations françaises face aux défis métropolitains*, Economica Anthropos, Paris.

Neuman, M. (2007) Multi-Scalar Large Institutional Networks in Regional Planning *Planning Theory and Practice*, **8**, 319–344.

Ohmae K. (1993) The Rise of the Region State, *Foreign Affairs* **72 (2)**, 78-87.

Park R.E., McKenzie R.D. and Burgess E. (1925) *The City: Suggestions for the Study of Human Nature in the Built Environment*. University of Chicago, Chicago, IL.

Parr J.B. (2005) Perspectives on the City –Region, *Regional Studies* **39**, 555-566.

Putnam R. (2000) *Bowling Alone: The collapse and revival of American community*, Simon and Schuster, New York.

Ravetz J. (2000) *City Region 2020. Integrated Planning for a Sustainable Environment*, Earthscan, London.

Rutten R. and Boekema F. (Eds.) (2007) *The Learning Region: Foundations, State of the Art, Future*, Edward Elgar, Cheltenham, UK.

Sassen S. (2001) *The Global City: New York, London, Tokyo*, Princeton University Press, Princeton. 2nd edition.

Sassen S. (2000) *Cities in a World Economy*, Pine Forge Press, Thousand Oaks.

Saxenian A. (1994). *The Regional Advantage: Culture and competition in Silicon Valley and Route 128*, Harvard University Press, Cambridge, MA.

Schön D. and Rein M. (1994) *Frame Reflection: toward the resolution of intractable policy controversies*, Basic Books, New York.

Scott A. (Ed.) (2001) *Global city-regions: Trends, theory, policy*, Oxford University Press, Oxford.

Seberg K. (Ed.) (2007) *The Making of Global City Regions*, Johns Hopkins University Press, Baltimore.

Simpson L. (2004) *Selling the city: gender, class, and the California growth machine, 1880-1940*, Stanford University Press, Stanford, CA.

Stone C. (1990) *Regime politics: Governing Atlanta, 1946-1988*, University of Kansas Press, Lawrence, KS.

Storper M. (1993) Regional worlds of Production: France, Italy, and the USA, *Regional Studies* **27**, 433-55.

Sudjic D. (1992) *The 100 Mile City*, Harcourt Brace, San Diego.

Taylor P. J. (2004) *World City Network: A Global Urban Analysis*, Routledge, London.

Thompson J. (1967) *Organizations in action: social science bases of administrative theory*, McGraw-Hill, New York.

Teitz, M. and Barbour, E. (2007). Megaregions in California: Challenges to Planning and Policy in Todorovich, P., ed. *The Healdsburg Research Seminar on Megaregions*. Cambridge, MA and New York: the Lincoln Institute on Land Policy and the Regional Plan Association, 7-19.

Transportation Research Board (2004) Transportation network modeling, *Transportation Research Record*, no. 1882.

Vicino, T., Hanlon, B., and Short, J. R. (2007) Megalopolis 50 Years On: The Transformation of a City Region, *International Journal of Urban and Regional Research* **31**, 344–67.

Weber, M. (1958) *The City*, translated and edited by Don Martindale and Gertrude Neuwirth, Free Press, Glencoe, Illinois.

The New Metropolis: Rethinking Megalopolis

ROBERT LANG and PAUL K. KNOX

LANG R. and KNOX P. K. The new metropolis: rethinking megalopolis, *Regional Studies*. The paper explores the relationship between metropolitan form, scale, and connectivity. It revisits the idea first offered by geographers Jean Gottmann, James Vance, and Jerome Pickard that urban expansiveness does not tear regions apart but instead leads to new types of linkages. The paper begins with an historical review of the evolving American metropolis and introduces a new spatial model showing changing metropolitan morphology. Next is an analytic synthesis based on geographic theory and empirical findings of what is labelled here the 'new metropolis'. A key element of the new metropolis is its vast scale, which facilitates the emergence of an even larger trans-metropolitan urban structure – the 'megapolitan region'. Megapolitan geography is described and includes a typology to show variation between regions. The paper concludes with the suggestion that the fragmented post-modern metropolis may be giving way to a neo-modern extended region where new forms of networks and spatial connectivity reintegrate urban space.

LANG R. and KNOX P. K. 新的大都市区：对特大城市的再思考，区域研究。本文探讨了大都市形态、尺度以及关联性之间的相互关系。文章回顾了由地理学家 Jean Gottmann, James Vance, 以及 Jerome Pickard提出的 "城市蔓延非但不会割裂区域反而会引发新型关联" 这一观点。文章首先追溯了美国大都市的发展历程，并引入一个新的空间模型来展示大都市变化的形态学。紧接着文章在地理学理论和实证研究基础上综合分析了 "新大都市" 的特征。新大都市的一个核心要素在于，其巨大的尺度有助于形成一个更大的跨大都市区城市结构-特大城市区域。文中对特大城市区域地理学进行了相关描述，同时还提供了其类型学来展现区域间差异。文章总结到：破碎的后现代的大都市区域可能会让位于以 "新现代" 方式扩展的区域，在这样的区域中新型网络和空间关联性再度将城市空间整合。

大都市形态学　新大都市　空间关联　巨型城市区域　空间模型　美国大都市

LANG R. et KNOX P. K. La nouvelle metropolis: repenser la mégapole, *Regional Studies*. Cet article examine les relations existant entre la forme, l'échelle et la connectivité métropolitaines. Il revisite l'idée, proposée en premier lieu par les géographes Jean Gottmann, James Vance et Jerome Pickard, selon laquelle la capacité d'expansion des villes ne démolit pas les régions, mais conduit plutôt à de nouveaux types de liens. L'article commence par un examen historique de la Metropolis américaine dans son évolution et introduit un nouveau modèle spatial montrant que la morphologie métropolitaine est en train de changer. Vient ensuite une synthèse analytique, fondée sur la théorie géographique et les résultats empiriques, de ce qui est étiqueté ici comme étant la 'nouvelle Metropolis'. Un élément clé de la nouvelle Metropolis est sa grande échelle, qui facilite l'émergence d'une structure urbaine trans-métropolitaine encore plus vaste – 'la région mégapolitaine'. La géographie mégapolitaine est décrite et inclut une typologie afin de montrer les variations entre les régions. L'article se termine en suggérant que la Metropolis post-moderne éclatée est peut-être en train de laisser la place à une région étendue néo-moderne dans laquelle les nouvelles formes de réseaux et de connectivité spatiale réintègrent l'espace urbain.

LANG R. und KNOX P. K. Die neue Metropole: ein Überdenken der Megalopole, *Regional Studies*. In diesem Beitrag wird die Beziehung zwischen der Form, dem Maßstab und der Konnektivität von Metropolen untersucht. Es wird ein frischer Blick auf die erstmals von den Geografen Jean Gottmann, James Vance und Jerome Pickard vorgebrachte Idee geworfen, wonach die urbane Ausdehnung nicht zum Auseinanderreißen von Regionen führt, sondern vielmehr zu neuen Arten von Verknüpfungen. Zu Beginn des Aufsatzes werfen wir einen historischen Rückblick auf die Entstehung der amerikanischen Metropole und führen ein neues räumliches Modell ein, in dem die sich wandelnde Morphologie der Metropole verdeutlicht wird. Als Nächstes stellen wir eine analytische Synthese vor, die auf der geografischen Theorie und den empirischen Ergebnissen im Zusammenhang mit dem hier als 'neue Metropole' bezeichneten Phänomen beruhen. Ein wesentliches Element der neuen Metropole liegt in ihrer gewaltigen Ausdehnung begründet, welche das Entstehen einer noch größeren transmetropolitanen Stadtstruktur begünstigt – der 'Megapolitanregion'. Es wird die megapolitane Geografie beschrieben, wozu auch eine Typologie gehört, mit der Abweichungen zwischen den einzelnen Regionen aufgezeigt werden. Wir schließen unseren Beitrag mit der Vermutung, dass die fragmentierte postmoderne Metropole von einer neomodernen erweiterten Region abgelöst werden könnte, in der neue Formen von Netzwerken und räumliche Konnektivität den urbanen Raum neu integrieren.

LANG R. y KNOX P. K. La nueva metrópolis: remodelar la megalópolis, *Regional Studies*. En este artículo analizamos la relación entre la forma, escala y conectividad metropolitanas. Revisamos la primera idea que aportaron los geógrafos Jean Gottmann, James Vance y Jerome Pickard de que la expansibilidad urbana no separa a las regiones sino que produce nuevos tipos de vínculos. En este ensayo hacemos primero una revisión histórica de los cambios en la metrópolis americana e introducimos un nuevo modelo espacial que muestra los cambios en la morfología metropolitana. A continuación aportamos una síntesis analítica basada en la teoría geográfica y los resultados empíricos de lo que aquí denominamos la 'nueva metrópolis'. Un elemento clave de la nueva metrópolis es su amplia escala que facilita la aparición de una estructura urbana transmetropolitana aún más grande: la 'región megapolitana'. Describimos la geografía megapolitana e incluimos una topología para mostrar las diferentes variaciones entre las regiones. Terminamos sugiriendo que la metrópolis postmoderna y fragmentada podría dar paso a una región neomoderna ampliada donde las nuevas formas de redes y conectividad espacial reintegren el espacio urbano.

INTRODUCTION

The main difference between an urban area at the scale of the Atlantic Urban Region [i.e. megalopolis] and the traditional metropolitan scale is that the emerging larger form has a multitude of major nodes whose areas of influence are likely to be autonomous. Nevertheless, the individual urban centers benefit from mutual proximity, and there is bound to be increased interaction.

(REGIONAL PLAN ASSOCIATION (RPA), 1967, p. 35)

then, sometime in the 1950s a 'city of realms' began to be evident, but what were the determinants of its structure? ... the process of parturition ... changed outlying areas from the suspected functional potential for semi-independent existence – first felt when suburbs began to be large and separate enough so some activities found in the central cities came to be replicated there – to actual semi-independent.

(VANCE, 1977, p. 410)

The evolution of metropolitan space remains fundamental in understanding the spatial organization of advanced economies. The above passages suggest that post-war US development produced a multi-nodal yet integrated urban structure at both the metropolitan and megapolitan scales. VANCE's (1977) 'urban realms' and GOTTMANN's (1961) 'megalopolis' (as interpreted by the RPA) highlight different dimensions of metropolitan scale and form, yet the two ideas are linked. Both offer the counter-intuitive notion that urban expansiveness does not tear regions apart but instead produces new types of connectivity.

This paper revisits these ideas, recasting Vance's concept of urban realms in the context of the extended contemporary scale of metropolitan regions. There have been significant changes in real estate investment in the USA in the past quarter century, in tandem with equally significant changes in the structure and functional organization of metropolitan regions. Traditional patterns of urbanization have been repealed as new rounds of economic restructuring, digital telecommunications technologies, demographic shifts, and neoliberal policies have given rise to new urban, suburban, and exurban landscapes. Urban regions have been stretched and reshaped to accommodate increasingly complex and extensive patterns of interdependency, while the political economy of metropolitan America has been reshaped in response to socio-economic realignments and cultural shifts. If the industrial metropolis was the crucible and principal spatial manifestation of what Ulrich Beck has dubbed the 'first modernity', contemporary metropolitan America may be viewed as an emergent spatial manifestation of a 'second modernity', in which the structures and institutions of 19th-century modernization are both deconstructed and reconstructed (BECK et al., 2003). Viewed in this way, traditional models of metropolitan structure and traditional concepts and labels – 'city', 'suburb', metropolises – are 'zombie categories'. According to BECK and WILLMS (2003):

zombie categories embody nineteenth-century horizons of experience, horizons of the first modernity. And because these inappropriate horizons, distilled into *a priori* and analytic categories, still mould our perceptions, they are blinding us to the real experience and ambiguities of the second modernity.

(p. 19)

Contemporary metropolitan America is characterized by a 'splintering urbanism' (GRAHAM and MARVIN, 2001) that severely challenges the nomothetic models of urban form and structure that for so long have been the staples of urban geography. As in the 'Mega-City Regions' of Europe (HALL and PAIN, 2006) and the USA (CARBONELL and YARO, 2005), the consequence is a dominant new form of urbanization: polycentric networks of up to 50 cities and towns, physically separate but functionally networked, clustered around one or more larger central cities, and drawing enormous economic strength from a new functional division of labour. This paper recasts the discussion of urban form and structure in the USA in terms of the 'New Metropolis' that is part of a network of 'Megapolitan Areas'.

Data used in this paper are derived from a larger research project at Virginia Tech on 'megapolitan' geography. The megapolitan concept has been developed in part to depict geographically where the next 100 million Americans will live (LANG and NELSON, 2007b). This analysis identified 20 emerging megapolitan areas that are based on the US Census Bureau's definition of a 'combined statistical area' (CSA). These megapolitan areas extend the census's current method several decades forward. The main criterion for a census-defined CSA is economic interdependence, as evidenced by overlapping commuting patterns. The same holds true for megapolitans. Based on projections of commuting, by 2010 the census will

likely show that Phoenix–Tucson in Arizona and Washington–Baltimore–Richmond (i.e. Washington DC, Maryland and Virginia) have become CSAs. In 2020, several more metropolitan areas will pass this threshold, and at mid-century all 20 megapolitan areas should officially be CSAs.

EVOLVING METROPOLITAN FORM

Until the mid-20th century, urban and metropolitan form could safely be conceptualized in terms of the outcomes of processes of competition for land and ecological processes of congregation and segregation, all pivoting tightly around a dominant central business district and transportation hub (Fig. 1a). During the middle decades of the 20th century, however, American metropolises were unbound by the combination of increased automobility, and the blossoming of egalitarian liberalism in the form of massive federal outlays on highway construction and mortgage insurance that underwrote the 'spatial fix' to the over accumulation crisis of the 1930s (CHECKOWAY, 1980; HARVEY, 1985; LAKE, 1995). The result was a massive spurt of city building and the evolution of dispersed, polycentric spatial structure, and the emergence of urban realms (Fig. 1b).

Urban realms

Initially, the shift to an expanded polycentric metropolis was most pronounced in the north-eastern USA,

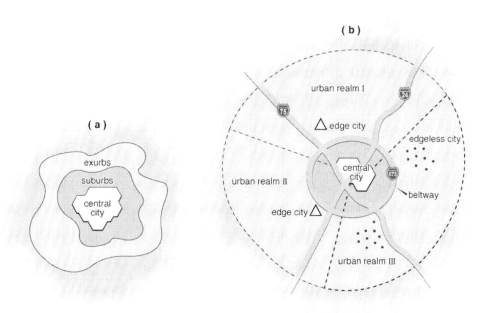

Fig. 1. Evolving 20th-century metropolitan form

and Gottmann captured the moment with his conceptualization of 'megalopolis'. It was not long, however, before observers noted the change elsewhere. MULLER (1976) was among the first to note the emergence of a new 'outer city'. VANCE (1977) argued that major metropolitan areas in the USA, such as Los Angeles in California, New York in New York State, and San Francisco, also in California, had grown so decentralized that they had become a series of semi-autonomous subregions, or 'urban realms'. Vance's basis for identifying different realms within metropolitan areas rested on several criteria. The first is the overall size of the region – the bigger the metropolis, the more plentiful and differentiated the realms. Next is an area's terrain and topography. Physical features such as mountains, bays and rivers often serve to delimit realms by directing the spread of urbanization into distinct and geographically defined areas. The third variable is the amount and type of economic activity contained within it. Realms can also be distinguished by either an overriding economic unification, such as the Silicon Valley in California, or shared employment centres as are identified by commuter sheds. Finally, the regional geography of transportation, as originally recognized by HOYT (1939), also plays a role in separating urban realms. This process began with trolley cars but is now centred on Interstate Highways, in particular metropolitan beltways. Beltways can either define the boundary of an area, as reflected by the expression of one being located 'inside the Washington beltway', or unify a realm as in the case of the LBJ (Freeway) Corridor north of downtown Dallas in Texas.

To Vance, urban realms are natural functions of the growth of cities; the city has changed structurally as a collection of realms, that has grown 'one stage beyond that of a metropolis' (VANCE, 1964, p. 78). The core–periphery relationship weakens as realms become more equal. The basic organization of the region becomes more cooperative as the shared urban and cultural identity of the urban realms creates what Vance called a 'sympolis' rather than a metropolis. For example, consider the relationship between Orange County and Los Angeles, California. Orange County is clearly part of Greater Los Angeles, but it also maintains a distinct and semi-autonomous identity as 'South Coast'. Orange County contributes significantly to the region's larger economy but mostly does not compete with Los Angeles. Industries such as the automotive design found at the Irvine Spectrum, a master-planned high-technology office park in the centre of the county, show this pattern. Several car companies chose the Spectrum for access to California trends and regard Orange County as 'the next capital of cool' (SKLAR, 2003). Orange's association with the Los Angeles helps makes this once sleepy suburban county cool and the larger Southern California region gains by additional economic activity.

Realms have their own subregional identities, such as those in the Los Angeles region such as South Coast (or Orange County) or the Inland Empire (Riverside and San Bernardino Counties). The realms around Los Angeles are so distinct that South Coast and the Inland Empire have their own subregional newspapers and airports. On a smaller, but emerging scale, a place such as the East Valley of Phoenix (with such major suburbs as Mesa, Tempe, Chandler and Gilbert) already has its own newspaper and will soon have a separate national airport from Phoenix. Finally, urban realms also show up in business names, such as South Coast Plaza, Inland Empire National Bank, or the *East Valley Tribune*.

LANG and HALL (2008) synthesized thinking on urban realms and offered four realm types based on a mix of social characteristics, built densities, and development age:

- Urban core realms: the original places of substantial 19th- and 20th-century development, including the region's major principal city and downtown.
- Favoured quarter realms: the most affluent wedge of a metropolitan area, containing upscale communities, luxury shopping, and high-end office districts.
- Maturing suburban realms: the areas of substantial late 20th-century and early 21st-century development that are rapidly filling in and will ultimately extend the edges of the metropolis.
- Emerging exurban realms: extended, rapidly growing, lower-density spaces that contain leapfrog development and will not be full extensions of the main metropolitan development for decades to come.

The relationship between these realm types plays a role in determining the overall megapolitan dynamic. Favoured quarters, such as Southern California's South Coast (Orange County), are often job rich, but have expensive housing. A less affluent maturing suburban realm, such as the Inland Empire (or Riverside and San Bernardino Counties), can develop a dependence on the favoured quarter. Thus, an important traffic pattern in Southern California is the commute between these two suburban realms. In fact, one of the biggest bottlenecks in the region's freeway system is along a mountain pass (known locally as 'The 91') that divides the two realms.

Exurban realms also serve a critical role in megapolitan formation. The 'mid'-exurban realms that emerge between two proximate metropolitan areas lie in the crosshairs of regional growth. It is in these places where commuters go in both directions and provide the linkages – based on a shared economy – that join metropolitan areas.

The new metropolitan form

Parallel with the development of urban realm theory were new models of metropolitan form. These concepts captured the ever-expanding scale and fracturing nature of the late 20th-century metropolis. In 1962, a now obscure urban thinker Jerome Pickard took Gottmann's megalopolis idea a step further and developed a national map of 'urban regions'.[1] PICKARD (1966) then followed up with an analysis of how US migration patterns were expanding these regions. In 1970, Pickard projected growth in urban regions to the year 2000 (Fig. 2). With remarkable precision Pickard predicted the basic frame of the nation's current pattern of urbanization. He also cleanly delineated between an urban region and a metropolitan area. An urban region, to PICKARD (1970), is:

> not necessarily a contiguous 'super city' but rather it is a region of high concentrations of urban activities and urbanized population.
>
> (p. 154)

From his original work on urban regions, PICKARD (1962) argued that urban regions were not simply an extended city:

> The largest urban region, sometimes called 'megalopolis', extends along the northern Atlantic seaboard from Portland, Maine to Washington, DC. A popular misconception has led to calling this a 'city 500 miles long'. It most definitely is *not* a single city, but a region of concentrated urbanism – a continuous zone of metropolises, cities, towns and exurban settlement within which one is never far from a city.
>
> (p. 3, original emphasis)

PICKARD (1970) also noted that:

> urban regions have evolved during the automobile era form multiple urban nodes that expanded very rapidly toward regional cities.
>
> (p. 154)

By Pickard's definition, an urban region is required to have a total population of 1 million people and an average population density of at least three times the national average (PICKARD, 1962).

Pickard was indeed a seer, but he was not alone in noting the role that post-war metropolitan expansion played in changing basic regional form. In 1980, geographer BRIAN J. L. BERRY (1980) argued that:

> urbanization, the process of population concentration, has been succeeded in the United States by counterurbanization, a process of population deconcentration characterized by smaller sizes, decreasing densities, and increasing homogeneity, set within a widening radii of national interdependence.
>
> (p. 13)

Moreover, Berry also identified new urban development at the 'intermetropolitan peripheries' (p. 16). These are the spaces that in many instances have boomed in the past three decades and are now what are called the 'mid corridor realms', as shown in Fig. 2.

Following Berry, LEWIS (1983) coined the term 'galactic metropolis' to capture the disjointed and decentralized urban landscapes of late 20th-century North America. The galactic metropolis is vast, with

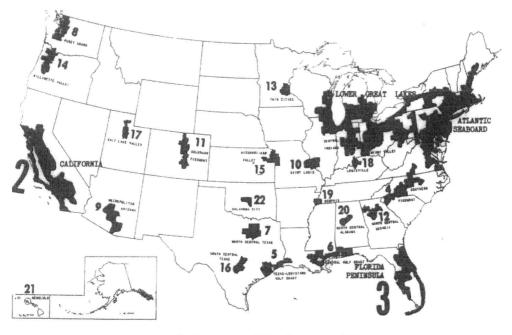

Fig. 2. Vance's projected US urban areas in 2000

varying sized urban centres, subcentres and satellites; it is fragmented and multinodal, with mixed densities and unexpected juxtapositions of form and function. The basic unit of the galactic metropolis includes a:

> cluster of space-consuming buildings near an interchange, all equally and easily accessible by car and truck, and all lavishly furnished with 'free' parking.
>
> (LEWIS, 1983, p. 31)

Looking at US cities established after 1915, Lewis found that every one had evolved in the 'galactic' form rather than with a traditional nucleated morphology (LEWIS, 1995). Lewis also found that even older, more established metropolitan areas have subsequently developed in this same direction, especially at their edges.

More recently, HALL (2001) identified six common types of nodes within the polycentric metropolitan form of developed economies:

- Traditional downtown centres: the hub of the traditional metropolis, now often the setting for the oldest informational services – banking, insurance, and government.
- Newer business centres: often developing in an old prestigious residential quarter and serving as a setting for newer services such as corporate headquarters, the media, advertising, public relations, and design.
- Internal edge cities: resulting from pressure for space in traditional centres and speculative development in nearby obsolescent industrial or transportation sites.
- External edge cities: often located on an axis with a major airport, sometimes adjacent to a high-speed train station, always linked to an urban freeway system.
- Outermost edge city complexes for back offices and research and development (R&D) operations (typically near major transport hubs 20–30 miles from the main core).
- Specialized subcentres: usually for education, entertainment, and sporting complexes, and exhibition and convention centres.

The edges of metropolitan areas have meanwhile generated an enormous literature, partly because of the sheer amount and pace of growth, and partly because of the innovative nature of much of the growth (TEAFORD, 2006). Historian ROBERT FISHMAN (1987) saw a fundamental change in metropolitan form as a result of the emergence of what he called the 'technoburb', metropolitan fabric that: 'lacks any definable borders, a center or periphery, or clear distinctions between residential, industrial or commercial zones' (p. 189) and 'can best be measured in counties[2] rather than city blocks' (p. 203). SUDJIC (1992) wrote about the '100-mile city'; while the challenges of characterizing evolving metropolitan fringes in contrast to mid-century suburbs ('sitcom suburbs') invoked a great variety of neologisms: 'postsuburbia', 'exurbia',

'exopolis', 'generica', 'satellite sprawl', 'mallcondoville', and so on. As much as anything, this flurry of terminology was a reflection of a clear shift from the central city–suburban and urban–suburban–rural frameworks associated with the industrial era and the Fordist city toward more complex and variable expressions of metropolitan form associated with the transition to post-industrial economic structures and the 'variable geometry' of more flexible forms of capital accumulation.

The novelty, complexity, and fluidity of contemporary metropolitan form has been the focus of the 'LA School', which vigorously challenged old assumptions about economic structure and space, leaning heavily on the deconstructive impulses of postmodernity as an explanatory framework (e.g. DEAR, 2002; DEAR and FLUSTY, 1998; SOJA, 2002). Drawing on the Los Angeles metropolitan region as both avatar and exemplar, the LA School has emphasized the disjointedness, disorder, and apparent variability of outcomes of metropolitan restructuring. Yet, an empirical comparison of the changing socio-economic structure (as measured by population density, rent, house values, and per capita income) of ten metropolitan areas (consolidated metropolitan statistical areas, or CMSAs)[3] in the USA between 1970 and 2000 suggests that 'stasis, rather than volatility, is a common pattern in the landscape' (HACKWORTH, 2005, p. 499). Hackworth's analysis affirmed the intensifying polycentricity of metropolitan America, along with the 'valorization' of the outer suburbs; while six of the ten metropolitan areas had evidently experienced pronounced reinvestment in their central core.

THE ANATOMY OF THE NEW METROPOLIS

With this background, one can draw on the broader literature, together with recent empirical analyses undertaken at the Metropolitan Institute at Virginia Tech, to posit an anatomy of contemporary metropolitan form: the New Metropolis (Fig. 3). Key to the polycentric structure of the New Metropolis are clusters of decentralized employment – where office employment is arguably the most significant element (LANG, 2003). In this context, edge cities are one of the most striking components of the New Metropolis.[4] Yet of more than 3 billion square feet of office space in the USA in the 13 largest US metropolitan areas in 2005, only 13% was in edge cities (LANG et al., 2006). Downtown settings accounted for 33%, while commercial corridors along major intra-metropolitan highways accounted for another 3.8%. Smaller clusters of office development within the urban envelope of principal cities accounted for an additional 5.2%, and secondary downtowns accounted for 1.2% of office space. But one of the

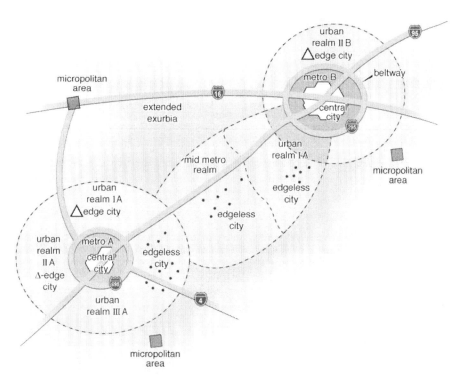

Fig. 3. The New Metropolis

most distinctive characteristics of the New Metropolis is the pattern of development in outer suburban and exurban areas, which accounted for more than 40% of total office space in settings that LANG (2003) has dubbed 'edgeless cities'. Edgeless cities may fill a county and might even be the dominant focus of commerce in whole urban realms. They are one step further removed in spatial logic from older city centres than edge cities.

The residential fabric of the New Metropolis is also distinctive in comparison with the integrated metropolis of the modern era (Fig. 1a). As the metropolitan areas have grown, their suburbs have changed, becoming quasi-urbanized, part of a new form of metropolitan development. In the New Metropolis the suburbs contain significant concentrations of poverty (SWANSTROM *et al.*, 2004), and have a growing share of the nation's single-person households (FREY and BERUBE, 2003) and seniors (FREY, 2003). The New Metropolis is also characterized by 'boomburbs' – fast-growing suburban jurisdictions with more than 100 000 residents that have maintained double-digit rates of population growth in recent decades (LANG and LEFURGY, 2007), and by extended tracts of exurban development with packaged, themed, and fortified subdivisions of private master-planned developments that provide

sequestered settings for competitive consumption – 'Vulgaria' (KNOX, 2005, 2007).

Megapolitan areas

But the most distinctive attribute of the New Metropolis, its signature feature, is its scale. Bound together through urban freeways, arterial highways, beltways, and interstate highways, the prototypical New Metropolis is rapidly emerging as part of a megapolitan region. Megapolitan regions are integrated networks of metropolitan areas, principal cities, and micropolitan areas. The US Census now recognizes a polynuclear 'principal city' category that lifts select suburbs to the status of big cities.[5] The census has also established a new 'micropolitan' category, for principal cities between 10 000 and 50 000 residents that are more populated than rural places, but smaller than big metros. Micropolitans fill in a large share of space in between metropolitan areas. In fact, metropolitan and micropolitan areas now cover over half the land area in the Continental USA between them (LANG and DHAVALE, 2006).

In the 1960s, Dallas and Fort Worth were clearly colliding, as were Washington and Baltimore by the 1980s. Now regions with more distant urban cores such as

Phoenix and Tucson, Tampa and Orlando in Florida, and San Antonio and Austin in Texas are beginning to exhibit the same pattern, only on a more extensive scale. The entire North Carolina Piedmont extending from Raleigh to Charlotte seems, to drivers on Interstate 85, as one continuous countrified city.

According to LANG and DHAVALE (2005), the USA has ten megapolitan regions (Table 1), with six in the eastern half of the country and four in the west. Megapolitan regions extend into 37 states, including every one east of the Mississippi River except Vermont. As of 2004, Megapolitan regions contained about one-fifth of all land area in the lower 48 states, but captured almost 70% of the total US population with over 205 million people. The 15 most populous US metropolitan areas are also found in megapolitan regions. By 2040, megapolitan regions are projected to gain over 85 million residents, or about three-quarters of national growth (LANG and NELSON, 2007b). To put this in perspective, consider that this area, which is smaller than north-west Europe, is about to add a population exceeding that of Germany's by mid-century. The costs of building the residential dwellings and commercial facilities to accommodate this growth could run over US$35 trillion by some estimates (NELSON, 2004; NELSON and LANG, 2007). Much of this

development will fill in the gaps between metropolitan areas, consolidating the links among principal cities and micropolitan areas within megapolitan regions.

Interstate highways are major structural elements in megapolitan development. Interstate 95, for example, plays a major role in megapolitan mobility from Maine in the north-east to Florida in the south-east. The West's bookend to I-95 is I-5, which runs through three separate megapolitan areas. Interstate 10 also links three megas – SoCal, Sun Corridor, and Gulf Coast. Interstate 85 forms the backbone of the Southern Piedmont, running from Raleigh in North Carolina south-west to Atlanta in Georgia.

Traditional measures of functional regions – commuter sheds, for example – are only partially relevant at the megapolitan scale. The areas are simply too big to make many daily trips possible between distant sections. However, data showing commutes of 50 and 100 miles each way indicate a growing number of people who journey to work between big megapolitan metros (LANG and NELSON, 2007a). According to the US Census Bureau, the number of 'extreme commuters' (or those who travel 90 miles or more to work) is growing (NAUGHTON, 2006). In 2005, 3.4 million people made such a commute, or double the number in 1990. In addition, the fastest growing commuting

Table 1. Megapolitans at a glance

Megapolitan area	Megapolitan states	Anchor metros	Signature industry	2000 and 2004 Presidential vote
Arizona Sun Corridor	Arizona	Phoenix–Tucson	Home building	Republican
Cascadia	Oregon, Washington	Seattle–Portland	Aerospace	Democratic
Florida Peninsula	Florida	Miami–Orlando	Tourism	Democratic/ Republican
Great Lakes Crescent	Illinois, Indiana, Kentucky, Michigan, Ohio, Pennsylvania, West Virginia, Wisconsin	Chicago–Detroit	Manufacturing	Democratic
Gulf Coast	Alabama, Florida, Louisiana, Mississippi, Texas	Houston–New Orleans	Energy	Republican
I-35 Corridor	Kansas, Missouri, Oklahoma, Texas	Dallas–Oklahoma City	Telecom	Republican
Megalopolis	Connecticut, Delaware, Massachusetts, Maryland, Maine, New Jersey, New York, Pennsylvania, Rhode Island, Virginia	New York–Washington, DC	Finance	Democratic
NorCal	California, Nevada	San Francisco–Sacramento	High-technology	Democratic
Piedmont	Alabama, Georgia, North Carolina, Tennessee, South Carolina, Virginia	Atlanta–Charlotte	Consumer banking	Republican
SoCal	California, Nevada	Los Angeles–Las Vegas	Entertainment	Democratic

departure time is between 05.00 and 06.00 hours, indicating a boom in long journeys to work (NAUGHTON, 2006). The percentage of people who participate in a regional economy without technically living in its officially designated metropolitan area is correspondingly rising (MORRILL *et al.*, 1999). But one question the US Census Bureau does not ask is the frequency of commutes – or the number of days in an average week that a worker reports to their place of employment. It may be that while commuting distances grow, the number of actual trips drops (LANG and NELSON, 2007a).

The changing nature of work is feeding this transition. In many fields workers simply need not be present in the office five days per week. The practice of 'hoteling' where employees 'visit' work infrequently and mostly work at home and/or on the road is common in high-technology firms and will soon spread to other sectors. This allows people the flexibility to live at great distance to work in remote exurbs or even a neighbouring metropolitan area. Innovations in and diffusion of broadband technology will even further drive this trend as the ability to conference visually into meetings improves to the point where it proxies face-to-face interaction. This is not to say that direct physical connectivity is unimportant. For one, it is hard to advance to senior management in most businesses without being plugged into office politics, which requires some 'face time' with key people. However, face-to-face interactions may become a more specialized type of exchange used for building trust, networking, or closing deals (SASSEN, 2002; THRIFT, 1996).

But commuting is just one aspect of regional cohesion at the megapolitan scale. Other integrating forces exist such as goods movement, business linkages, cultural commonality, and physical environment. A megapolitan region could parallel a sales district for a branch office. Or, in the case of the Northeast Megalopolis or the Florida Peninsula, it can be a zone of fully integrated toll roads where an 'E-Z Pass' (Northeast) or 'SunPass' (Florida) works across multiple metropolitan areas. More importantly, they have become the basis for economic regions with distinctive economic, political and cultural profiles where functional interdependencies exist among companies in the strongly communicative branches in the top end of the tertiary sector – banks, financial services and insurance companies, law firms and advertising industry. Table 1 profiles some basic elements of the ten megapolitan regions, including a thumbnail of their economy and politics. Note that the 'signature industry' may not be the largest in the region, but instead is the one whose image is most easily identified with leading metros in the megapolitan region. Table 1 also shows the mega 'anchor metros'. These metros are often the biggest in the megapolitan region and maintain strong social and business links with each other. The political leanings by

mega are based on the results of the 2000 and 2004 Presidential elections.

Megapolitan regions vary in spatial form and scale. Some exhibit a corridor (or linear) form, while others spread out into vast urban galaxies. Arizona's Sun Corridor, for example, forms a definite corridor structure and covers a fairly modest area (Fig. 4). Table 2 shows how the corridor megapolitan form fits within the hierarchy of urban complexes that exist throughout the USA. The types are listed by their scale, starting with metropolitan areas and moving up to massive 'megaplexes'.

The Dallas–Ft Worth 'metroplex' forms an extended metropolitan area where the two major nodes lay some 30 plus miles apart. Until the development of the Dallas–Ft Worth (DFW) Airport[6] at the midpoint in the metroplex, Dallas and Ft Worth functioned as two different worlds. But DFW helped integrate the region so thoroughly that one now has a hard time distinguishing between the two places.

Just beyond a metroplex in scale are the 100 mile-plus anchor cities, such as Phoenix and Tucson (or the Sun Corridor), which is labelled a 'corridor megapolitan' in Table 2. In this new metropolis era, the commuting patterns between these places will join some under the Census's new CSA category by 2010, with Phoenix–Tucson being a leading candidate.

Above the corridor scale are the 'galactic megapolitans' (named in part based on LEWIS's, 1983, definition). These urban complexes spread broadly over dozens and even hundreds of counties and form a vast web of metropolitan areas that are linked by overlapping commuter sheds and business networks. Leading examples are the Piedmont and Great Lakes megapolitan regions.

Finally, there are megaplexes, which comprise the largest urban complexes in the USA. An example is the pairing between Southern California and Arizona's Sun Corridor. Despite being separated by miles of desert, SoCal and the Sun Corridor are linked by goods movement along several rail lines and two Interstates (I-8 and I-10). The west side of the Sun Corridor, which is most proximate to SoCal, has a land market shaped by access to these transportation corridors. In fact, a place such as Goodyear in Arizona along I-10 has a booming market for warehousing linked to the Port of Los Angeles.[7] SoCal and the Sun Corridor share many other affinities, including linked housing markets (as Californians seek lower cost locations), similar master-planned development practices, integrated business networks (especially in defence contracting and goods movement), and a similar Western Sun Belt climate and lifestyle.

US Census Bureau's 'combined statistical areas' (CSAs)

As noted above, the US Bureau of the Census uses a new metropolitan geography – the CSA – that approximates the corridor megapolitan concept

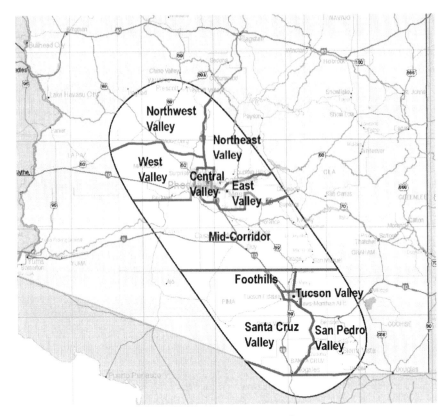

Fig. 4. *The Arizona Sun Corridor*

developed by Virginia Tech. CSAs combine at least two metropolitan (or micropolitan) areas into a single unit that share a regional economy based on commuting patterns.

LANG and NELSON (2007a) developed a method to predict new CSAs in advance of the census by looking at the commuting patterns of recent movers into proximate metropolitan areas. They found that many new residents come from neighbouring metropolitan areas and often still maintained jobs in the original region. People who worked in one metro and lived in another were the glue that linked regions into CSAs and were driving the trend toward megapolitans. LANG and NELSON (2007a) also used commuter data to show that megapolitans maintain economic connectivity at a threshold at half the level the census uses to define CSAs. To qualify as a CSA, two metros must share at least 15% of commuters in a linking county.

Table 2. *Metropolitan hierarchy*

Types	Description	Examples
Metropolitan	Current definition of the Census Bureau	Pittsburgh; Boise
Metroplex	Two or more metropolitan areas that share overlapping suburbs but principal cities do not touch	Dallas–Ft Worth; Washington–Baltimore
Corridor megapolitan	Two or more metropolitan areas with anchor principal cities between 75 and 150 miles apart that form an extended linear urban area along an Interstate	Arizona Sun Corridor (Phoenix–Tucson); SanSac (San Francisco–Sacramento)
Galactic megapolitan	Three or more metropolitan areas with anchor principal cities over 150 miles apart that form an urban web over a broad area that is laced with Interstates	Piedmont; Great Lakes Crescent
Megaplex	Two megapolitan areas that are proximate and occupy common cultural and physical environments and maintain dense business linkages	Megalopolis and Great Lakes Crescent; Sun Corridor and SoCal

In the study by Lang and Nelson, megapolitan areas share at least 15% of new commuters (1995 onward) via a linking county.

The census treats commuting patterns as the key variable in identifying an economically integrated space. It has used this measure since metropolitan areas were first officially defined by the census in 1949. Commuting is taken as a proxy for a host of other variables such as retail and housing markets. For example, if job losses occur in one metropolitan county, then the residents of a neighbouring metro county who commute to these jobs will be impacted. It will also affect their ability to purchase goods and services and afford housing. Commuting, therefore, reveals much larger patterns of economic integration at the megapolitan scale.

At the moment, no megapolitan area meets the 15% threshold to form CSAs. But this research will establish how close many corridor megapolitans come to this commuting level. A quick test of the Phoenix–Tucson megapolitan shows that Pinal County, which is in the southern part of the Phoenix region, had 9% of its workers commuting to Pima County (metropolitan Tucson) in 2000. Therefore, Phoenix–Tucson was just 6 percentage points away from official recognition by the census in 2000 as a CSA. Given the dynamic nature of these metropolitan areas, the Phoenix–Tucson megapolitan area may have already crossed into CSA status, but this status would not be assigned until after the 2010 Census. Other corridor megapolitan areas that could qualify as CSAs 2010 include: Phoenix–Tucson; Los Angeles–San Diego; San Francisco–Sacramento; Washington–Baltimore–Richmond; Tampa–Orlando; New Orleans–Baton Rouge; San Antonio–Austin; and Chicago–Milwaukee.

As Pickard understood in the 1960s, planning for the future involves more than simply projecting population growth. It also means considering what new urban forms might emerge along with metropolitan expansion:

> Regional urbanism will eventually force us to a new level of thinking ... Washington and Baltimore must plan for the eventual binding of their suburban and commuter zones into an interlocking mesh. Dallas and Fort Worth are already meshing, whether willing or not, and Miami and Fort Lauderdale are merged with West Palm Beach into a continuously developed urbanized strip 80 miles in length.
>
> (PICKARD, 1962, p. 3)

The megapolitan geography outlined in the present paper is based on an extrapolation of existing trends. It draws on the US Bureau of Census's metropolitan statistical categories and methods to predict which urban areas will combine into corridor megapolitan areas. By 2020, and perhaps even 2010, metroplexes where the anchor cities lay 100 miles or more apart

will be officially recognized by the US government. As Pickard noted, such an extended metropolis will require new thinking. In 1962, it was shocking to imagine that Dallas and Fort Worth were merging. But this reality is now so mundane that the idea that the two places were ever really separate seems dated. Several decades from now the same might be true of dozens more even larger metropolitan twins. Now is the moment to consider the implications of such a future and plan for a 21st-century megapolitan area that dwarfs previous urban regions in scale and complexity.

A REASSERTION OF MODERNITY?

Metropolitan expansion and regional integration on this scale invites a reconsideration of the traditional separation of urban and regional scales in the analysis and theorizing of spatial organization. It also suggests that one needs to look beyond locally bounded processes of competition for land, ecological processes of congregation and segregation, and broader impulses of postmodernity for an appropriate interpretative framework. In this context, the New Metropolis, along with the evolving network of world cities (TAYLOR, 2004), and increasing evidence of 'glocalization' – the simultaneous shift from the traditional institutions and agencies of governance and development upward to the global economy and downward to non-profits and local actors (SWYNGEDOUW, 2004) – is consistent with the idea of a reassertion of the processes of modernization that are:

> wrestling free from the cocoon in which the managed capitalism and planned modernity of the postwar era had tried to contain them.
>
> (SWYNGEDOUW, 2005, p. 126)

The challenge is to identify new analytic categories that help in understanding and theorizing the spatial outcomes of this second modernity. There is already a debate on typologies of settlement categories (BERUBE et al., 2005; CHAMPION and HUGO, 2004; CROMARTIE and SWANSON, 1996; FREY, 2004), and the US Census Bureau has extended its traditional categories to identify combined statistical areas and micropolitan areas. The census has also tried to capture the changing dynamic of metropolitan area growth by softening its central city definition to include such former suburbs as Scottsdale in Arizona and Thousand Oaks in California (LANG et al., 2005; LANG and LEFURGY, 2006). But this geography may already be dated by the emergence of even larger-scale and networked urban complexes. The US Census Bureau needs to rethink completely some basic dimensions of its categories to show the emergent functional relationships of the new 21st-century metropolis.

In this regard, there is an emerging research agenda focused on the megalopolis. Organizations such as the Lincoln Institute of Land Policy and the Regional Plan

Association are actively promoting scholarship on what they term 'megaregions' (RPA, 2007). Virginia Tech is one of several universities that now conduct studies on what it calls megapolitan areas. Researchers at Georgia Tech and the University of Pennsylvania have examined the Piedmont and Northeast megaregions, while Arizona State University will soon release a report on the Sun Corridor (LANG and HALL, 2008).

CONCLUSION: FORCES CONSTRAINING MEGAPOLITAN EXPANSION

While US megapolitan growth has occurred unabated in the past and will likely continue so for the next several decades, there are some threats on the horizon that might significantly curtail further expansion. The first such threat is climate change – in particular the prospects of sea level rise and severe drought. Places such as South Florida and the Gulf Coast are especially vulnerable to shifts in ocean levels and could see large sections of their built areas flooded. The need to redevelop and secure these areas would draw investment away from the metropolitan edge.

Global warming can also cause drought (INTER-GOVERNMENTAL PANEL ON CLIMATE CHANGE (IPCC), 2007), which would have a major impact on megapolitan growth in the US West. Urban development in the West relies on a series of reservoirs and aqueducts to deliver water to its arid cities. A warming trend could reduce this water supply in two ways. The first is that it will raise elevations in which snow packs occur. This will shrink the run off in the Colorado System, which provides much of the water to the West. Climate shift could also disrupt the much-needed summer monsoon rains in the West, further damping available water. Clearly, careful stewardship of water is needed in order to sustain megapolitan growth in the face of global warming.

Resource constraints may also dampen or at least alter the form that urban growth takes worldwide. The key variable is the cost and availability of energy. There is a growing concern that the world might have reached a point at which half its total oil has been consumed – a point known as 'peak oil' (SIMMONS, 2006). There have been several near-hysterical treatments of this topic. The most notable is by social critic James Howard Kunstler, who practically roots for an enduring energy crisis in the hopes that it kills suburban development in the USA. KUNSTLER (2005), a neo-Malthusian, makes a series of highly mechanistic and technologically deterministic assumptions that do not factor human agency into the equation. By contrast, it is assumed that energy constraints may present some challenges to growth, but that market adjustments and creative adaptation of green technology (e.g. plug-in hybrid cars) will mostly mitigate the impact of reduced hydrocarbon capacity.

More probable forces altering future growth patterns are changes in demographics, taste, and public policy.

NELSON and LANG (2007) show how a combination of preference shifts and an older population will produce a greater share of US housing being built in denser settings. The new market for denser housing development combined with public policies that promote smart growth outcomes such as more traditional neighbourhood form and farm land preservation will reshape the metropolis. But it is assumed that most of the new development will be suburban in location if not conventionally suburban in form. The edges will still grow, yet they might take on a more village-like character than the endless sea of tract-style subdivisions that so dominated the US built environment at the end of the 20th century.

NOTES

1. In the 1960s, Pickard was the Research Director for the Urban Land Institute (ULI) in Washington, DC. Pickard produced his series on urban regions under a grant from the Ford Foundation to study 'dimensions of metropolitanism'. The project produced remarkably accurate projections of American metropolitan growth patterns, including correctly predicting the rise of the Sun Belt, which Pickard referred to as 'exotic' regions because they were so different in look and form from urban areas in the Northeast and Midwest.

2. US counties vary considerably in size. The biggest is San Bernardino County, California, which includes the Mojave Desert and is bigger than many Eastern US states. The smallest county is Arlington, Virginia, across the Potomac River from Washington, DC, which is no bigger than a small city. Mid-range counties run 200–800 square miles in size.

3. A Consolidated Metropolitan Statistical Area is the US Census Bureau's old definition for the largest statistical areas. It was replaced in 2003 by a CSA measure. A CSA is defined as two or more adjacent micro- and metropolitan areas that have an employment interchange measure of at least 15% in 2000.

4. Defined by GARREAU (1991, following LEINBERGER, 1988) as consisting of at least 5 million square feet of office space and 600 000 square feet of retail space. Other criteria include a place with more jobs than people; and a reputation for commerce.

5. A principal city replaces the old central city designation in the US Census Bureau's 2003 redefinition of American urban space. The loss of the word 'central' is significant because it reflects the fact that the major cities in the new metropolis might no longer lie in the centre of the region.

6. DFW was the first 'super regional' airport and has been followed by Atlanta's Hartsfield Airport and Denver International Airport. A little noticed quirk in the accounts of the John F. Kennedy assassination is the fact that Kennedy had actually flown into Dallas Love Field from Fort Worth Airport, hinting that before DFW the region was less fully integrated than today.

7. This information was relayed to Robert Lang by a city planner from Goodyear on 12 March 2006.

REFERENCES

BECK U., BONSS W. and LAU C. (2003) The theory of reflexive modernization, *Theory, Culture, and Society* **20**, 1–33.

BECK U. and WILLMS J. (2003) *Conversations with Ulrich Beck*. Polity, New York, NY.

BERRY B. J. L. (1980) Urbanization and counterurbanization in the United States, *Annals of the American Academy of Political and Social Science* **451**, 13–20.

BERUBE A., KATZ B. and LANG R. (Eds) (2005) *Redefining Urban and Suburban America: Evidence from Census 2000*, Vol. 2. Brookings Institution Press, Washington, DC.

CARBONELL A. and YARO R. D. (2005) American spatial development and the new megalopolis, *Land Lines* **17**, 1–4.

CHAMPION A. and HUGO G. (Eds) (2004) *New Forms of Urbanization: Beyond the Urban–Rural Dichotomy*. Ashgate, Burlington, VT.

CHECKOWAY B. (1980) Large builders, federal housing programs, and postwar suburbanization, *International Journal of Urban and Regional Research* **4**, 21–45.

CROMARTIE J. and SWANSON L. (1996) *Defining Metropolitan Areas and the Rural–Urban Continuum: A Comparison of Statistical Areas Based on County and Sub-County Geography*. ERS Staff Paper No. 9603. Department of Agriculture, Washington, DC.

DEAR M. (Ed.) (2002) *From Chicago to LA: Making Sense of Urban Theory*. Sage, Thousand Oaks, CA.

DEAR M. and FLUSTY S. (1998) Postmodern urbanism, *Annals of the Association of American Geographers* **88**, 50–72.

FISHMAN R. (1987) *Bourgeois Utopias: The Rise and Fall of Suburbia*. Basic, New York, NY.

FREY W. (2003) Melting pot suburbs: a study of suburban diversity, in KATZ B. and LANG R. (Eds) *Redefining Urban and Suburban America: Evidence from Census 2000*, Vol. 1, pp. 155–180. Brookings Institution Press, Washington, DC.

FREY W. (2004) The fading of city-suburb and metro–nonmetro distinctions in the United States, in CHAMPION A. and HUGO G. (Eds) *New Forms of Urbanization: Beyond the Urban–Rural Dichotomy*, pp. 110–131. Ashgate, Aldershot.

FREY W. and BERUBE A. (2003) City families and suburban singles: an emerging household story, in KATZ B. and LANG R. (Eds) *Redefining Urban and Suburban America: Evidence from Census 2000*, Vol. 1. Brookings Institution Press, Washington, DC.

FREY W., WILSON J. H., BERUBE A. and SINGER A. (2004) *Tracking Metropolitan America into the 21st Century: A Field Guide to the New Metropolitan and Micropolitan Definitions*. Brookings Institution Metropolitan Policy Program, Living Cities Census Series (November), Washington, DC.

GARREAU J. (1991) *Edge City: Life on the New Frontier*. Doubleday, New York, NY.

GOTTMANN J. (1961) *Megalopolis: The Urbanized Northeastern Seaboard of the United States*. Twentieth-Century Fund, New York, NY.

GRAHAM S. and MARVIN S. (2001) *Splintering Urbanism*. Routledge, London.

HACKWORTH J. (2005) Emergent urban forms, or emergent post-modernisms? A comparison of large U. S. metropolitan areas, *Urban Geography* **26**, 484–519.

HALL P. (2001) Global city-regions in the 21st century, in SCOTT A. J. (Ed.) *Global City-Regions: Trends, Theory, Policy*, pp. 59–77. Oxford University Press, New York, NY.

HALL P. and PAIN K. (2006) *The Polycentric Metropolis. Learning from Mega-city Regions in Europe*. Earthscan, London.

HARVEY D. (1985) *The Urbanization of Capital: Studies in the History and Theory of Capitalist Urbanization*. Johns Hopkins University Press, Baltimore, MD.

HOYT H. (1939) *The Structure and Growth of Residential Neighborhoods in American Cities*. Federal Housing Administration, US Government Printing Office, Washington, DC.

INTERGOVERNMENTAL PANEL ON CLIMATE CHANGE (IPCC) (2007) *Climate Change 2007*. IPCC, Geneva.

KNOX P. L. (2005) Vulgaria: the re-enchantment of suburbia, *Opolis* **1**, 34–47.

KNOX P. L. (2007) Schlock and awe. the American dream, bought and sold, *American Interest* **2**, 58–67.

KUNSTLER J. H. (2005) *The Long Emergency: Surviving the End of Oil, Climate Change, and Other Converging Catastrophes of the Twenty-first Century*. Atlantic Monthly, New York, NY.

LAKE R. (1995) Spatial fix 2: the sequel, *Urban Geography* **16**, 189–191.

LANG R. (2003) *Edgeless Cities: Exploring the Elusive Metropolis*. Brookings Institution Press, Washington, DC.

LANG R. E., BLAKELY E. J. and GOUGH M. Z. (2005) Keys to the new metropolis: America's big, fast-growing suburban counties, *Journal of the American Planning Association* **71**, 381–391.

LANG R. E. and DHAVALE D. (2005) *Megapolitan Areas: Exploring a New Trans-Metropolitan Geography*. Census Report No. 05:01 (July). Metropolitan Institute at Virginia Tech, Alexandria, VA.

LANG R. E. and DHAVALE D. (2006) Micropolitan America: a brand new geography, in BERUBE A., KATZ B. and LANG R. E. (Eds) *Redefining Cities and Suburbs: Evidence from Census 2000*, Vol. 3, pp. 237–258. Brookings Institution Press, Washington, DC.

LANG R. E. and HALL J. S. (2008) *The Sun Corridor: Planning Arizona's Megapolitan Area*. Morrison Institute of Public Policy, Tempe, AZ.

LANG R. E. and LEFURGY J. L. (2007) *Boomburbs: The Rise of America's Accidental Cities*. Brookings Institution Press, Washington, DC.

LANG R. E. and NELSON A. C. (2007a) *Beyond Metroplex: Examining Commuter Patterns at the Megapolitan Scale*. Lincoln Institute for Land Policy, Cambridge, MA.

LANG R. E. and NELSON A. C. (2007b) America 2040: the rise of the megapolitans, *Planning* **January**, 7–12.

LANG R. E., SANCHEZ T. and LEFURGY J. (2006) *Beyond Edgeless Cities: A New Classification System for Suburban Business Districts*. National Association of Realtors, Washington, DC.

LEINBERGER C. B. (1988) The six types of urban village cores, *Urban Land* **47**, 24–27.

LEWIS P. (1995) The urban invasion of rural America: the emergence of the galactic city, in CASTLE E. N. (Ed.) *The Changing American Countryside: Rural People and Places*, pp. 39–62. University Press of Kansas, Lawrence, KS.

LEWIS P. F. (1983) The galactic metropolis, in PRATT R. H. and MACINKO G. (Eds) *Beyond the Urban Fringe*, pp. 60–91. University of Minnesota Press, Minneapolis, MN.

MORRILL R., CROMARTIE J. and HART G. (1999) Metropolitan, urban and rural commuting areas: toward a better depiction of the United States settlement system, *Urban Studies* **20**, 727–748.

MULLER P. (1976) *The Outer City: Geographical Consequences of the Urbanization of the Suburbs*. Resource Paper. Association of American Geographers, Washington, DC.

NAUGHTON K. (2006) The long and grinding road, *Newsweek* **1 May**, 41–44.

NELSON A. C. (2004) *Toward A New Metropolis: The Opportunity to Rebuild America*. Brookings Institution Metropolitan Policy Program Survey Series (December), Washington, DC.

NELSON A. C. and LANG R. E. (2007) The next 100 million: reshaping America's built environment, *Planning* **January**, 3–6.

PICKARD J. P. (1962) Urban regions of the United States, *Urban Land* **April**, 3–10.

PICKARD J. P. (1966) U.S. urban regions: growth and migration patterns, *Urban Land* **May**, 3–10.

PICKARD J. P. (1970) Is megalopolis inevitable?, *The Futurist* **October**, 151–156.

REGIONAL PLAN ASSOCIATION (RPA) (1967) *The Region's Growth: A Report of the Second Regional Plan*. RPA, New York, NY.

REGIONAL PLAN ASSOCIATION (RPA) (2007) *America 2050: A Prospectus*. RPA, New York, NY.

SASSEN S. (2002) *Global Networks, Linked Cities*. Routledge, New York, NY.

SIMMONS M. R. (2006) *Twilight in the Desert: The Coming Saudi Oil Shock and the World Economy*. Wiley, Hoboken, NJ.

SKLAR D. L. (2003) The next capital of cool, *Irvine World News* **20 February**.

SOJA E. (2002) *Postmetropolis: Critical Studies of Cities and Regions*. Blackwell, Oxford.

SUDJIC D. (1992) *The 100-Mile City*. Harcourt Brace, New York, NY.

SWANSTROM T., CASEY C., FLACK R. and DREIER P. (2004) *Pulling Apart: Economic Segregation Among Suburbs and Central Cities in Major Metropolitan Areas*. Brookings Institution Metropolitan Policy Program, Washington, DC.

SWYNGEDOUW E. (2004) *Glocalizations*. Temple University Press, Philadelphia, PA.

SWYNGEDOUW E. (2005) Exit 'post' – the making of 'glocal' urban modernities, in READ S., ROSEMANN J. and VAN ELDIJK J. (Eds) *Future City*, pp. 125–144. Spon, London.

TAYLOR P. J. (2004) *World City Network: A Global Urban Analysis*. Routledge, New York, NY.

TEAFORD J. (2006) *The Metropolitan Revolution*. Columbia University Press, New York, NY.

THRIFT N. (1996) *Spatial Formations*. Sage, London.

VANCE J. E. JR (1964) *Geography and Urban Evolution in the San Francisco Bay Area*. Institute of Government, University of California, Berkeley, CA.

VANCE J. E. JR (1977) *This Scene of Man: The Role and Structure of the City in the Geography of Western Civilization*. Harper's College Press, New York, NY.

Looking Backward, Looking Forward:
The City Region of the Mid-21st Century

PETER HALL

HALL P. Looking backward, looking forward: the city region of the mid-21st century, *Regional Studies*. Emerging as a serious tool of analysis in the United States around 1950, the city region concept was increasingly applied in a European context after 1980. Since 2000, it has evolved further with recognition of the polycentric Mega-City Region, first recognized in Eastern Asia, but now seen as an emerging urban form both in Europe and the United States. The paper speculates on the main changes that may impact on the growth and development of such complex urban regions in the first half of the 21st century, concluding that achieving the goal of polycentric urban development may prove more complex than at first it may seem.

HALL P. 回顾与前瞻：二十一世纪中叶的城市区域，区域研究。城市区域的概念作为一项重要的分析工具始于上世纪五十年代的美国，并于 1980 年后开始逐渐应用于欧洲背景。自 2000 年以来，随着多中心巨型城市区域的出现 - 这一城市形态首先在东亚萌芽，目前正在欧洲与美国兴起 - 城市区域这一概念也发生了进一步演变。其中的某些主要变化可能会在 21 世纪上半页影响上述复杂城市区域的增长与发展，对此本文进行了一一阐释并得出结论：多中心城市发展目标的实现可能会比人们最初预想的更为复杂。

预测　城市区域　空间发展

HALL P. Une rétrospective et une prospective: la cité-région du milieu du 21ième siècle, *Regional Studies*. La notion de la cité-région, qui a vu le jour comme outil d'analyse important aux Etats-Unis aux alentours de 1950, est appliquée de plus en plus au contexte européen après 1980. Depuis l'an 2000, elle se développe suite à la reconnaissance de la mégacité-région polycentrique. Cette dernière a été reconnue pour la première fois en Asie de l'Est. Actuellement, on la considère comme une forme urbaine naissante à la fois en Europe et aux Etats-Unis. L'article spécule sur les principaux changements qui pourraient avoir un impact sur la croissance et le développement de telles régions urbaines complexes pendant la première moitié du 21ième siècle. En guise de conclusion, on affirme que la réalisation du développement urbain polycentrique pourrait s'avérer plus difficile que l'on n'avait pu prévoir au départ.

HALL P. Blick zurück, Blick nach vorne: die Stadtregion in der Mitte des 21. Jahrhunderts, *Regional Studies*. Das Konzept der Stadtregion entstand in den fünfziger Jahren als ernsthaftes Analyseinstrument in den USA und fand nach 1980 zunehmend auch im europäischen Kontext Anwendung. Seit dem Jahr 2000 hat es sich mit der Anerkennung der polyzentrischen Megastadtregion weiterentwickelt, einer Form, die zuerst in Ostasien anerkannt wurde, aber inzwischen auch in Europa und den USA als entstehende urbane Form angesehen wird. In diesem Beitrag wird über die wichtigsten Veränderungen gemutmaßt, die sich in der ersten Hälfte des 21. Jahrhunderts auf das Wachstum und die Entwicklung dieser komplexen urbanen Regionen auswirken könnten, mit dem Fazit, dass sich die Verwirklichung des Ziels der polyzentrischen Stadtentwicklung als komplexer erweisen könnte als zunächst angenommen.

HALL P. Mirando al pasado, mirando al futuro: la región metropolitana en la mitad del siglo XXI, *Regional Studies*. El concepto de la región metropolitana, que surgió como herramienta seria de análisis en los Estados Unidos alrededor de los cincuenta, se aplicó cada vez más al contexto europeo después de 1980. Desde 2000, ha avanzado aún más con el reconocimiento de la región policéntrica mega-ciudad, reconocida por primera vez al este de Asia pero ahora vista como una forma emergente urbana tanto en Europa como en los Estados Unidos. En este artículo se prevén los principales cambios que podrían repercutir en el crecimiento y el desarrollo de tales regiones urbanas complejas en la primera mitad del siglo XXI, concluyendo que lograr el objetivo de desarrollo urbano policéntrico podría ser más complejo que lo que podría parecer en un primer momento.

INTRODUCTION

This paper serves two purposes. First, taking up themes in the Editorial Introduction, it analyses the concept of the city region in the academic and professional literature since its first emergence in the mid-20th century and its evolution into the 'Mega-City Region' concept in the first years of the 21st century. The city region concept has hugely changed the ways in which urban analysts seek to understand the changing spatial dynamics of urban areas; the Mega-City Region concept is about to have equally momentous intellectual implications. This first section is highly technical and analytical. Second, using this dual analytic framework, it speculates on the likely further development of the city region over approximately the first half of the new century. This second section, quite deliberately, is speculative, drawing in empirical work where possible, going beyond it where necessary. No attempt is made to introduce any formal forecasting methods, since the necessary research is not available. Rather, the argument will be developed that long-term spatial trends have proved fairly robust and are likely to continue thus in the future. This gives reasonable certainty, which is all that can be expected, that one can project these trends to produce a probable picture of the mid-21st-century city region.

Throughout the paper, the primary emphasis is on trends in Europe, because of the relative richness of recent research on the European city region. However, parallels will be made with other highly developed and highly urbanized regions of the world: North America and Pacific Asia. Incidental attention will also be paid to the developing economies.

FROM CITY REGION TO MEGA-CITY REGION

The concept of a city region first appears in the classic work of Patrick Geddes, *Cities in Evolution* (GEDDES, 1915). In it, Geddes argued that in certain regions of the world – particularly Europe and North America – individual cities and towns were already coagulating into so-called *conurbations*. It is, however, clear from Geddes' detailed descriptions that he saw this as a purely physical phenomenon. This concept was later adopted officially by the United Kingdom (in the Census definitions of conurbations), and in France (the similar concept of the *agglomeration urbaine*). In contrast, the modern concept of the city region is specifically not defined in physical or morphological terms; neither are such regions based on administrative units, though administrative units must usually be used to define them. Rather, they are defined on the basis of what Manuel Castells has called the 'Space of Flows': flows of people, information, or goods, on a *regular* basis, for instance daily commuting, or weekly shopping or reading a local paper (CASTELLS, 1989). They are thus Functional Urban Regions (FURs).

The best-known example of such a system of regions is the American Metropolitan Statistical Area (MSA): a functionally defined urban region that extends beyond the physically built-up area to encompass all the areas that have regular daily relationships with a core city. This originated in official nomenclature in 1949, in the Standard Metropolitan Area (SMA; later, in 1959, the Standard Metropolitan Statistical Area (SMSA)); then, in 1983, the Metropolitan Statistical Area (MSA); then, in 1990, the Metropolitan Area (MA), and so widely accepted there as a statistical base; finally, in 2000, as the Core Based Statistical Area (CBSA), including Metropolitan and (a new concept) Micropolitan Statistical Areas. However, these are variants on a common concept which has remained the same for over half a century. In its latest (2000) manifestation, a Core Based Metropolitan (or Micropolitan) Statistical Area consists of the following:

- A *core area* containing a substantial population nucleus.
- Plus *adjacent communities* having *a high degree of social and economic integration* with that core.
- And comprising *one or more entire counties*.

Further:

- Each CBSA must contain at least one urban area of 10 000 or more population.
- Each Metropolitan Statistical Area must contain at least one urbanized area of 50 000 or more inhabitants.
- Each Micropolitan Statistical Area must have at least one urban cluster of at least 10 000 but less than 50 000 population.
- The county (or counties) in which at least 50% of the population resides within urban areas of 10 000 or more population, or that contain at least 5000 people residing within a single urban area of 10 000 or more population, is the *Central County* (Counties).
- Additional *outlying counties* are included in the CBSA if they meet specified requirements of commuting to or from the central counties.

New England has no counties, so here, a similar set of areas is developed, using cities and towns: New England City and Town Areas (NECTAs)

This produces a total (at the last redefinition) of 362 Metropolitan Statistical Areas and 560 Micropolitan Statistical Areas. Fig. 1 shows the MSAs at this last (2000) revision.

Extending the Metropolitan Area concept to Europe

As long ago as 1968, work at the London School of Economics for the Royal Commission on Local Government in England (the Redcliffe–Maud Commission) adopted the American Metropolitan Area concept and applied it to South East England (ROYAL COMMISSION ON LOCAL GOVERNMENT IN ENGLAND, 1968). But, applied to the actual task of reorganizing local government, it proved somewhat of a Procrustean Bed: fitting reasonably well in the shire counties of midland England, it was less satisfactory in less densely populated areas such as East Anglia, where the FUR does not produce a sufficiently large unit in terms of population to be efficient in providing local government services (HALL, 1969). However, the concept was then applied nationally in studies that led in 1973 to publication in the book *The Containment of Urban England* (HALL *et al.*, 1973). There, too, it

gave good results across much of the country but less satisfactory results in sparsely populated rural areas like Devon and Cornwall or the Lake District.

In 1980, Hall and Hay extended the concept to Europe. They defined and analysed data for a set of 539 uniform Functional Urban Regions (FURs) in Western Europe, and a decade later a larger follow-up study by Cheshire and Hay, funded by the European Commission, updated and deepened the work for a set of 229 larger FURS in the then twelve-Member European Community area, and conducted a further detailed analysis of a subset of 53 FURS (HALL and HAY, 1980; CHESHIRE and HAY, 1989).

This and subsequent work (CHESHIRE, 1995, 1999; CHESHIRE and CARBONARO, 1996; MAGRINI, 1999), though updating the data base from the 1990 Census round, had to rely on the original FUR definitions based on data from the 1970 Census round or nearest equivalent. In consequence, over time the definitions became in many cases out of date and misleading. This was demonstrated in the work of the GEMACA group (INSTITUT D'AMÉNAGEMENT ET D'URBANISME DE LA RÉGION ILE DE FRANCE (IAURIF), 1996), which showed, for example, that while the boundaries of the Paris urban region had remained relatively stable to 1991, those of London had expanded

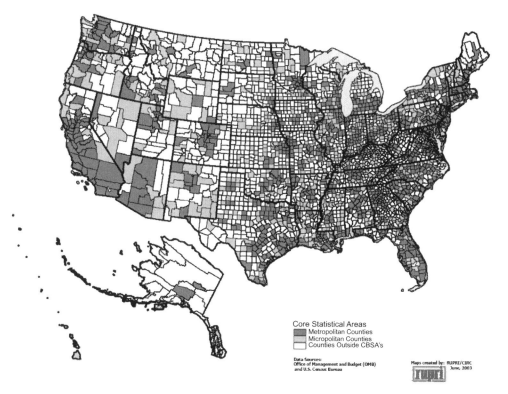

Fig. 1. US core-based statistical areas, 2000

substantially. In the United States, the equivalent MSAs are regularly redefined on the basis of the latest Census and other data.

The Mega-City Region: a new spatial concept

This concept was taken up and further adapted in the POLYNET study (HALL and PAIN, 2006). POLYNET, however, seeks to analyse a new urban phenomenon, in course of formation in the most highly urbanized parts of the world: the *Mega-City Region*. The term comes from Eastern Asia, where it was originally applied to areas like the Pearl River Delta and Yangtze River Delta regions of China, the Tokaido (Tokyo−Osaka) corridor in Japan, and Greater Jakarta (LIN and MA, 1994; McGEE and ROBINSON, 1995; SIT and YANG, 1997; HALL, 1999). It is a new form: a series of anything between twenty and fifty cities and towns, physically separate but functionally networked, clustered around one or more larger central cities, and drawing economic strength from a new functional division of labour. These places exist both as separate entities, in which most residents work locally and most workers are local residents, and as parts of a wider functional urban region connected by dense flows of people and information along motorways, high-speed rail lines, and telecommunications cables. It is no exaggeration to say that this was the emerging urban form at the start of the 21st century.

But Mega-City Regions are not exclusively an Asian phenomenon. Recent American work has identified ten 'megalopolitan areas' housing 197 million people, almost 68% of the entire US population (LANG and DHAVALE, 2005; SHORT, 2007; LANG and KNOX, in this issue). Mega-City Regions exist also in Europe. The outstanding European examples, analysed in the comparative POLYNET study (HALL and PAIN, 2006), are the Greater South East region around London, Central Belgium, Dutch Randstad, RhineRuhr and Rhine-Main in Germany, and Northern Switzerland. But many other parts of Europe have developed corridors of intense urbanization along major transport spines, as in the Rhône Valley south of Lyon (France), or the Emilia-Romagna region of Italy. In a few cases (as in South East England) planning policy has played a conscious role in this; elsewhere, again, it seems to have been a spontaneous evolution.

The expression 'Mega-City' may recall the earlier term coined by Jean Gottmann in his book *Megalopolis: The Urbanized Northeastern Seaboard of the United States* (GOTTMANN, 1961). But there is a subtle distinction. As defined by Gottmann fully in his celebrated 1961 study of the Boston-to-Washington corridor, Megalopolis was:

> an almost continuous stretch of urban and suburban areas from southern New Hampshire to northern Virginia and from the Atlantic shore to the Appalachian foothills.
>
> (GOTTMANN, 1961, p. 3)

That suggested a *physical* definition, like that of Geddes earlier: a continuously urbanized area. In response to criticism, Gottmann made it clear that he meant something different: Megalopolis was 'the cradle of a new order in the organization of inhabited space' (GOTTMANN, 1961, p. 9), defined in terms of Standard Metropolitan Statistical Areas; in other words a *functional* definition.

The Mega-City Region arises from a process of extremely long-distance deconcentration from one or more major cities stretching up to 150 kilometres from the centre, with local concentrations of employment surrounded by overlapping commuter fields, and served mainly by the private car. The precise spatial details vary from country to country according to culture and planning regime: in the United States, lower-density and less regulated with 'Edge Cities' or 'New Downtowns' on greenfield sites, exclusively accessed by the private car; in Europe, medium-density, regulated through green belts and other constraints, and centred on medium-sized country market towns or planned new towns (GARREAU, 1991; SCOTT, 2001).

The POLYNET study analysed and compared the functioning of eight such regions in Europe:

- *South East England*, where London is now the centre of a system of some thirty to forty centres within a 150-kilometre radius.
- *Belgian Central Cities* comprising Brussels and a surrounding ring of large- and medium-sized cities, with a high degree of interdependence and a total population of approximately 7 million.
- *The Randstad* in the Netherlands, encompassing the cities of Amsterdam, The Hague, Rotterdam and Utrecht, but now extending outwards to include the cities of Almere, Amersfoort and Breda.
- *RhineRuhr* is one of the world's largest polycentric Mega-City Regions, embracing thirty to forty towns and cities with a total population of some 10 million people, in this case with no obvious 'core city'.
- *The Rhine-Main region* of Germany, encompassing core cities of Frankfurt am Main, Wiesbaden, Mainz, and Offenbach, but extending widely outwards as far as Limburg in the north, Aschaffenburg in the east, Darmstadt in the south, and Bad Kreuznach in the west.
- *The European Metropolitan Region (EMR) Northern Switzerland*, an incipient 'Mega-City Region' extending in discontinuous linear pattern from Zürich and its region westwards towards Basel.
- *Greater Dublin*, within a 50−60-kilometre radius, but particularly northward along the Dublin−Belfast corridor.
- The *Paris Region* represents a special case: through the 1965 Schéma Directeur, outward decentralization pressures have been accommodated in new city

concentrations within the agglomeration, with little impact on surrounding rural areas. But recent research shows that the region's economic core is not the historic Ville de Paris, but a 'Golden Triangle' bounded by the city's western *arrondissements*; La Défense; and the suburbs of Boulogne–Billancourt and Issy-les-Moulineaux (BECKOUCHE, 1999, HALBERT, 2002a, 2002b).

In the POLYNET study, Mega-City Regions are defined as aggregations of smaller constituent city regions: Functional Urban Regions (FURs). These comprise a *core* defined in terms of employment size and density, and a *ring* defined in terms of regular daily journeys (commuting) to the core; the concept is very similar to the Metropolitan Statistical Area (MSA) widely employed in the United States Census and other sources, and used by Lang and Knox as building blocks. The *Mega-City Region* is then defined in terms of contiguous FURs, and is thus similar to the so-called Consolidated Metropolitan Statistical Area (CMSA) used in the United States. Contiguity is the sole criterion. There may be functional relations (cross-commuting) between the constituent FURs, or there may not; this would emerge only in the course of the analysis. To be more specific:

- *Functional Urban Regions (FURs)*: comprise a *core* defined in terms of employment size and density, and a *ring* defined in terms of regular daily journeys (commuting) to the core. Cores are defined in terms of Nomenclature des Unités Territoriales Statistiques (NUTS) 5 units (the smallest units for which published data are generally available), on the basis of: seven or more workers per hectare, and a minimum of 20 000 workers in either single NUTS 5 unit or in contiguous NUTS 5 units. Rings also use NUTS 5 units, where possible, and are defined on the basis of 10% or more of the residentially based workforce commuting daily to the core.[1] Where they commute to more than one core, they are allocated to the core to which most commuters go.
- *The Mega-City Region (MCR)*: these are defined in terms of contiguous FURs, and thus similar to the so-called Consolidated Metropolitan Statistical Areas (CMSAs) used in the United States.

The underlying hypothesis of the POLYNET study was that falling costs of transportation and (more particularly) communication, combined with new informational agglomeration economies, lead to the emergence of a highly complex 'space of flows' (CASTELLS, 1989, p. 344) within the 'Mega-City Region': there is a pervasive geographical deconcentration within these regions, from the heavily urbanized areas which form their cores, including most of the capital cities of North West Europe (London, Paris, Brussels), with the most severe losses occurring where urban decentralization is reinforced by industrial decline and the loss of port activities. The

gainers are smaller metropolitan areas within the outer parts of the same regions, which have been among the fastest-growing urban areas in Europe; in the very largest and densest urban regions (South East England, Dutch Randstad), there is a process of long-distance relative deconcentration from the largest central cities to wide rings of medium-sized cities in the surrounding rural areas.

This process of 'concentrated deconcentration' generates a progressive redistribution of functions: in the core city or cities, continuing concentration of higher-order service functions (financial and business services, design services, media, higher education, health, and so on); in secondary cities, growth of more routine functions (research and development, high-technology manufacturing; niche roles, such as university cities) (LLEWELYN-DAVIES *et al.*, 1996). The entire complex, however, achieves major agglomeration economies through clustering of activities, not in any one centre, but in a complex of centres with some degree of functional differentiation between them.

These trends reflect underlying economic realities. Globalization and the shift to the informational economy give special value to large cities as centres for efficient face-to-face information exchange. They are the locations of the major hub airports and the high-speed train stations; they also are hubs for commuter traffic. But they also experience some economic disadvantages: high rents, congestion, pollution, the costs of attracting middle- and junior-level staff. So certain activities ('back offices', research and development) tend to migrate outwards: to corridors leading to the airports, to suburban train stations, to country towns in the surrounding ring. Paradoxically, the more these central core cities succeed in the global economy, the more they will tend to irrigate the growth of other cities in their localities. Hence, logically, the development of polycentric Mega-City Regions around these principal cities.

However, the critical central feature of all such complexes is that their constituent parts are linked by flows: of people, of goods and – increasingly important – of information. The central feature of the POLYNET research was its attempt to measure and evaluate information flows in the knowledge economy – specifically, in the Advanced Producer Services (APS) – both through telecommunications and face-to-face, and both internal (node to node) and external. How are these flows of information reshaping relationships within these Mega-City Regions? In particular, are functional relationships between top-level and other centres changing? To what extent are these other centres dependent on concentrations of service industries in the top-level core cities? How far do lower-level centres in each region connect directly with similar places in other regions, bypassing the top cities? How do these flows differ as between polycentric Mega-City Regions (like the Dutch Randstad or RhineRuhr) and more 'monocentric' regions like Paris?

This is intrinsically difficult, because some of the most significant information – for instance, on telephone or email traffic – is commercially sensitive. In any case, it will tell us only about the sizes of the flows, not their content or, most critically, their quality. For this reason, quantitative data need to be supplemented and deepened by qualitative information derived from interviews with the agents who create the flows: a time-consuming and difficult research task, dependent on fine judgement (PAIN and HALL, 2007).

FORECASTING THE FUTURE CITY REGION

The question logically arises: how far are these deep-seated geographical processes likely to change during the coming half-century? Are there underlying structural changes – technological, economic, social, cultural – that could cause a basic disjuncture, a breach, with recent past trends? Or, in contrast, are there features that could actually exacerbate the processes, speeding them up?

Experience of previous exercises in forecasting (WELLS, 1902; HALL, 1963, 1977) suggests that forecasting tends to consist of two elements, one of which is relatively easy because it depends on long-term trends that are only occasionally shaken up by wars and other disasters, the other part of which is fundamentally difficult because it focuses on the very few key developments that will prove to change many if not most of the assumptions. These may be scientific, like the Human Genome project and its outcomes, which are still unfolding; technical, like the personal computer of 1976–1881 and the World Wide Web of 1989–1992; they may also be political, like the Russian revolutions of 1917 and 1990, or the establishment of the European Union in 1957, which change the entire shape of world affairs. They are inherently difficult to predict. John D. Barrow, Professor of Mathematical Sciences at the University of Cambridge, reminds us that, looking back fifty years:

> None of the greatest discoveries in the astronomical sciences were foreseen. ... Perhaps scientists are as blinkered as the politicians and economists who failed to foresee the fall of the Iron Curtain and the climatic implications of industrialisation. ... Nothing truly revolutionary is ever predicted because that is what makes it revolutionary.
>
> (BARROW, 2006, p. 36)

However, occasionally forecasters have achieved singular successes by imaginatively seizing upon key trends at their very outset. At the beginning of the 20th century, in a non-fiction work titled *Anticipations of the Reaction of Mechanical and Scientific Progress Upon Human Life and Thought* (1902), H. G. WELLS foresaw both the coming of the motorways and their impact on space and location in Britain. All of the southern half of the country, he said, would become a single urban region, tied together by the motorways and by other 'nervous connections'. He did not get every particular right: he forecast pneumatic parcels tubes, instead we have different 'nervous connections' in the form of fax and electronic mail. But he went on to argue that without the competition of motor traffic, 'the existing type of railways' would be unlikely to 'attempt any very fundamental change in the direction of greater speed or facility'. A century later, all over Europe and in parts of Pacific Asia, railway systems have achieved an extraordinary renaissance in the form of high-speed trains: the Japanese Shinkansen, the French TGV, the British Inter-City 125s, the Italian Direttisima. During the 21st century, they promise to do what motorways failed to do: to shrink geographical space, and thus tie not only half of Britain, but also much of Europe, into a single polycentric Megalopolis.

From this discussion, one can recast the argument of the second half of the paper. There are basic parameters, for the most part reflecting long and deep structural trends, which are reasonably predictable. There is the possibility of a drastic event, whether natural or triggered by human action – global conflict, a pandemic – but the likelihood of this is impossible to predict. Relatedly, there is the possibility of a parametric shift because of a trend that results in a step function: over the next half century, the implications of global warming represent a probable example.

BASIC PARAMETERS

Environment

The strong scientific consensus is that global warming will bring a shift in climate, making the climate of Southern England or the Netherlands rather like that of Bordeaux today, or that of Northern Norway like that of Western Europe. That would be within the span of historic variation; historical geographers tell us that was the position about the time of the Crusades (11th–13th centuries). This will change lifestyles, and may well speed up the processes of mass migration, increasing pressures to move out of a desiccating Africa into a temperate Western Europe. But it will be accompanied by a rise in sea level that will, by 2050, begin to threaten many large coastal areas – London, the Dutch Randstad, New York, Tokyo, and many others – with inundation. There are possible ways of managing such a sea rise actively being explored in the Netherlands: they are drastic, involving the deliberate flooding of substantial areas which would effectively have to be depopulated (KOLBERT, 2006). It seems likely that Dutch methods will be generally adopted in the low-lying North Sea areas where three of the Mega-City Regions of North West Europe are found. This has implications for the future outward expansion of these regions, for instance, the Thames Gateway corridor east of London. It is likely to divert the bulk of the expansion into higher-lying areas, but it is unlikely to curb their growth overall.

Demography

One difficult question is the possibility of an extraordinary – and, therefore, difficult-to-predict – life-changing event such as a new plague or a new strain of drug-resistant disease, marking a return to the days before antibiotics and penicillin. Avian influenza, mutating to humans, is presently the most obvious. There could be discoveries of new toxins with serious effects on health, long after they had taken effect on a mass scale (BLANC, 2006).

More likely, almost to the point of certainty, is that – as an outcome of the Human Genome project and its continuation – there will be quantum jumps in our ability to treat certain kinds of disease, above all cancers, over and above the steady improvements that have been based on our current medical knowledge. Already, over the last twenty years of the 20th century, one begins to see significant attacks on the big killers such as coronary disease, where the statins are having a major effect, and various kinds of cancer – for instance, brachytherapy for prostrate cancer, the main cause of death for elderly men, followed by easily available drug treatments. The consequence could be an appreciable lengthening of the life span (JHA, 2006). Francis Collins, Director of the United States National Human Genome Project, has predicted that:

> It is possible that half-a-century from now, the most urgent question facing our society will not be 'How long can humans live?' but 'How long do we want to live?'
>
> (COLLINS 2006, p. 36)

A first impact of these medical improvements, if indeed they transpire, would be on current population projections, which indicate substantial declines in the populations of a number of European countries (HALL and PFEIFFER, 2000). In Europe, fertility in many countries and regions is already well below replacement levels and populations are firmly projected to begin to fall: between 2005 and 2050, in Italy from 57.5 million to 48 million, in Germany from 83 million to 76 million, and across the European Union from 455 million to 432 million. In most European countries the rate of immigration necessary to counteract these trends, several million a year into the major European countries, is not conceivable economically or socially – though both the United Kingdom and Spain have seen rapid immigration from within the European Union, taking the Spanish population from 40 million to 47 million in only eight years from 2000 to 2008. With these notable exceptions, Europe faces the prospect of shrinking nations and shrinking cities, with severe consequences for rising costs of social services and falling tax revenues to pay for them. The same transition will occur drastically in China after 2015, when the working-age population will start to fall and the numbers of old people will start to rise: from 38% in 2005 to 58% in 2024, when fully three-quarters of all households will be childless; the total population will begin to decline rapidly from 2019.

Medical advances may slow the projected rate of decline, but they are unlikely to reverse it in many European countries. In the process, they will generate a second consequence: the ageing of populations. In Italy, where by 2025 the median age will already be fifty, between 2005 and 2050 the working-age population is projected to fall by 20% and the numbers of old people (sixty-five or older) to rise by 44%, doubling the dependency ratio (the numbers of old people to those of working age) from 32% to 67% in less than half a century. The position for Spain is even more drastic, for the entire European Union only slightly less so. (The rate of immigration necessary to counteract these trends, several million a year into the major European countries, is not conceivable economically or socially.) This will further worsen the burden of dependency, through an increase in the 'old old', the really dependent and expensive-to-treat old. One obvious answer, adopted fully by the United States and more tentatively by the United Kingdom, is to raise and eventually abolish the mandatory retirement age, effectively releasing the increasingly active 'young old' to share the burden of catering for the 'old old'. At the same time, there is likely to be considerable geographical resorting of the population by age. Most notable, and already observable, is the migration of older retired people to areas of more favourable climate and lower living costs, as on the Mediterranean coast of Europe or the desert states of the United States, where they tend to form age-segregated colonies. This has been a major factor in the growth of extended Mega-City Regions like Phoenix (Arizona) or Las Vegas (Nevada) or the Texas Urban Triangle (Dallas–Fort Worth–Houston–Austin–San Antonio), which have enjoyed phenomenal rates of growth through the 1980s and 1990s – albeit somewhat restrained by the recession of 2007–2008 (KNOX, 2008; NEUMAN and BRIGHT, 2008).

Sociology, culture

Immigration, associated with the huge migration pressures that will be created along Europe's southern and eastern flanks, will almost certainly continue to bring flows of people, whether legal or semi-legally tolerated or illegal, into the neighbouring areas of low increase – above all the urban areas of Southern, Western and Central Europe. The population of Spain increased by 5 million between 2000 and 2007, all due to immigration, mainly of young men from Africa and Eastern Europe. The vast majority of these immigrants have gone into the major cities – London, Paris, Amsterdam, Madrid, New York, Miami, Los Angeles, Toronto, Vancouver – where they have already changed the overall ethnic and cultural composition of the population. Although diversity will increase almost everywhere, it will take an extreme form in these cities, with minorities forming a majority of populations: a position already being reached in some of them by the early 21st century.

The question then is whether cities can integrate these increasingly diverse populations. Exiling ethnic–cultural groups to live segregated from the mainstream in 1960s high-rise suburbs, where increasingly no one with a choice is willing to live, can prove a recipe for social disaster, as the French experience has so closely shown. The critical index here is the degree of such segregation, which we should be measuring across cities. New research in the United Kingdom gives encouraging news: between 1991 and 2002, in forty-eight out of fifty-six major urban areas in England, segregation declined, in six others it increased marginally, and in one of the two remaining ones the numbers were negligible anyway (UK OFFICE OF THE DEPUTY PRIME MINISTER (ODPM), 2006, p. 153). However, recent experience in the United Kingdom does not give confidence that this will axiomatically lead to a reduction in extremism.

Urban educational systems will play a crucial role here, integrating successive generations of immigrant children. As emphasized by Amartya Sen (SEN, 2006), it will prove commonplace to adopt a double or a treble identity: we will feel ourselves both Dutch, or British, or French (and for that matter citizens of Rotterdam or Londoners or Parisians) and simultaneously European. But this could be compromised if urban schools become ethnically and culturally segregated, as appears to be happening in some European cities. These factors are relevant because the degree of integration of urban societies will in part determine the rate of out-migration from them into surrounding rural areas, with significant outcomes for urban form and structure. Simultaneously with immigration from outside, as is already observable in European as well as American cities, there is a large compensating out-migration of older-settled, locally born groups including the children of earlier generations of immigrants. The destinations will include distant climatically favoured regions, but also the outermost parts of the Mega-City Regions of which these cities form the centres. Thus, there are likely to be increasing socio-cultural distinctions and divisions within these regions, as well as between them and the rest of their national territories.

Technology

The most important technological developments, as in the recent past, will occur in the field of Information and Communication Technology (ICT). Here the problem is to estimate the likelihood of really fundamental, or pervasive, technological change akin to the development of the integrated circuit or the internet. Two in particular would appear to promise fundamental

prizes but to be highly uncertain: the development of direct man–machine interface ('Google in the Head'), representing a fundamental prosthetic aid to the human brain, and the creation of realistic three-dimensional synthetic environments (artificial experiences). Both would depend on fundamental scientific advances in physics and biology, not presently on the radar. But there are small-scale signs – for instance, in the ability of computers to help remedy sensory loss – which suggest possible ways forward. Ray Kurzweil, a member of an eighteen-strong team of scientists, entrepreneurs, and thinkers convened by the United States National Academy of Engineering (NAE) to report to the 2008 American Association for the Advancement of Science (AAAS) annual meeting in Boston, Massachusetts, confidently forecast that:

> Intelligent nanorobots will be deeply integrated in the environment, our bodies and our brains, providing vastly extended longevity, full-immersion virtual reality incorporating all of the senses . . . and enhanced human intelligence.
> (JHA, 2008)

Other experts appear more doubtful.

The significance of these advances, as with those that have recently occurred, lies in their impact on the pattern of human communication, above all the potential for substituting for face-to-face interaction. This is further discussed below.

Economy

The long process of economic and social change in progress for much of the last fifty years, certainly for the last thirty years, can reasonably be expected to continue. Its main components are the globalization of the economy, the transition from a manufacturing to an informational mode of production, the feminization of the labour force, the destructuring of firms and the development of flexible specialization, and the critical importance of both education and training for entry into the labour force. They are so commonplace that no extended discussion is needed. What is important, as elsewhere in this exercise, is to trace their consequences forward, particularly for the spatial organization of economic activity.

Globalization and deindustrialization are an accomplished fact, converting national economies in the advanced urbanized world from ones with a sizeable manufacturing sector to one in which manufacturing occupies niche markets and the majority of the workforce earns a living by trading in information of one kind or another. There are now parallel pressures both to offshore service production and to substitute capital for labour in the informational services, reducing the demand for routine clerical labour. It will equally affect education, rendering much of the present teaching force redundant, though it should allow some of them to retrain to do the new jobs, which are producing the new programmes and offering personal interaction with students, both on-line and face-to-face.

There are indications of fundamental changes in urban employment patterns, with a 'disappearing middle' of junior and middle-level clerical jobs, many occupied by women who in some cases have become the sole breadwinners in their households, and increasing numbers of highly paid jobs in business services, including not only the commercially related ones such as law and accountancy and public relations, but also in the design professions like architecture, engineering and planning, fashion and industrial design; in high-level command and control functions; in the creative and cultural industries, ranging from live performing arts though galleries and museums to the print and electronic media; in education and research, health services for an ageing and health-conscious population, and tourism of both the business and leisure forms. They will be disproportionately located in the cities, even in the hearts of the cities. There will also be increasing numbers of unskilled minimum-wage jobs in the personal service sector, thus perpetrating and intensifying the unequal income distribution already evident, especially in major cities; research on London suggests that there the top 10% of the income distribution are increasing their incomes much more rapidly than the rest, and so are drawing steadily away from the mean (BUCK *et al.* 2002).

A continuing question is the future of that section of the population – estimated as between 15% and 20% of the potential workforce – who so lack basic education that they become effectively unemployable. Here, attitudes play a major role: recent research in the United Kingdom shows that white boys from traditional blue-collar backgrounds are more prone to drop out of education than more highly motivated ethnic minorities (UK CABINET OFFICE, SOCIAL EXCLUSION TASK FORCE, 2008). This is compounded by educational ghettoization: as schools compete more and more as rival consumer products, even encouraged to do so by policy (as in the United Kingdom), some of them are bound to fail and to start servicing only an extremely deprived and underperforming catchment area. Statistical evidence from England shows clearly that this educational apartheid is occurring particularly in the big cities where good schools compete to attract the best students (SUTTON TRUST, 2005; HIGHER EDUCATION FOUNDING COUNCIL FOR ENGLAND (HEFCE), 2007; DORLING *et al.*, 2007). And this means that family background is compounded by neighbourhood effects, as working-class children, especially boys, become locked into a culture of low aspiration and low achievement (UK CABINET OFFICE, SOCIAL EXCLUSION TASK FORCE, 2008). One challenge for planning will be to find ways of breaking up and dispersing such islands of concentrated deprivation. This is relevant because such areas generate very negative perceptions, helping to precipitate urban outflows from inner city areas to more affluent, increasingly distant, suburbs.

Consumption

Though such income inequalities are likely to persist, long-term trends suggest that across the developed world average incomes could increase three to four times by 2050. Assuming that consumption patterns and preferences remain constant, the average household of 2050 would then live like the very rich of 2000, with a large house or apartment, at least one car for every adult, and at least one second home, perhaps in some exotic and distant place.

The complication is that consumption patterns will have been altered by technology, in ways that cannot easily be foreseen. An unimaginable wealth of education and entertainment will come directly into the home at the touch of a button. Providing such value-added services will become a major industry in its own right. But all this electronic information is highly unlikely to reduce the need for travel, for precisely the same reasons as suggested above for production. If someone watches an electronic opera or rock concert, that creates a desire to see and hear the live performance; buyers of Microsoft's computerized art gallery will develop an irresistible desire to see the originals in the Louvre or the Uffizi. As in production, so in consumption, the information technology only in part substitutes for face-to-face; in part, it actually generates new demands for face-to-face. The spatial implication is that the growth of remote electronic consumption will do nothing to reduce the demand for direct consumption of cultural products, which are disproportionately concentrated in the largest (and oldest) cities. In Europe, urban tourism accounts for 35% of international travel, with an annual average growth of 4% over the last ten years; according to the European Travel Monitor (ETM), urban tourism has a market share of 18%, which is growing Europe-wide (EUROPEAN COMMISSION, 2000). Christopher Law shows that of more than thirty leading urban tourist destinations worldwide, virtually all are in old-established major cities, half of them in Europe (LAW, 2001, p. 10). Since this increases the demands on central urban spaces, the likelihood is increased pressure on other activities (including permanent residences) to relocate to lower-cost peripheral locations.

IMPLICATIONS FOR CITY REGIONS: INFORMATION TECHNOLOGY AND FACE-TO-FACE COMMUNICATION

Thus, a critical question, whether in the production or the consumption sphere, is the likely impact of e-communication on the need for direct face-to-face experience. Frances Cairncross's book *The Death of Distance: How the Communications Revolution Will Change Our Lives* (CAIRNCROSS, 1997) does not mean the death of the city: the most critical exchange of information still occurs through face-to-face contact, as in conferences (HALL, 2003). The people who market e-communication like to create a myth that we can now work anywhere. But this proves to be untrue in practice. Stephen Graham and Simon Marvin in their book *Telecommunications and the City: Electronic Spaces, Urban Places* (1996) show that for France, over a period of 150 years from 1830 to 1980, as telecommunication traffic grew, so did personal traffic grow in the same proportion (GRAHAM and MARVIN, 1996, p. 262). That would be surely true, if similar data were available intercontinentally, internationally, or within another country: personal transport increases with electronic communication. Potentially, electronic services will reduce both the need and the desire to travel, and this almost certainly will mean that many people no longer need to work a five-day week or whatever the 2050 equivalent will be. We can already see this in the work patterns of free professionals like university teachers or consultants, who have become nomadic workers. And, as large corporations increasingly become virtual, subcontracting out many of their functions to specialist providers and providing hot-desk space for a residual peripatetic workforce, this process must grow exponentially. Already, in 2009 the typical professional worker might start the day with a couple of hours at home, go into a local hot-desk office for a meeting – or might equally well meet in a rented hotel suite, go on by train or air for a similar meeting and dinner in Europe, and then retire into a hotel room that is fitted up as a home office, from which he or she can communicate freely by any kind of information technology including videophone and instant access to any kind of information. But this will become more and more commonplace as more people join the informational class.

A paradox thus arises. Though the information technology revolution will potentially reduce the need and desire for face-to-face contact, in practice it is likely to produce the reverse: the growth in information exchange will bring with it a necessity for more and more face-to-face. Therefore, a key question is where this activity will happen. The answer lies in the locational demands of the advanced business services which dominate the 21st-century economy. These are part of Manuel Castells's 'space of flows' (CASTELLS, 1989, 1996). In work comparing London, Paris, New York and Tokyo (LLEWELYN-DAVIES *et al.*, 1996), we distinguished four key sectors of the metropolitan economy: Finance and Business, Power and Influence (Government and Corporate Headquarters), Tourism, and Creative and Cultural Industries; many key activities (hotels, restaurants; museums, art galleries; the media) occupy the interstices between these four sectors. And the study showed that although some activities move out, other activities grow to take their place (Figs 2a and 2b). Key global cities are now growing so remarkably because of the concentration in them of the key economic drivers: not merely in the advanced producer services, but also advanced consumer services (conferences; cultural tourism) which in practice are often difficult to distinguish.

We may make such face-to-face encounters in traditional city centres, or in edge city centres. All the evidence, even from high priests of cyberspace like Bill Gates or Bill Mitchell of MIT (GATES, 1995; MITCHELL, 1995), suggests that city centres will retain their unique role in providing the most efficient locations for much of this activity, simply because of the accumulated weight of interrelated functions that have historically accrued there, and because radially oriented transport systems focus on them. Again, limited empirical evidence suggests that the hierarchy of cities in Europe has not changed only in one or two significant respects (notably, the rise of Madrid) in the last forty years; as suggested below,

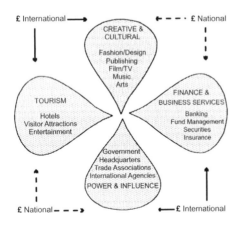

Fig. 2a. *Four key sectors in world cities*
Source: LLEWELYN-DAVIES *et al.* (1996)

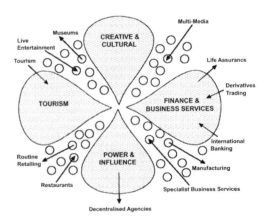

Fig. 2b. *Four key sectors in world cities: interstitial activities and trends*
Source: LLEWELYN-DAVIES *et al.* (1996)

Eastern European capital cities may well see similar rises in the overall hierarchy over the next half century, but otherwise the system is likely to change only slowly.

Therefore, the need is to understand how information moves in order to achieve face-to-face communication. Over longer distances it will continue to move by air, through the great international airports (SHIN and TIMBERLAKE, 2000). There is significant correspondence between this list and another from recent research by the Globalization and World Cities (GaWC) group, which shows the urban hierarchy of the informational or knowledge economy (TAYLOR, 2004). This is only to be expected. The main new technological influence is likely to be the development of the high-speed train system, which in Europe will be largely in place shortly before 2010, connecting cities in North West and West Central Europe, in Spain and in Italy – and will be completed during the following decade with linkages through the Pyrenees and the Alps (HALL, 1995, 2009). This will carry conventional steel wheel on steel rail trains, capable of speeds up to 350 kilometres per hour (220 miles per hour) on new dedicated tracks and about 200 kilometres per hour (125 mph) on older conventional tracks; this will represent an overland speed limit for the foreseeable future. Extensive experience in Europe and Japan teaches that these trains will take about 80–90% of traffic up to about 500 kilometres and about 50% up to about 800 kilometres; the most recent evidence from France suggests that these figures may be underestimates (PEPY and LEBOEUF, 2005; PEPY and PERREN, 2006). Further, given that they have been shown to produce a fraction of the carbon dioxide (CO_2) of equivalent flights, there will be the strongest possible environmental incentive to transfer to them for all but long-haul flights.

Thus, in Europe, as early as 2020, high-speed trains will connect all the principal cities of Europe from Bari (Southern Italy) right up to Glasgow (Scotland) and Umeå (Sweden), and virtually all traffic between key city pairs, up to at least the 500 kilometre limit – Madrid and Barcelona, Naples and Milan, Milan and Paris, Munich and Cologne, Cologne and Brussels, Brussels and London, Brussels and Paris, Copenhagen and Stockholm – will go by rail. The longer-distance traffic – Southern to Northern Europe, far West Europe to far East Europe, as well, of course, as intercontinental traffic – will largely remain in the air, and a critical planning question will then become the linkages at the airports between the two systems. Efficient and easy links between the two modes already exist at Europe's most advanced airports: Amsterdam, Frankfurt, Paris-Charles de Gaulle. These places are likely to become effectively new urban centres, as Dejan Sudjic (SUDJIC, 1992) has suggested, not only attracting conference centres, exhibition centres and hotels, but also becoming major shopping centres, as at London's new Heathrow Terminal Five. So they will compete with traditional downtown areas as business hubs.

There are two other recent developments that relate closely to the evolution of high-speed train systems. One, especially in Europe, is the regional metro: a network of fast trains connecting medium-sized towns, up to 100 kilometres distant, through city centres to towns on the other side. Stockholm has developed such a system around Lake Mälar; Copenhagen–Malmö have built an international system via the new Öresund link, opened in 2000; London's Thameslink project will connect cities up to 150 kilometres distant; Switzerland is networking the entire country in this fashion. In Japan the extensive commuter rail systems around Tokyo and Osaka have a similar character, though they did not usually extend across city centres; in the United States the San Francisco (California) BART system was designed to perform a similar function and may yet achieve it, if future extensions complete the original grand design. The other – first in the German city of Karlsruhe, in 1992, and now spreading to many other cities – is the development of tram–train systems, allowing urban tram (streetcar) networks to operate on railway systems which extend their radius widely into the surrounding region (HALL, 2007, 2008). Together these act as agents – in effect, alternative technologies – for the development of a polycentric city region structure, whereby cities, towns and villages are connected to central inter-city high-speed train interchanges. Ironically, however, this structure closely resembles the concept of the Social City, in Ebenezer Howard's visionary book titled *To-Morrow: A Peaceful Path to Real Reform* (1898) (HOWARD, 1898/2003).

A critical question for this paper, clearly, is the precise effect of these new networks on urban form. Trains connect centres to centres; they always have been remarkable agents of urban centralization, unlike airports and orbital motorways which disperse functions centrifugally. The question is whether inner-urban or suburban stations can similarly act as development foci. The Japanese experience at Shin Yokohama and the Swedish experience at Stockholm Syd suggest they can; the United Kingdom is about to test the theory in the Thames Gateway stations at Stratford in East London and Ebbsfleet just beyond the London boundary in Kent. The result is likely to be the emergence of variants of Joel Garreau's book titled *Edge City: Life on the New Frontier* (GARREAU, 1991), some such places being located at airport-to-rail transfer points, others serving as the points of relationship between high-speed trains and the outer ends of metropolitan transit systems. Precursors, in existence or about to be built, include Paris-Charles de Gaulle, Paris Marne–La-Vallée (Disneyland Paris), Amsterdam Zuid and Amsterdam Schiphol, Stratford International and Ebbsfleet International on the United Kingdom's High-Speed One. Serving as nodes for major new developments, they will compel urbanists to think about the words they use casually: centrality and urbanity.

Progressive European cities such as Freiburg, Zürich, Amsterdam, Copenhagen and Barcelona have developed strong policies to maximize access to opportunities by walking and cycling and public transport and minimizing the need to use the car, giving priority to these virtuous forms of movement and deliberately subsidizing public transport while making private motoring much more expensive. These cities have mixed-use, walking–scale neighbourhoods linked by conventional public transport, including the regional metro systems mentioned above, or by new systems such as automated car travel (CERVERO, 1998). Extending this to the city-regional scale, the suggestion is that – at least in European Mega-City Regions – an urban settlement structure will emerge, suggested by the late Michael Breheny and the late Ralph Rookwood in the United Kingdom, or Peter Calthorpe in the United States: a beads-on-a-string structure, developed along strong public transport corridors (BREHENY and ROOKWOOD, 1993; CALTHORPE, 1993), which recall Howard's vision of a century earlier.

However, the threat of global warming is hugely intensifying the pressures to develop a zero emission vehicle (ZEV) at affordable purchase and running costs, and also an automated Personal Rapid Transit system vehicle which would act as an alternative to, even a successor to, the private car; in 2008, all the major producers are beginning to market such vehicles, and this can be only the beginning of a major change (HALL and PFEIFFER, 2000). The resulting irony is that most of the objections to the motor car would then be removed, encouraging yet further decentralization out of our cities, as H. G. Wells forecast in 1902. One particularly difficult problem for forecasting is to guess which of these contrary scenarios is more likely. At least until 2020, more likely beyond 2030, conventional cars are likely to survive and are likely to be the subject of ever more stringent physical and fiscal controls.

IMPLICATIONS FOR URBAN SYSTEMS: THE EUROPEAN CASE

What might be the impacts of these developments on national or supra-national urban systems? And how might policy seek to shape the process? Europe presents a particularly interesting case. At the macro or Europe-wide scale, the dominant feature is the contrast between the Pentagon – the area bounded by London, Paris, Milan, Munich and Hamburg – with its dense cluster of cities closely networked through air, high-speed-train and telecommunications links, and forming the cores of extensive Mega-City Regions (London, Paris, Frankfurt, Luxembourg, Brussels, Amsterdam), and the 'gateway' or 'regional capital'

cities in the more peripheral European regions, each dominating a large but less densely populated territory (Dublin, Edinburgh, Copenhagen, Stockholm, Helsinki, Berlin, Vienna, Rome, Madrid, Lisbon, Ljubljana, Budapest, Prague, Warsaw and Tallinn). These latter cities invariably act as regional airport hubs, with a range of long-distance destinations (Copenhagen, Madrid) and as the hubs of sub-continental high-speed train systems (Madrid, Rome, Copenhagen); they have a wide variety of global service functions, especially where they dominate linguistic regions (Madrid and Barcelona for Latin America). The larger ones have also spawned extensive surrounding city regions.

As DAVOUDI (2003) has argued, in Europe the concept of polycentricity is not merely an analytical tool; in the 1999 European Spatial Development Perspective (ESDP), it has also become a *normative* concept, a principle to be achieved through policy intervention. And this is to be achieved at a European scale: policy should seek to divert growth from the cities of the Pentagon to more remote growth centres, the intermediate-size gateway cities that proved relatively dynamic in the 1980s and 1990s – not least because several of them (Dublin, Lisbon, Madrid, Athens) received fairly massive aid from European Union structural funds. But the paradoxical outcome is that while official policy has promoted urban polycentricity at the European scale, it has resulted in increasing monocentricity at the national scale, as national political and/or commercial capitals increasingly dominate the picture. This has been obvious in the cases of Dublin, Madrid and Lisbon in the 1980s and 1990s; it is equally evident for Prague, Budapest, Warsaw or Tallinn in the first decade of the 21st century. As a result, during the coming half-century many of these cities also are likely to develop large surrounding Mega-City Regions.

Given this basic fact, as these extended city regions develop, experience from the older-developed ones suggests the wisdom of a policy of 'deconcentrated concentration', guiding decentralized growth, wherever possible, on to selected development corridors along strong public transport links, including high-speed 'regional metros' or even along true high-speed lines such as London–Ashford, Amsterdam–Antwerp or Berlin–Magdeburg. These would not be corridors of continuous urbanization, but rather clustered urban developments, at intervals, around train stations and key motorway interchanges offering exceptionally good accessibility. Some could be at considerable distances, up to 150 kilometres, from the central metropolitan city.

But it needs to be emphasized, finally, that 'morphological polycentricity', which refers to the regional distribution of towns and cities of different sizes, is not at all the same as 'functional polycentricity', which refers to flows of information (business travel and communication, especially face-to-face) and the organization of firms. Interview evidence in the POLYNET study paradoxically suggests morphological polycentricity – as in the Dutch Randstad – may be associated with rather weak intra-regional functional linkages, while the very degree of global concentration in London (regarded as a monocentric area in the North West Metropolitan Area (NWMA) Spatial Vision), was found to produce the most concrete evidence of regional functional polycentricity. Yet this too is associated with uneven development, in the form of an east–west economic imbalance in South East England: the area west of London is found to contain many more independent nodes, with a greater degree of functional independence, than the area to the east. It is functional polycentricity that proves more significant, and it is not axiomatic that it yields either more competitive or more sustainable outcomes than its opposite, monocentricity (or primacy) (HALL and PAIN, 2006, ch. 18).

At whatever spatial scale, spatial planning strategies cannot impose rigid blueprints. They can only suggest broad desirable directions; since the ESDP (in whatever form it survives by 2050) may well continue to be advisory, and the principle of subsidiarity will still apply, implementation will come mainly at national, regional and local levels. And there can be no firm guarantee as to outcomes: increasingly cities will compete directly in a global marketplace, and it can and should be no part of planning strategy to discourage this process. But the European Union will play an increasingly valuable role in coordinating efforts at these other levels, and in managing a variety of funds which can help shape them.

CONCLUSION

The Mega-City Region is the emerging urban form at the start of the 21st century and is likely, on all realistic scenarios, to become steadily more dominant in the course of the next half century. But that leaves open a number of important questions for spatial policy.

The first is that Mega-City Regions vary very greatly in location, scale, urban form, and economic base. As the POLYNET study showed for North West Europe, some (South East England, Paris Region) are based on a single dominant core city; others (Randstad, RhineRuhr) are truly more polycentric in a physical sense, while others occupy an intermediate position between these two poles. Even more significantly, some (RhineRuhr, Central; Belgium) contain significant elements of the old manufacturing economy, while others (South East England, Paris, Rhine-Main) have largely completed the transition to the new knowledge economy based on informational services. In parts of Europe (Northern England, Scotland, Rhine-Ruhr) it appears that central 'core' cities are in course of making a successful transition while other smaller places are not. Here, between the growing economy of the core cities and the rural areas

outside, from which many of the core city workers commute each day, old single-industry towns form a solid ring characterized by higher unemployment, lower gross value added, higher deprivation indices, and lower property values (SIMMIE et al., 2006; HALL, 2007). There is still an open question as to the future of these places. Perhaps, as some observers suggest – and as is observable in Eastern Germany – they are destined to undergo long-term shrinkage (LEUNIG et al., 2007; MACE et al., 2004).

The second point is that because of differences in scale and location, there is no necessary firm agreement as to the minimum scale necessary to constitute such a region. Thus, in North West England, spatial strategy calls for the recognition of three 'City Regions' – in effect, Mega-City Regions: Greater Manchester, Merseyside (Greater Liverpool), and Central Lancashire (Blackpool, Preston, Blackburn with Darwen, Accrington, and Burnley–Nelson–Colne) (NORTHWEST REGIONAL DEVELOPMENT AGENCY (NWDA) and CENTRE FOR CITIES AT IPPR, 2006). But, while the first two are demonstrating positive economic transformation and falling levels of deprivation based on the recovery of their core cities, the third – which has no core city – does not. There is a suggestion here of a complex process of spatial differentiation, manifesting itself as an 'archipelago economy' (VELTZ, 2000; DORLING and THOMAS, 2004): a few central islands dominated by the sharp peaks of the core city economies, and lower peripheral islands in perpetual danger of economic inundation.

The third point is that in such a pattern, wide bordering rural areas may effectively be brought into the orbit of the Mega-City Region, as more affluent urbanites continue to work in the cities (particularly the core cities) but reside and dispose of their incomes in rural locations. This, however, is an uneven process: research in the United Kingdom shows that the spatial orbit of more affluent professional and managerial workers, whether for residential search into the countryside or for entertainment opportunities back in the cities, is far wider than that of their lower-income counterparts (HARDING and ROBSON, 2006). One may therefore increasingly need to think in terms of a variable geometry when one deals with the spatial perceptions that help build these increasingly complex urban artefacts. And – again assuming no radical disjuncture in economic growth and income distribution – this complexity can only grow over the coming decades.

NOTE

1. The threshold levels depend on the size of national building blocks, that is, the size of NUTS 5 units. They required modification on the basis of local knowledge and experience.

REFERENCES

BARROW J. D. (2006) John D. Barrow forcasts the future, *New Scientist* **18 November**.

BECKOUCHE P. (Ed.) (1999) *Pour une métropolisation raisonnée: Diagnostic social et économique de l'Ile-de-France et du Bassin Parisien*. Préfecture d'Ile-de-France, Datar; La Documentation Française, Paris.

BLANC P. D. (2006) *How Everyday Products Make People Sick: Toxins at Home and in the Workplace*. University of California Press, Berkeley, CA.

BREHENY M. and ROOKWOOD R. (1993) Planning the sustainable city region, in BLOWERS A. (Ed.) *Planning for a Sustainable Environment*, pp. 150–189. Earthscan, London.

BUCK N., GORDON I., HALL P., HARLOE M. and KLEINMAN M. (2002) *Working Capital: Life and Labour in Contemporary London*. Routledge, London.

CAIRNCROSS F. (1997) *The Death of Distance: How the Communications Revolution Will Change Our Lives*. Orion, London.

CALTHORPE P. (1993) *The Next American Metropolis: Ecology, Community, and the American Dream*. Princeton Architectural Press, Princeton, NJ.

CASTELLS M. (1989) *The Informational City: Information Technology, Economic Restructuring and the Urban-Regional Process*. Basil Blackwell, Oxford.

CASTELLS M. (1996) *The Information Age: Economy, Society, and Culture*, Vol. I: *The Rise of the Network Society*. Blackwell, Oxford.

CERVERO R. (1998) *The Transit Metropolis: A Global Inquiry*. Island, Washington, DC.

CHESHIRE P. C. (1995) A new phase of urban development in Western Europe? The evidence for the 1980s, *Urban Studies* **32**, 1045–1063.

CHESHIRE P. C. (1999) Cities in competition: articulating the gains from integration, *Urban Studies* **36**, 843–864.

CHESHIRE P. C. and CARBONARO G. (1996) Urban economic growth in Europe: testing theory and policy prescriptions, *Urban Studies* **33**, 1111–1128.

CHESHIRE P. C. and HAY D. G. (1989) *Urban Problems in Western Europe: An Economic Analysis*. Unwin Hyman, London.

COLLINS F. (2006) Francis Collins forecasts the future, *New Scientist* **2578**(18 November 2006).

DAVOUDI S. (2003) Polycentricity in European spatial planning: from an analytical tool to a normative agenda, *European Planning Studies* **11**, 979–999.

DORLING D. RIGBY J., WHEELER B., BALLAS D., THOMAS B., FAHMY E., GORDON D. and LUPTON R. (2007) *Poverty, Wealth and Place in Britain, 1968 to 2005*. Policy Press for the Joseph Rowntree Foundation, Bristol.

DORLING D. and THOMAS B. (2004) *People and Places: A 2001 Census Atlas of the UK*. Policy Press, Bristol.

EUROPEAN COMMISSION (2000) *Towards Quality Urban Tourism: Integrated Quality Management (IQM) of Urban Tourist Destinations*. Enterprise Directorate-General, Tourism Unit, Brussels.

GARREAU J. (1991) *Edge City: Life on the New Frontier*. Doubleday, New York, NY.

GATES W. (1995) *The Road Ahead*. Viking, London.

GEDDES P. (1915) *Cities in Evolution*. Williams & Norgate, London.

GOTTMANN J. (1961) *Megalopolis: The Urbanized Northeastern Seaboard of the United States*. Twentieth Century Fund, New York, NY.

GRAHAM S. and MARVIN S. (1996) *Telecommunications and the City: Electronic Spaces, Urban Places*. Routledge, London.

HALBERT L. (2002a) *Services aux entreprises: vers une nouvelle géographie économique métropolitaine*. Note Rapide Number 8, Bilan Stratégique du SDRIF. Institut d'Aménagement et d'Urbanisme de la Région Ile de France (IAURIF), Paris.

HALBERT L. (2002b) *Les emplois supérieurs en Ile-de-France. Vers de nouvelles polarités?* Note Rapide Number 12 Bilan Stratégique du SDRIF. Institut d'Aménagement et d'Urbanisme de la Région Ile de France (IAURIF), Paris.

HALL P. (1963) *London 2000*. Faber & Faber, London.

HALL P. (1969) Geography: illogical? (The Maud Report examined), *New Society* **19 June**, 954–955.

HALL P. (1977) *Europe 2000*. Duckworth, London.

HALL P. (1995) A European perspective on the spatial links between land use, development and transport, in BANISTER D. (Ed.) *Transport and Urban Development*, pp. 65–88. E&FN Spon, London.

HALL P. (1999) Planning for the mega-city: a new Eastern Asian urban form?, in BROTCHIE J., NEWTON P., HALL P. and DICKEY J. (Eds) *East–West Perspectives on 21st Century Urban Development: Sustainable Eastern and Western Cities in the New Millennium*, pp. 3–36. Ashgate, Aldershot.

HALL P. (2003) The end of the city? 'The Report of My Death was an Exaggeration', *City* **7**, 141–152.

HALL P. (2007) The revolution starting at Platform 3A, *Town and Country Planning* **76**, 38–39.

HALL P. (2008) Catching up with our visions, *Town and Country Planning* **77**, 444–449.

HALL P. (2009) Magic carpets and seamless webs: opportunities and constraints for high-speed trains in Europe. *Built Environment* **35**, 59–69.

HALL P. and HAY D. (1980) *Growth Centres in the European Urban System*. Heinemann, London.

HALL P. and PAIN K. (2006) *The Polycentric Metropolis: Learning from Mega-City Regions in Europe*. Earthscan, London.

HALL P. and PFEIFFER U. (2000) *Urban Future 21: A Global Agenda for Twenty-first Century Cities*. E&FN Spon, London.

HALL P., THOMAS R., GRACEY H. and DREWETT R. (1973) *The Containment of Urban England*, 2 vols. George Allen & Unwin, London.

HARDING A. and ROBSON B. (2006) *A Framework for City-Regions*. Office of the Deputy Prime Minister (ODPM), London.

HIGHER EDUCATION FOUNDING COUNCIL FOR ENGLAND (HEFCE) (2007) *Young Participation in Higher Education in the Parliamentary Constituencies of Birmingham Hodge Hill, Bristol South, Nottingham North and Sheffield Brightside*. Report to the HEFCE by the University of the West of England and the School of Education, University of Nottingham (available at: http://www.hefce. ac.uk/pubs/rdreports/2007/rd16_07/rd16_07.pdf).

HOWARD E. (1898/2003) *To-Morrow: A Peaceful Path to Real Reform* [1898], Edited with an Introduction, Commentary and Postscript, HALL P., HARDY D. and WARD C. Routledge, London.

INSTITUT D'AMÉNAGEMENT ET D'URBANISME DE LA RÉGION ILE DE FRANCE (IAURIF) (1996) *North-West European Metropolitan Regions: Geographical Boundaries and Economic Structures*. IAURIF, Paris.

JHA A. (2006) The future of old age, *The Guardian* **8 March**.

JHA A. (2008) Live longer, live better: futurologists pick top challenges of next 50 years, *The Guardian* **16 February**.

KNOX P. N. (2008) *Metroburbia, USA*. Rutgers University Press, Piscataway, NJ.

KOLBERT E. (2006) *Field Notes from a Catastrophe*. Bloomsbury, London.

LANG R. E. and DHAVALE D. (2005) America's megalopolitan areas, *Land Lines: Newsletter of the Lincoln Institute of Land Policy* **17**, 1–4.

LAW C. M. (2001) *Urban Tourism and the Growth of Large Cities*, 2nd Edn. Continuum, London.

LEUNIG T., SWAFFIELD J. and HARTWICH O. M. (2007) *Cities Limited*. Policy Exchange, London.

LIN G. C. S. and MA L. J. C. (1994) The role of towns in Chinese regional development – the case of Guangdong Province, *International Regional Science Review* **1**, 75–97.

LLEWELYN-DAVIES, UCL BARTLETT SCHOOL OF PLANNING and COMEDIA (1996) *Four World Cities*. Comedia, London.

MACE A., GALLENT N., HALL P., PORSCH L., BRAUN R. and PFEIFFER U. (2004) *Shrinking to Grow? The Urban Regeneration Challenge in Leipzig and Manchester*. Institute of Community Studies, London.

MAGRINI S. (1999) The evolution of income disparities among the regions of the European Union, *Regional Science and Urban Economics* **29**, 257–281.

MCGEE T. G. and ROBINSON I. (Eds) (1995) *The Mega-Urban Regions of Southeast Asia*. University of British Columbia Press, Vancouver, BC.

MITCHELL W. J. (1995) *City of Bits: Space, Place, and the Infobahn*. MIT Press, Cambridge, MA.

NEUMAN M. and BRIGHT E. (Eds) (2008) *The Texas Urban Triangle: Framework for Future Growth*. Texas A&M University, College Station, TX.

NORTHWEST REGIONAL DEVELOPMENT AGENCY (NWDA) and CENTRE FOR CITIES AT IPPR (2006) *Cities Northwest*. NWDA, Warrington.

PAIN K. and HALL P. (2007) Informational quantity versus informational quality: the perils of navigating the space of flows, *Regional Studies* **42**, 1065–1077.

PEPY G. and LEBOEUF M.(2005) Le TGV au XXIème siècle: rompre sans dénaturer, *Revue Générale des Chemins de Fer* **May**, 7–27.

PEPY G. and PERREN B. (2006) 25 Years of the TGV, *Modern Railways* **October**, 67–74.

ROYAL COMMISSION ON LOCAL GOVERNMENT IN ENGLAND (1968) *Research Studies 1: Local Government in South East England*. Greater London Group, London School of Economics and Political Science/HMSO, London.

SCOTT A. J. (Ed.) (2001) *Global City-Regions: Trends, Theory, Policy*. Oxford University Press, Oxford.

SEN A. (2006) *Identity and Violence: The Illusion of Destiny*. W. W. Norton, New York, NY.

SHIN K.-H. and TIMBERLAKE M. (2000) World cities in Asia: cliques, centrality and connectedness, *Urban Studies* **37**, 2257–2285.

SHORT J. R. (2007) *Liquid City: Megalopolis Revisited*. Resources for The Future Press/Johns Hopkins University Press, Washington, DC.

SIMMIE J. *et al.* (2006) *State of the English Cities: The Competitive Economic Performance of English Cities*. Department for Communities and Local Government (DCLG), London.

SIT V. F. S. and YANG C. (1997) Foreign-investment-induced exo-urbanisation in the Pearl River Delta, China, *Urban Studies* **34**, 647–677.

SUDJIC D. (1992) *The 100 Mile City*. Andre Deutsch, London.

SUTTON TRUST (2005) *Rates of Eligibility for Free School Meals at the Top State Schools*. Sutton Trust, London.

TAYLOR P. J. (2004) *World City Network: A Global Urban Analysis*. Routledge, London.

UK CABINET OFFICE, SOCIAL EXCLUSION TASK FORCE (2008) *Aspiration and Attainment Amongst Young People in Deprived Communities: Analysis and Discussion Paper*. December 2008. Cabinet Office, London.

UK OFFICE OF THE DEPUTY PRIME MINISTER (ODPM) (2006) *State of the English Cities*, 2 Vols. ODPM, London.

VELTZ P. (2000) *Mondalisation Villes et Territoires: L'Économie d'Archipel*, 3rd Edn. PUF, Paris.

WELLS H. G. (1902) *Anticipations of the Reaction of Mechanical and Scientific Progress Upon Human Life and Thought*. Chapman & Hall, London.

The 21st-Century Metropolis: New Geographies of Theory

ANANYA ROY

ROY A. The 21st-century metropolis: new geographies of theory, *Regional Studies*. This paper calls for 'new geographies' of imagination and epistemology in the production of urban and regional theory. It argues that the dominant theorizations of global city-regions are rooted in the EuroAmerican experience and are thus unable to analyse multiple forms of metropolitan modernities. By drawing on the urban experience of the global South, the paper presents new conceptual vectors for understanding the worlding of cities, the production of space, and the dynamics of exurbanity. It makes the case that such area-based knowledge deepens recent theoretical attempts to articulate a relational study of space and place.

ROY A.21 世纪的大都市区：新的地理学理论，区域研究。本文认为在城市区域理论领域需要提出"新地理学"假设及相关认识论。 文章指出，目前主导全球城市区域理论的是基于欧美经验的分析，因此无法用于分析大都市区现代化的多元表现形式。随即文章以南部城市实践为例，向读者展示了一种用以理解城市全球化、空间产生以及超城市性 (exurbanity) 活力的新型概念矢量。这 一尝试表明，基于地方的知识能够加深和补充目前关于空间与场所关联性研究理论。

新地理学 城市特征 城市理论 城市化 城市主义 第三世界城市

ROY A. Les métropoles du XXIe siècle: nouvelle géographie de la théorie, *Regional Studies*. Cet article appelle à de nouvelles géographies de l'imagination et de l'épistémologie pour la production de théories urbaines et régionales. Il avance que les théorisations dominantes des villes-régions du monde sont enracinées dans l'expérience euro-américaine et sont donc incapables d'analyser les formes multiples de la modernité des métropoles. En s'appuyant sur l'expérience urbaine du Sud, cet article présente de nouveaux vecteurs conceptuels pour comprendre la mondialisation des villes, la production d'espaces et la dynamique de l'exur-banisation. Il prétend que la connaissance basée sur la région approfondit de récentes tentatives théoriques visant à expliquer une étude relationnelle de l'espace et de la place.

ROY A. Die Metropole im 21. Jahrhundert: neue Geografien der Theorie, *Regional Studies*. In diesem Artikel werden 'neue Geografien' der Fantasie und Epistemologie bei der Entwicklung von urbanen und regionalen Theorien gefordert. Es wird argu-mentiert, dass die dominanten Theoretisierungen der globalen Stadtregionen in der euro-amerikanischen Erfahrung verwurzelt sind, weshalb sie sich nicht zu einer Analyse der multiplen Formen von metropolitanen Modernitäten eignen. Durch eine Nutzung der urbanen Erfahrungen im globalen Süden werden im Artikel neue konzeptuelle Vektoren für das Verständnis der Weltentwicklung von Städten, der Produktion von Raum und der Dynamik der Exurbanität vorgestellt. Es wird argumentiert, dass sich durch ein solches gebietsbasiertes Wissen die jüngsten theoretischen Versuche der Artikulation einer relationalen Studie von Raum und Ort vertiefen lassen.

ROY A. La metrópolis del siglo XXI: Nuevas geografías de la teoría, *Regional Studies*. En este artículo abogo por unas 'nuevas geografías' de la imaginación y la epistemología en la producción de la teoría urbana y regional. Postulo que las teorizaciones dominantes de las regiones ciudades globales tienen sus raíces en la experiencia euroamericana y por tanto no son capaces de analizar las diversas formas de modernidades metropolitanas. Basándome en la experiencia urbana del sur global, en este artículo presento los nuevos vectores conceptuales para comprender el desarrollo mundial de las ciudades, la producción del espacio y las dinámicas de la exurbanidad. Expongo que tales conocimientos de áreas incrementan los recientes intentos teóricos de articular un estudio relacional del espacio y el lugar.

DISLOCATING THE CENTRE

The territories of the metropolis, with its social topographies, economic energies, and political machineries, is once again on the theoretical and policy agenda. This time the interest lies in the extended conurbations of the 'city-region', in the fading of city into countryside, in the frontiers that trail into the horizon, and in the vast blotches of sprawl that defy census boundaries and categories. Of course, this is a resurgent rather than wholly new interest. Urban historians have long been interested in precisely such conurbations, be they those of the feudal age where economic and political identities of freedom and serfhood were embedded in the localities of city and countryside; or those of early 20th-century social-democratic capitalism when there was a lively imagination for managing the relationship between city and countryside, an imagination that today would possibly be named 'sustainability'.

The present paper argues that it is time to rethink the geographies of urban and regional theory. Much of the theoretical work on city-regions is firmly located in the urban experience of North America and Western Europe. This is not unusual. It is part of a canonical tradition where theory is produced in the crucible of a few 'great' cities: Chicago, New York, Paris, and Los Angeles – cities inevitably located in EuroAmerica. It is time to rethink the list of 'great' cities. While the 20th century closed with debate and controversy about the shift from a 'Chicago School' of urban sociology to the 'Los Angeles School' of postmodern geography, the urban future already lay elsewhere: in the cities of the global South, in cities such as Shanghai, Cairo, Mumbai, Mexico City, Rio de Janeiro, Dakar, and Johannesburg. Can the experiences of these cities reconfigure the theoretical heartland of urban and metropolitan analysis?

The cities of the global South, when visible in urban theory, are usually assembled under the sign of underdevelopment, that last and compulsory chapter on 'Third World Urbanization' in the urban studies textbook. They are the sites at which capital accumulation and democratic governance happen under 'special circumstances' (STREN, 2001, p. 205). They are the mega-cities, bursting at the seams, overtaken by their own fate of poverty, disease, violence, and toxicity. They constitute the 'planet of slums', with its 'surplus humanity' and 'twilight struggles' (DAVIS, 2004, p. 13). Davis's apocalyptic imagination of the Global Slum is only the newest variant in the high-pitched narration of the crisis of mega-cities. It is thus that

ROBINSON (2002) has launched an unrelenting critique of the geography of urban theory, sharply noting the enduring divide between 'First World' cities (read: global cities) that are seen as models, generating theory and policy, and 'Third World' cities (read: mega-cities) that are seen as problems, requiring diagnosis and reform. Against the 'regulating fiction' of the First World global city, ROBINSON (2003, p. 275) calls for a robust urban theory that can overcome its 'asymmetrical ignorance'.

The present paper seeks to articulate new geographies of urban theory. Doing so requires 'dislocating' the EuroAmerican centre of theoretical production; for it is not enough simply to study the cities of the global South as interesting, anomalous, different, and esoteric empirical cases. Such forms of benign differencemaking keep alive the neo-orientalist tendencies that interpret Third World cities as the heart of darkness, the Other. It is argued that the centre of theorymaking must move to the global South; that there has to be a recalibration of the geographies of authoritative knowledge. As the parochial experience of EuroAmerican cities has been found to be a useful theoretical model for *all* cities, so perhaps the distinctive experiences of the cities of the global South can generate productive and provocative theoretical frameworks for *all* cities. The critique of the EuroAmerican hegemony of urban theory is thus not an argument about the inapplicability of the EuroAmerican ideas to the cities of the global South. It is not worthwhile to police the borders across which ideas, policies, and practices flow and mutate. The concern is with the limited sites at which theoretical production is currently theorized and with the failure of imagination and epistemology that is thus engendered. It is time to blast open theoretical geographies, to produce a new set of concepts in the crucible of a new repertoire of cities. In putting forward such an argument, the paper suggests a rather paradoxical combination of specificity and generalizability: that theories have to be produced *in* place (and it matters *where* they are produced), but that they can then be appropriated, borrowed, and remapped. In this sense, the sort of theory being urged is simultaneously located and dis-located.

The theoretical agenda that can be engendered by such new geographies of theory will now be briefly outlined. As perceptively noted by JONAS and WARD (2007, p. 170), the city-region is often conceptualized as a building block of the global economy. In the work of SCOTT (2001), for example, the city-region heralds a new phase of capitalist territorial development and is thus the key space of accumulation, competition, and governance. Such a framework links up in important ways with the dominant narrative of global/world cities. Pioneered by SASSEN (1991) and KNOX and TAYLOR (1995), but partly derivative of CASTELLS's (1996) theories of 'spaces of flows', this narrative maps a hierarchy of city-regions. This is agglomeration economics writ large. But it is also a Darwinian ecology of cities: the survival of the fittest in the keen competition of network capitalism. In the alpha–beta–gamma worldwide rankings, 'mega-cities' are usually off the map, seen as 'big but powerless' entities, while global/ world cities are presented as nodes of a globalization that is unidimensionally driven by finance capital.

Such a conceptualization falls short in several ways. First, as JONAS and WARD (2007, p. 170) note, the city-region literature is silent on 'how new territorial forms are constructed politically and reproduced through everyday acts and struggles around consumption and social reproduction'. It is thus that JARVIS (2007) calls for closer attention to the practices and politics of 'care' that make possible the economic production of city-regions. Second, as PURCELL (2007) argues, the research on city-regions is thin in its engagement with issues of democracy. The focus on economic competitiveness tends to elide the terrain of political struggle and subject-making through which space is lived and negotiated. For this reason, the only two essays under the heading 'Questions of Citizenship' in SCOTT's (2001) edited volume, *Global City-Regions* – one by HOLSTON (2001) and the other by ISIN (2001) – tell an unusual story of informality, populism, social movements, and Islamicist politics. The story is unusual not because these phenomena are unusual, but rather because they have thus been rendered in the normalized narrative of global city-regions. Central to such shortcomings then is what AMIN (2004, p. 35) calls a 'territorial' reading of regions, one that is premised on the assumption that there is a well-defined territory that can be controlled and managed and that thus reduces politics to 'managerial localism'. Building on the work of Massey, AMIN (2004, pp. 38–39) calls for a 'relational' or 'topological' reading of regions, such that the local is viewed as a 'field of agonistic engagement' with 'different scales of politics/social action'.

In the present paper, Amin's call for a topological reading of regions is linked with Robinson's call for an end to the asymmetrical ignorance of urban and regional theory. It is argued that while it is necessary to articulate a 'relational' theory of place, such an articulation is well served by the production of theory in the context of the global South. Such an enterprise does not entail 'adding' the experience of the global South to already existing frameworks of the city-region. For example, there is new work that seeks to illuminate the city-regions of the developing world (SEGBERS, 2007) but which strives to fit these spaces into the predictable forms and hierarchical rankings of the global/world city theory of Sassen and Taylor. The paper is less interested in the additive or predictive assimilation of the Southern experience into the theory of city-regions. Instead, it aims to convince that a serious study of the global South can dislodge what AMIN (2004, pp. 33–34) terms the 'hegemonic territorial imaginary of the world' and instead reveals 'an excess of spatial composition'. The present paper thus moves away from the term 'city-region' and instead seeks to create an agenda for the study of the 21st-century metropolis that is focused on a variety of dynamic topologies and deep relationalities: the worlding of cities, the production and politics of space, and exurbanity and extraterritoriality. What is at stake here is not the mapping of bounded and located city-regions but rather an analysis of the heterogeneity and multiplicity of metropolitan modernities.

NEW GEOGRAPHIES OF THEORY: STRATEGIC ESSENTIALISMS

The EuroAmerican academy has a rather unique institution called 'area studies'. Formulated in a Cold War era, 'area studies' signifies the geopolitics of knowledge. Intending to produce 'area studies specialists', this field of training grounds disciplinary identities in the deep understanding of world-regions. More recently, there has been a rethinking of area studies such that the emphasis is no longer on 'trait geographies' but rather on 'process geographies' (APPADURAI, 2000a): in other words, on the forms of movement, encounter, and exchange that confound the idea of bounded world-regions with immutable traits.

It is proposed that 'area studies', especially when understood through the lens of 'process geographies', can help forge new geographies of urban theory. At the very least it makes possible an understanding of the area-based production of knowledge – how and why particular concepts are produced in particular world-areas. Such a venture makes possible an understanding of the diverse specificity of urbanism and metropolitanism and also facilitates useful comparative inquiries. It is in this spirit that the present author and Nezar AlSayyad, under the auspices of a Ford Foundation 'Crossing Borders' project, brought together scholars of urban informality who work in Latin America, South Asia, and the Middle East (ROY and ALSAYYAD, 2003). It was demonstrated that the conceptualization of urban informality had emerged in the Latin American context, such that it was not possible to separate this theoretical framework from its area studies origins. But it was possible to recognize the distinctive types of theorization that were being enabled by the study of urban informality in other world-regions, such as the Middle East and South Asia, and it was possible for scholars and practitioners working in each area context to learn from the other.

In this paper the agenda is more ambitious. On the one hand, an 'area studies' framework yields a *located* urban theory, rich in the grounded realities of world-areas. This is necessary and imperative. On the other hand, when the 'area studies' framework is itself complicated as 'process geographies', then it is possible to think about a *dis-located* urban theory that far exceeds its geographic origins. OLDS (2001b) thus rightly notes that:

> the large regions which dominate the current maps for area studies are not permanent geographical facts. They are problematic heuristic devices for the study of global geographic and cultural processes.
>
> (p. 129)

This type of an 'area studies' framework can be seen as producing 'strategic essentialisms': authoritative knowledge that is fine-grained and nuanced but exceeds its empiricism through theoretical generalization. Such forms of essentialism and dislocation, it is argued, are needed to dismantle the dualisms that have been maintained between global cities and mega-cities, between theory and fieldwork, and between models and applications. It is not enough for one's understanding of the 21st-century metropolis simply to make visible the cities of the global South. It is not even enough to exceed the visibility of crisis and catastrophe. It is instead necessary to view *all* cities from *this* particular place on the map.

These places on the map and the views they afford will now be briefly discussed. This discussion is broached with the explicit recognition that each world-area is a heuristic device rather than a permanent geographical fact. The present coverage of different world-areas is thus highly selective and strategic rather than comprehensive. It is also particularly concerned with theoretical work that not only is area based, but also is focused on the urban and metropolitan experience. In other words, this brief overview is a glimpse of how the 'urban question' is broached in distinctive ways in and across different world-areas. It will become quickly evident that such urban questions are simultaneously located and dislocated, affording both a view of a place on the map as well as of a topology and relationality that redraws the map itself.

Latin America

The empirical and theoretical structure that emerges from Latin America is one concerned with the conditions of urban citizenship. Most recently, there has been considerable scholarship on forms of marginality and inequality in cities such as Buenos Aires and Rio de Janeiro (AUYERO, 2000; PERLMAN, 2003). Such patterns of impoverishment and deprivation are seen to be produced by geographies of separation, by the Latin American 'city of walls' (CALDEIRA, 2001). At the same time, Latin Americanists are intrigued by the possibilities of 'insurgent citizenship' (HOLSTON, 1999).

What are the ways in which the urban poor claim and appropriate space and livelihood, thus challenging the unequal terms of citizenship that have been laid down in Latin American city-regions? Such questions are of particular relevance and urgency in Latin America today, with the popularity of leftist political regimes and with reinvented forms of populism. Will Chavez's Caracas be a just city? Can Morales live up to his promise of a remedy for the enduring poverty of the Bolivian countryside? Can Brazil transform its socio-spatial hierarchies through the institutionalization of participatory democracy? But such questions also speak to a longer tradition of Latin American theory: the work of the *dependistas*. Articulated as a counterpoint to modernization theory and its claims of growth poles, spatial equilibrium, and trickle-down growth, dependency theory asserts the persistence of core—periphery geographies, including parasitic primate cities and involutionary informal economies. For dependency theorists this underdevelopment is actively produced by the modes of dependency through which Latin America is inserted into the world economy (FRANK, 1967; CARDOSO and FALETTO, 1979). In the 1970s, an urban dimension was added to dependency theory. Most notably, CASTELLS (1983) put forward the idea of the 'dependent' city as a space of social mobilizations but one where these energies were often co-opted by the populist politics of patronage. While the potential of social movements was there, insurgency and radical social change were rarely realized. Dependency then was not simply an external condition, perpetuated through neocolonial forms of development and globalization, but it was also an internal condition, the reproduction of inequality in the struggle for the Latin American city.

South Asia

The corpus of work on South Asian cities is more limited. In this 'area studies' terrain the exposition of the 'agrarian question' has been much more thorough than that of the 'urban question'. More recently, there has been what RAO (2006) calls an 'urban turn' in South Asianist scholarship. Theorists of the postcolonial nation are increasingly concerned with the forms of 'political society' (CHATTERJEE, 2006) that find expression in the city. As in the case of Latin American urbanism, there is a sustained engagement with the violences, marginalities, and erasures of the South Asian city (APPADURAI, 2000b). But there is also an interest, even optimism, about the possibilities of urban citizenship, what APPADURAI (2002) calls 'deep democracy'. It is worth noting that the South Asian debates about urban politics and citizenship have a unique theoretical signature. If Latin American urban analysis is steeped in the legacies of dependency theory, then the South Asian scholarship is shaped by the traditions of postcolonial theory, and particularly that South Asian variant of postcolonial analysis: subaltern studies. Postcolonialism, of course, is more than the study of colonial and after-colonial societies. It is above all a critical theory of subjectivity and power. South Asia thus yields a window on forms of agency and subjectivity that go well beyond theories of populism and patronage and democracy. Whether located in the colonial city or the contemporary city, the South Asian debates are fundamentally concerned with the hegemonic production of urban subjects and subjecthood. Studies of the South Asian colonial city are thus as concerned with the aesthetic registers of beauty and hybridity as they are occupation and destruction (DUTTA, 2006). Studies of the contemporary South Asian city are thus concerned with the ways in which subaltern subjects consent to and participate in projects of urban redevelopment and urban inequality (ROY, 2003). An inevitable theoretical companion to such work is a radical reflection on the conditions under which scholarship can or cannot represent such subjects: can the subaltern speak?

East Asia

Postcolonial theory produced in the context of East Asia is substantially different than that produced in Latin America or South Asia. So are the implications for urban theory. While Latin American theory has been focused on dependency and South Asian theory on subaltern identities, the scholarship of East Asia has instead been concerned with 'arbitrage': the negotiation and mediation of economic globalization and cultural cosmopolitanism. Provocatively argued by ABBAS (2000, p. 783), arbitrage is the East Asian variant of the term 'glocalization', and indicates strategies that capitalize on differences in scales, spaces, and zones: 'everyday strategies for negotiating the disequilibria and dislocations that globalism has created' (ABBAS, 2000, p. 786). It is in this sense that Abbas reads Hong Kong as a 'para-site', shaped by its geographies of dependency, colonialism, and para-colonialism, but also wielding the capacity to mediate global flows of capital, bodies, ideas, desires, and aspirations. East Asian urban theory thus draws attention to the polytemporal and polyvalent productions of global modernity, as in the conceptualization of 'modern' (1920s) and newly 'modern' (1990s) Shanghai. The idea of a 'Shanghai modern' (LEE, 2001), inevitably colonial but ineluctably cosmopolitan, is a powerful theoretical claim. It creates a framework of globalized urbanism that is more differentiated and nuanced than both *dependista* mappings and global city ecologies.

Africa

For a while, the Africanist literature on cities echoed the themes of Latin American urbanism: peasants in the city, world-systems structures of dependency and underdevelopment, informalization under conditions of neoliberal globalization. Or, the scholarship tackled particular geopolitical conditions, such as the apartheid and post-apartheid city. More recently, a more ambitious project of theorizing African urban spaces and subjects has emerged. The first mandate is to understand capitalism in African cities not simply as social relations of production but as forms-in-circulation (NUTTALL and MBEMBE, 2005, p. 2000). This study of circulations – the circulation of racialized bodies, of migrant bodies, of value, of commodities, of superstitions, of rumours, of bribes, of used goods – creates a dizzying sense of the urban economy. It is thus that SIMONE (2004a) reframes urban infrastructure as 'people as infrastructure', indicating the contingent and fleeting circulations and transactions through which African cities are reproduced. The second mandate is to link such forms-in-circulation to African modernities. What are the ways in which African cities can be understood not as 'failed' cities but rather as cities of aspirations and expectations, the 'city yet to come' (SIMONE, 2004b)? What are the ways in which the 'figure of the subject in the time of crisis' can be understood as the arbiter of metropolitan modernities (MBEMBE and ROITMAN, 2003)?

Middle East

The Middle East is a complex epistemological terrain. It is perhaps the only 'area' in 'area studies' that is not a geographical territory but rather a social construct. Middle of what and east of where (ALSAYYAD and ROY, 2003, p. 2)? In this sense, the idea of the Middle East makes evident the social (read: orientalist) construction that underlies all geographies and geographical facts. It is the ultimate heuristic device, one that calls into question the ways in which one's theories are 'world'. The boundaries of the Middle East are constantly reworked – spilling over into North Africa, extended in the public imagination to sites of conflict, and often conflated with the contours of predominantly Muslim societies, even those as far-flung as Afghanistan. Within these ambiguous and expanding borders there are also emerging and significant traditions of urban and metropolitan theory. As in the case of South Asia, the violences of Middle East nationalisms have led to a careful analysis of how the city can embody the cruelties, separations, and erasures of nation-making: from the ethnocracy of Zionist settlements (YIFTACHEL, 2006), to the politically sanctioned fiefdoms of multicultural Beirut, and to the 'urbicide' that is at work in various occupied territories (GRAHAM, 2004). Most recently, a bolder effort has been afoot. The self-styled 'Cairo School' has launched a study of cosmopolitanisms and modernities located in the globalized Middle East, examining the heteronomous landscapes of malls, gated communities, Islamicized public spaces, and informal settlements (SINGERMANN and AMAR, 2006).

Here, then, is a rich and complex landscape of concepts and theoretical traditions. But the aim of this paper is something more than the documentation of empirical richness and regional diversities. How can regionally produced concepts be deployed as 'strategic essentialisms', simultaneously located and dislocated? How can the theories embedded in 'area studies' retain their geographic coordinates but also cross borders and travel as dynamic vectors of new theoretical conversations and exchanges?

CONCEPTS FOR THE 21ST-CENTURY METROPOLIS

It was noted above that the dominant narrative shaping the study of global city-regions is the global/world city theory of Sassen and Taylor. This section revisits this framework, but through the conceptual vectors that have emerged from 'area studies'. It is shown that there are other ways of 'worlding' cities and that these geographies of connections give a more relevant and dynamic theory of the 21st-century metropolis. Two other strands of theorization that are often mobilized are also engaged to make sense of the contemporary urban experience. The first, led by HARVEY (1989) and SMITH (1996), presents a Marxist analysis of urban accumulation and regulation. Particularly beholden to Lefebvre, it seeks to explain the production of space through forms of urban redevelopment and gentrification. The concern here is not only with uneven spatial development, but also with modes of regulation that manage and displace the crises of capitalism, as in the work of BRENNER (2004), BRENNER and THEODORE (2002), and JESSOP (1994). The second strand, often dubbed the 'Los Angeles school', traces the explosion and implosion of the metropolis: the exurban landscapes of the exopolis (SOJA, 1992), the enclaves of the fortress city (DAVIS, 1990), and the border geographies of the 'postborder' city (DEAR and LECLERC, 2003). In a Debordian analysis of late capitalism, this framework draws attention to the symbolic economies of the city-region: the alienation of production, reproduction, and regulation in the spectacle that is the postmodern metropolis (SORKIN, 1992). Through an engagement with new geographies of theory, it is sought to update and rework these theorizations.

Worlding of cities

In urban theory, the analytical practice of 'worlding' is dominated by the framework of global cities and world cities. This ecology of globalization pays attention to the circuits of finance capital and informational capital but ignores other circuitries of the world economy. It is not surprising then that global/world cities mapping drops all other cities from the map, arguing that they are structurally irrelevant to the functioning of economic globalization (ROBINSON, 2002). But the immense body of work being done in various world-regions indicates that there are many other ways of 'worlding' cities and that these are of crucial significance in the world economy. For example, theorists of 'transnational urbanism' are examining the ways in which gentrification and urban redevelopment are embedded in global property markets, the globalization of Lefebvre's 'production of space' (OLDS, 2001a). Others are studying 'transnationalism from below', the practices and strategies of migrants as they cross borders and produce space (SMITH, 2001). Particularly significant is the work of JACOBS (1996) on postcolonial urbanism. Jacobs interprets global cities such as London as 'postcolonial' cities and shows how London's colonial past shapes its contemporary spaces – in 'ethnic enclaves', in struggles over urban redevelopment, and in negotiations over cultural identity. This is the unstable and profound 'edge of empire', one that exists not at the margins, but rather at the heart of the global city. Similarly, MITCHELL's (2004) study of globalized Vancouver reveals contestations over urban space that are also contestations around nation and homeland. Vancouver's Pacific Rim urbanism, driven by wealthy and middle-class Chinese transnational entrepreneurs, disrupts the models/myths of assimilation and interculturalism that constitute Canadian citizenship.

Such forms of 'worlding' are crucial because they move urban theory from the mapping of 'world cities' to the historicized analysis of 'world systems'. The global/world cities framework asserts a hierarchy of cities but is unable to account fully for the materialization of such a hierarchy, and even less so in relation to the long histories of colonialism and imperialism. Space is a 'container' in these theoretical reports; its 'production' remains unexplained (SMITH, 2002). For example, TAYLOR (2000), following Braudel, rightly notes that capitalism is a world of multiple monopolies and that global/world cities represent a 'monopoly of place'. This is a refreshing recalibration of the rather simplistic narrative of 'agglomeration economies'. Yet, Taylor is unable to explain the formation of such power configurations and monopolistic complexes. The frameworks of transnational urbanism and postcolonial urbanism ply precisely such explanatory power. Through a study of imperial geographies, Jacobs can explain the production of London as a global city. Through and analysis of Pacific Rim elites, Olds can account for the global accumulation that is taking place in Vancouver. But it is interesting to note that even this work remains centred in 'First World' cities, though they represent an important effort to transnationalize and globalize the study of these cities. While such efforts at 'worlding' cities are of considerable significance, a second type of 'worlding' is being proposed that is less conventional.

The 'worlding' of cities has typically adopted a core−periphery model of globalization. This is the case with neo/liberal frameworks and this is the case with post/colonial frameworks. However, 'area studies' research indicates an urgent need to rethink the model of core and periphery. APPADURAI (1996) suggests a theory of 'scapes': overlapping, disjunctive orders (mediascapes, ethnoscapes, financescapes) as an analytics of globalization and as an alternative to core–periphery mappings. However, his theme of 'scapes' narrates globalization as a process of deterritorialization without taking into account the rather obvious forms of *re*territorialization that are at work in the world system. A 'worlding' of cities has now to take account of multiple cores and peripheries, and more provocatively has to note the emergence of core–periphery structures *within* the global South. Two examples of such 'worlding' will be cited.

The first is the case of global circuits of domestic work that link 'peripheries' such as the Philippines to 'cores' such as Hong Kong and Singapore. It is a well-established fact that there is a gender order to the geographies of late capitalism. EHRENREICH and HOCHSCHILD (2003) bestow the term 'Global Woman' on the labouring bodies (maids, nannies, sex workers, assembly line workers) through which global accumulation is facilitated and reproduced. The valuation and exchange of these bodies takes place not only in South–North flows, but also in South–South flows. The work of CONSTABLE (1997) and YEOH *et al.* (2000) details the feminization and racialization of domestic service in Hong Kong and Singapore, such that maidhood becomes synonymous with national and gender typifications (in these cases, usually with the type 'Filipina'). The Philippines, on the one hand, facilitates the 'export' of its women and relies heavily on their remittances, but on the other hand, gingerly negotiates wages and working conditions with Hong Kong and Singapore, and is often threatened with the spectre of 'returned' Filipinas.

The second is the case of the routes of migration, lines of evacuation, and exchanges of commodities that connect the cities of sub-Saharan Africa to cities such as Mumbai, Dubai, Bangkok, Kuala Lumpur, and Jeddah, elaborated by SIMONE (2001) in an illuminating article titled 'On the worlding of African cities'. Africans deploy 'the city as a resource for reaching and operating at the level of the world' (p. 22), thereby creating everyday strategies of 'worlding', a 'worlding from below'. Some of these circuits 'spin out and link themselves to the more conventional migratory paths' of Europe and North America (p. 22), but many of them remain connected primarily to other sites in the global South. These networks are facilitated not by the usual agents and firms of finance capital and informational capital, but by other equally relevant economic and social agents, in this case, the 'zawiyyah' or Sufi brotherhood. It is worth reading the following passage from SIMONE (2001, p. 28) as a counterpoint to the Darwinian mappings produced by the global/world cities framework:

Thus in Treichville, where I visited a Tidiane *zawiyyah* in 1993, a large world map was placed on a wall in one of the common rooms. On the map, hundreds of cities were circled with magic markers and 'tagged' with numbers. On a table below the map were heavily worn and numbered cardboard files corresponding to the numbers on the map. In these files were various lists of names of followers living in these cities with brief profiles of each one.

Such forms of 'worlding' move one away from simple core–periphery models of globalized urbanization. Instead, one is left with what ONG (1999) terms 'differentiated zones of sovereignty'. The 21st-century metropolis arbitrates this geography of multiplicity and differentiation. And in doing so it is, as Abbas would have one imagine, a 'para-site'. It is dependent on the circuits of global capital and yet it also produces and mediates these circuits.

Production of space

There is a sophisticated body of theory on the 'production of space', Lefebvre's shorthand for the ways in which surplus value is produced through the commodification and exchange of space. Of course, for Lefebvre, the production of space also takes place through representations of space (the abstract spatial conceptions of experts and planners), through the everyday, lived experience of space, and through the collective meanings of representational spaces. However, the primary appropriation of his work has centred on how property capital, once deemed to be a 'secondary' circuit, is today a 'primary' circuit, notable not simply for its role in expanded reproduction, but rather for its central role in the production of value (SMITH, 2002) and in the ever-expanding frontier of primitive accumulation (HARVEY, 2005). From such a conceptualization follows a host of corollary concepts about forms of regulation and formations of space. SMITH (1996) characterizes the contemporary city as 'revanchist', with zero tolerance for the urban poor. HARVEY (1990) charts the shift from 'urban managerialism' to 'urban entrepreneurialism', noting that the state is now an agent, rather than regulator, of the market. GRAHAM and MARVIN (2001) demonstrate that such productions of space yield a highly uneven metropolitan landscape, a 'splintering urbanism' of 'secessionary networked spaces' and 'black holes'. But of course it is this unevenness that makes possible new rounds of gentrification and urban redevelopment, with the revalorization of devalorized property (SMITH, 1996). The 'regulation' theorists (BRENNER and THEODORE, 2002) designate such practices as a 'spatial fix', whereby the crisis of over-accumulation is remedied through investments in new sites of value.

These theoretical positions have been produced in the context of the EuroAmerican urban experience. This is not to say that this analysis is not applicable to the cities of the global South. Indeed, it is highly relevant. The argument is less about transnational relevance and more about the scope and range of analysis. By being embedded in the EuroAmerican urban experience, this theoretical work bypasses some of the key ways in which the production of space takes place in other urban and metropolitan contexts. Further, this 'other' experience has considerable relevance for EuroAmerican city-regions and can provide insights into hitherto unexplained processes in these cities. One such mode of the production of space is highlighted: informality. 'First World' urban and metropolitan theory is curiously silent on the issue of informality. Or there is a tendency to imagine the 'informal' as a sphere of unregulated, even illegal, activity, outside the scope of the state, a domain of survival by the poor and marginalized, often wiped out by gentrification and redevelopment. But a large body of 'Third World' literature provides a sophisticated and rather different understanding of informality. It is worth highlighting three contributions of this analytical framework.

First, informality lies within the scope of the state rather than outside it. It is often the power of the state that determines what is informal and what is not (PORTES et al., 1989). And in many instances the state itself operates in informalized ways, thereby gaining a territorialized flexibility that it does not fully have with merely formal mechanisms of accumulation and legitimation. These too are, to borrow a term from BRENNER (2004), 'state spaces'. For example, the rapid peri-urbanization that is unfolding at the edges of the world's largest cities is an informalized process, often in violation of master plans and state norms but often informally sanctioned by the state (ROY, 2003). This means that informality is not an unregulated domain but rather is structured through various forms of extra-legal, social, and discursive regulation. Second, informality is much more than an economic sector; it is a 'mode' of the production of space (ROY and ALSAYYAD, 2003). Informality produces an uneven geography of spatial value thereby facilitating the urban logic of creative destruction. The differential value attached to what is 'formal' and what is 'informal' creates the patchwork of valorized and devalorized spaces that is in turn the frontier of primitive accumulation and gentrification. In other words, informality is a fully capitalized domain of property and is often a highly effective 'spatial fix' in the production of value and profits. Third, informality is internally differentiated. The splintering of urbanism does not take place at the fissure between formality and informality but rather, in fractal fashion, within the informalized production of space. With the consolidation of neoliberalism, there has also been a 'privatization of informality'. While informality was once primarily located on public land and practised in public space, it is today a crucial mechanism in wholly privatized and marketized urban formations, as in the informal subdivisions that constitute the peri-urbanization of so many cities (ALSAYYAD and ROY, 2003, p. 4). These forms of informality are no more legal than squatter settlements and shantytowns. But they are expressions of class power and can thus command infrastructure, services, and legitimacy in a way that marks them as substantially different than the landscape of slums.

Such issues are obviously of pressing concern for the cities of the global South where informality is often the primary mode of the production of 21st-century metropolitan space. But they are also of relevance to *all* cities because they draw attention to some key features of urbanism: the extralegal territoriality and flexibility of the state; modes of social and discursive regulation; and the production of differentiated spatial value. In this sense, informality is not a pre-capitalist relic or an icon of 'backward' economies. Rather, it is a capitalist mode of production, par excellence.

An equally significant contribution of the 'informality' framework to one's understanding of the 21st-century metropolis is the insight into forms of mobilization, agency, and resistance. Urban theory has long been concerned with the ways in which the poor and marginalized act in the face of power. However, it has been better able to explain acts of power than acts of resistance, as in concepts of growth machines, political regimes of redevelopment, modes of regulation, and urban entrepreneurialism. The 'Third World' literature on informality is a treasure-trove of conceptual work on the 'grassroots' of the city, and is thus able to expand considerably the analysis of 'urban politics' or 'metropolitics'. For example, BAYAT (2000) working in the context of Middle East cities, delineates the repertoire of tactics through which urban 'informals' appropriate and claim space (the influence of DE CERTEAU, 1984, is obvious). This 'quiet encroachment of the ordinary' by subaltern groups, according to him, creates a 'street politics' that shapes the city in fundamental ways. Similarly, CHATTERJEE (2006), writing about Indian cities, makes a distinction between 'civil' and 'political' societies. For him, civil society groups make claims as fully enfranchised citizens, a 'bourgeois governmentality' if you will. Political society on the other hand are the claims of the disenfranchised and marginalized, what APPADURAI (2002) has termed 'governmentality from below'.

Perhaps the most complex articulations of agency and subaltern subjecthood come from a growing body of work on African cities. On the one hand, this literature is concerned with the 'figures of the subject in the time of crisis', with 'registers of improvisation' where 'every law enacted is submerged by an ensemble of techniques of avoidance, circumvention, and envelopment' (MBEMBE and ROITMAN, 2003, p. 114). Here informality becomes a mode of subjectivity, a way of 'operating more resourcefully in underresourced cities'; cities thereby become 'pirate towns' (SIMONE, 2006, p. 357); and infrastructure must be understood not as steel and concrete but rather as fields of action and social networks (SIMONE, 2004a). On the other hand, this framework is more than an analysis of poverty and necessity. MBEMBE (2004, p. 378) thus designates it as an analytics of 'superfluity'. It is an analysis of the very material basis of the 'social' – of the ways in which the 'social' must be understood as 'the locus of experiment and artifice' rather than 'a matter of order and contract' (MBEMBE and NUTTALL, 2004, p. 349). How else can one understand situations where order is an artifice and the contract is an experiment, where contract is an artifice and order is an experiment? In his critique of this work, WATTS (2005) despairs:

> Is this 'really about a "collective system" or a desperate search for human agency (improvisation, incessant convertability) in the face of a neoliberal grand slam? Open and flexible, if provisional, is what used to be called self-exploitation'.

(p. 184)

But this is perhaps the point. The Africanist debates about agency, subjectivity, and politics defy the easy categorizations of power and resistance. Under conditions of crisis, the subaltern subject is simultaneously strategic and self-exploitative, simultaneously a political agent and a subject of the neoliberal grand slam.

Exurbanity and extraterritoriality

The 21st-century metropolis is a chameleon. It shifts shape and size; margins become centres; centres become frontiers; regions become cities. BAUDRILLARD (1986) writes of this process: 'They have not destroyed space; they have simply rendered it infinite by the destruction of its centre' (p. 99). The 21st-century metropolis makes a fool of census jurisdictions, of the mappings of city and suburbs, and confounds the easy narratives of regional change, including those that emphasize agglomeration and innovation. For the last two decades, the 'Los Angeles school' of urban theory has been tracing this explosion and implosion of metropolitan formations, a geography that is more appropriately imagined as 'exopolis' (SOJA, 1992) or as the 'postborder city' (DEAR and LECLERC, 2003). While the 'Los Angeles school' has been effective in analysing the symbolic economies of the postmodern metropolis, the concern here is with a very specific dimension of exurbanity: the relationship of city and nation. Drawing on the experiences of cities of the global South, it is argued that exurban geographies are deeply implicated in the making of the nation and, therefore, exceed the scale of city-regions. In this sense, they are 'extraterritorial' spaces.

The 'extraterritorial' metropolis is evident in various contexts. For DEAR and LECLERC (2003), the 'postborder city' is a 'transnational megalopolis' that exceeds not only metropolitan jurisdictions, but also national borders. The 'postborder city' is something more than a vast metropolis and something more than cross-border exchanges. It is an 'integrated city-region, or

regional city, that just happens to be bisected by an international border' (p. xii). At the same time, this city-region is not contiguous territory; the suburbs of its inner cities lie across national borders, in the villages of Latin America (DAVIS, 1999). In other words, the 'postborder city' subsumes national space-making within the territory of the metropolis. It thus transcends the border and yet it also recreates multiple borders at multiple, scattered sites. The 'postborder city' is after all also a 'fortress city' (DAVIS, 1990). When Baudrillard writes that exurbanity is American and America is exurban, he does not mean that this is uniquely American territory. Instead, he is suggesting that it is in the space of exurbanity that the 'utopia' of the American nation is achieved and that it is here that the violences accompanying such a utopia are most clearly traced.

There are other manifestations of the 'transnational megalopolis'. The extended metropolitan forms that are emerging in Southeast Asia, what LAQUIAN (2005) calls 'mega urban regions', are not only conurbations of city and countryside, but also spaces of transnational accumulation and development. Kuala Lumpur's Multimedia Super Corridor, created by Mahathir's Vision 2020, stretches 38 miles from Kuala Lumpur International Airport to the Petronas Towers and city centre. This spatial plan is a shorthand for transnational ambitions, a 'Cyberjaya' metropolis that can harness the benefits of informational capitalism and stretch the Kuala Lumpur metropolitan region to meet up with the development boom in neighbouring Singapore. But it is also anchored by a deeply nationalistic set of aspirations, including the new town capital 'Putrajaya' complete with an architectural aesthetics that conveys the image of a globalized, and yet distinctively Malaysian, modernity. Malaysia's cultural slogan after all is 'Malaysia, Truly Asia', a modernity of multicultural intermingling and a postcolonial harmony of colonial landmarks and hypermodern spatialities.

This dialectic of nationalism and transnationalism, of territoriality and extraterritoriality, is also sharply obvious in Shanghai. ABBAS (2000, p. 778) interprets early 20th-century Shanghai as the 'cosmopolitanism of extraterritoriality'. Indeed, *fin-de-siècle* Shanghai was a city of *inter*national interests and settlements, an ensemble of French, America, and British territories. The metropolis was thus simultaneously territorial and extraterritorial, with different (national) rules and norms shaping each swath of settlement. *Fin-de-millénaire* Shanghai is similarly cosmopolitan. The question is whether its extraterritoriality is similarly pronounced. Is the speed and intensity of transnational investments, including those by the overseas Chinese, creating an extraterritorial metropolis? Is Shanghai located in place and time, or is it a city of elsewhere, the city that is yet to come? Is it possible to interpret Shanghai as an expression of Chinese modernity if the very category of 'Chinese-ness' is bound up with flexible citizenship, diasporic identity, and transnational accumulation (ONG, 1999)? And yet is not Shanghai a distinctive project of a distinctive sort of national/nationalistic state anchored by the same types of colonial nostalgia and postcolonial hyperboles as Kuala Lumpur?

To read the extraterritorial in the territories of the metropolis is crucial. Equally crucial is the reading of the national in the transnational megalopolis. Such readings make visible formations of power and governance and forms of accumulation and dispossession. The most obvious example is the extra/territoriality and trans/nationalism of the Israeli settlements in the West Bank. Designated by NEWMAN (1996) as instances of suburban and exurban 'colonization', these settlements (which are in effect 'informal subdivisions') manifest the extraterritorial power of the state of Israel. Each time a settlement is established, Israeli infrastructure and law extends to this site, thus creating a metropolitan form that is not only ethnocratic (YIFTACHEL, 2006), but also one of splintered sovereignty (SEGAL and WEIZMAN, 2003). There is perhaps only one other contemporary example of such intense forms of extraterritoriality: the territorial formations of American military bases that now puncture the national territories of American allies and occupied countries – the 'America towns' of Iraq, Afghanistan, Okinawa, South Korea, Italy, and the Philippines (GILLEM, 2004). To keep pace with such geographies, one needs an urban and metropolitan theory that is simultaneously located and dis-located.

METROPOLITAN MODERNITIES

The study of the 21st-century metropolis is inevitably a study of modernity (ROBINSON, 2006). In urban and metropolitan theory, modernity has been firmly located in the EuroAmerican city. It is the experience of Paris, London, Vienna, New York, Chicago, and Los Angeles that defines the contours of the modern and postmodern. The cities of the global South are for the most part seen to be inheritors of a backward modernity, the 'modernism of underdevelopment' (BERMAN, 1982), or aspiring to mimic and copy EuroAmerican modernities. In recent years a strikingly different analysis of urban modernities has emerged. There are at least three variations in this emerging framework.

The first is the argument that modernity (and its violences) is everywhere. Writing against the efforts to frame 'Third World' cities through the master tropes of slums and disorder, NUTTALL and MBEMBE (2005) boldly assert that African cities and their residents are 'full participants in metropolitan modernity'. In a 'sameliness as worldliness' argument, they note that lavish urbanism is everywhere, including in Africa; and slum life is everywhere; including in America. The second is an imagination about 'alternative' modernities (GAONKAR, 2001), the sense that while modernity is everywhere, distinctive sorts of 'native' modernities are produced under conditions of 'alterity' and difference. There is thus a Shanghai modern, a Bengali modern, a Cairo cosmopolitan. The third is a bolder argument, for it 'dislocates' the very production of modernity. In particular, it calls into question the Western origins of modernity, arguing instead that it is important to take seriously the emergence of the modern outside the geography of the West and in the circuits of production and exchange that encircle the world (MITCHELL, 2000). It is in this sense that CHAKRABARTY (2000) 'provincializes Europe' and ROBINSON (2003) calls for the application of such 'postcolonial' perspectives to the study of cities and territories.

The present paper has sought to sketch the first outlines of a more worldly theory of the 21st-century metropolis. In doing so, it has drawn heavily upon the third strand of modern imaginings: a 'worlding' of cities such that the standard geographies of core and periphery are disrupted and dislocated. In such a world, Vancouver and San Francisco are the peripheral outposts of a dynamic Pacific Rim urbanism centred in the para-site, Hong Kong, and extending to Beijing and Shanghai with labour and outsourcing hinterlands in the Philippines, Cambodia, Chinese economic zones, and Vietnam. In such a world, Dubai is the lodestone of desires and aspirations, the icon of supermodernity in the backbreaking trudge of transnational migration from the villages of Egypt, Bangladesh, Indonesia, and Pakistan. It is surely an 'evil paradise' of 'fear and money', a 'dreamworld of neoliberalism' (DAVIS, 2006; DAVIS and MORK, 2007), but it is also an articulation of an Arab modernity where more is at stake than what DAVIS (2006, p. 53) designates as the 'monstrous caricature of futurism'. It is the place at which the distinctions between the black economy and global finance capital are erased, where city and nature are violently fused, and where the feudalism of an emirate meets up with an open cosmopolitanism.

This paper has also inscribed the 'worlding' of cities with the arguments of 'worldliness' – that while distinctive and alternative modernities are produced in multiple urban sites, such experiences can speak to and inform one's analysis of other places. While much of urban theory has managed a traffic of ideas that routes concepts from EuroAmerica to the global South, there is an urgency and necessity to chart more intricate roots and routes. It is in this sense that the study of informality in Latin America can tell something profound about political regimes and politics in *all* cities. It is in this sense that the registers of metropolitan wealth, transience, and disposability in African cities can tell something profound about agency and subjectivity in *all* cities. The extraterritoriality of the 21st-century metropolis demands such analytical work, a theory that is simultaneously located and dislocated.

There are, of course, limitations to such an approach. Placing the 21st-century metropolis in its different world-areas runs the risk of reifying territorial jurisdictions and geopolitical stereotypes, of producing a classificatory scheme that can obscure topologies and relationalities. However, when such world-areas are approached as 'process' rather than 'trait' geographies, and when the knowledge produced about these areas is seen as a 'strategic essentialism' rather than as a generalization, a more dynamic imagination and epistemology is possible. At the very least, such an approach can dramatically reconfigure the signifier, 'global', that seems to have become an ubiquitous presence in the theorization of city-regions. It is known how to map the 'global' through Darwinian hierarchies of city-regions; much less is known about the complex connections, exchanges, and references through which cities (everywhere) are worlded. The world is not flat, and it is time to produce a more contoured knowledge of its cities.

Acknowledgements – The author wishes to thank Angela Hull, Michael Neuman, and two anonymous reviewers for their useful comments. The author is particularly grateful to Ryan Centner, PhD candidate in Sociology, and Sylvia Nam, PhD student in City & Regional Planning, at the University of California–Berkeley. Their research assistance was invaluable in shaping this paper and its arguments.

REFERENCES

ABBAS A. (2000) Cosmopolitan de-scriptions: Shanghai and Hong Kong, *Public Culture* **12**, 769–786.

ALSAYYAD N. and ROY A. (2003) Prologue/dialogue, in ROY A. and ALSAYYAD N. (Eds) *Urban Informality: Transnational Perspectives from the Middle East, South Asia, and Latin America*. Lexington Books, Lanham, MD.

AMIN A. (2004) Regions unbound: towards a new politics of place, *Geografiska Annaler: Series B, Human Geography* **86**, 33–44.

APPADURAI A. (1996) *Modernity at Large: Cultural Dimensions of Globalization*, University of Minnesota Press, Minneapolis, MN.

APPADURAI A. (2000a) Grassroots globalization and research imagination, *Public Culture* **12**, 1–19.

APPADURAI A. (2000b) Spectral housing and urban cleansing: notes on millennial Mumbai, *Public Culture* **12**, 627–651.

APPADURAI A. (2002) Deep democracy: urban governmentality and the horizon of politics, *Public Culture* **14**, 21–47.

AUYERO J. (2000) The hyper-shantytown: neoliberal violence(s) in the Argentine slum, *Ethnography* **1**, 93–116.

BAUDRILLARD J. (1986) *America*. Verso, New York, NY.

BAYAT A. (2000) From 'dangerous classes' to 'quiet rebels': the politics of the urban subaltern in the global south, *International Sociology* **15**, 533–557.

BERMAN M. (1982) *All That Is Solid Melts Into Air*. Simon & Schuster, New York, NY.

BRENNER N. (2004) *New State Spaces: Urban Governance and the Rescaling of Statehood*. Oxford University Press, New York, NY.

BRENNER N. and THEODORE N. (2002) Cities and the geographies of 'actually existing neoliberalism, *Antipode* **34**, 349–379.

CALDEIRA T. (2001) *City of Walls: Crime, Segregation, and Citizenship in Sao Paulo*. University of California Press, Berkeley, CA.

CARDOSO F. H. and FALETTO E. (1979) *Dependency and Development in Latin America*. University of California Press, Berkeley, CA.

CASTELLS M. (1983) *The City and the Grassroots*. University of California Press, Berkeley, CA.

CASTELLS M. (1996) *The Rise of the Network Society*. Blackwell, Cambridge.

CHAKRABARTY D. (2000) *Provincializing Europe: Postcolonial Thought and Historical Difference*. Princeton University Press, Princeton, NJ.

CHATTERJEE P. (2006) *The Politics of the Governed: Reflections on Popular Politics in Most of the World*. Columbia University Press, New York, NY.

CONSTABLE N. (1997) *Maid to Order in Hong Kong: An Ethnography of Filipina Workers*. Cornell University Press, Ithaca, NY.

DAVIS M. (1990) *City of Quartz: Excavating the Future in Los Angeles*. Vintage, New York, NY.

DAVIS M. (1999) Magical urbanism: how Latinos reinvent the big city, *New Left Review* **234**, 3–43.

DAVIS M. (2004) Planet of slums: urban involution and the informal proletariat, *New Left Review* **26**, 5–34.

DAVIS M. (2006) Fear and money in Dubai, *New Left Review* **41**, 47–68.

DAVIS M. and MORK D. B. (Eds) (2007) *Evil Paradises: Dreamworlds of Neoliberalism*. New Press, New York, NY.

DE CERTEAU M. (1984) *The Practice of Everyday Life*. University of California Press, Berkeley, CA.

DEAR M. and LECLERC G. (Eds) (2003) *Postborder City: Cultural Spaces of Bajalta California*. Routledge, New York, NY.

DUTTA A. (2006) *The Bureaucracy of Beauty*. Routledge, New York, NY.

EHRENREICH B. and HOCHSCHILD A. (Eds) (2003) *Global Woman: Nannies, Maids, and Sex Workers in the New Economy*. Metropolitan Books, New York, NY.

FRANK A. G. (1967) *Capitalism and Underdevelopment in Latin America*. Monthly Review Press, New York, NY.

GAONKAR D. P. (Ed.) (2001) *Alternative Modernities*. Duke University Press, Durham, NC.

GILLEM M. (2004) America town: building the outposts of empire. Unpublished PhD dissertation, Department of Architecture, University of California at Berkeley, Berkeley, CA.

GRAHAM S. (Ed.) (2004) *Cities, War, and Terrorism: Towards an Urban Geopolitics*. Blackwell, Cambridge.

GRAHAM S. and MARVIN S. (2001) *Splintering Urbanism: Networked Infrastructures, Technological Mobilities, and the Urban Condition*. Routledge, London.

HARVEY D. (1989) *The Urban Experience*. Johns Hopkins University Press, Baltimore, MD.

HARVEY D. (1990) *The Condition of Postmodernity*. Blackwell, Cambridge.

HARVEY D. (2005) *The New Imperialism*. Oxford University Press, New York, NY.

HOLSTON J. (Ed.) (1999) *Cities and Citizenship*. Duke University Press, Durham, NC.

HOLSTON J. (2001) Urban citizenship and globalization, in SCOTT A. J. (Ed.) *Global City-Regions: Trends, Theory, Policy*, pp. 325–347. Oxford University Press, New York, NY.

ISIN E. F. (2001) Istanbul's conflicting paths to citizenship: Islamization and globalization, in SCOTT A. J. (Ed.) *Global City-Regions: Trends, Theory, Policy*, pp. 349–370. Oxford University Press, New York, NY.

JACOBS J. (1996) *Edge of Empire: Postcolonialism and the City*. Routledge, New York, NY.

JARVIS H. (2007) Home truths about care-less competitiveness, *International Journal of Urban and Regional Research* **31**, 207–214.

JESSOP B. (1994) Post-Fordism and the state, in AMIN A. (Ed.) *Post-Fordism: A Reader*, pp. 251–279. Blackwell, Cambridge.

JONAS A. and WARD K. (2007) Introduction to a debate on city-regions: new geographies of governance, democracy and social reproduction, *International Journal of Urban and Regional Research* **31**, 169–178.

KNOX P. and TAYLOR P. (1995) *World Cities in a World-System*. Cambridge University Press, Cambridge.

LAQUIAN A. (2005) *Beyond Metropolis: The Planning and Governance of Asia's Mega Urban Regions*. Johns Hopkins University Press, Baltimore. MD.

LEE L. (2001) Shanghai modern: reflections on urban culture in China in the 1930s, in GAONKAR D. P. (Ed.) *Alternative Modernities*, pp. 86–122. Duke University Press, Durham, NC.

MBEMBE A. (2004) Aesthetics of superfluity, *Public Culture* **16**, 373–405.

MBEMBE A. and NUTTALL S. (2004) Writing the world from an African metropolis, *Public Culture* **16**, 347–372.

MBEMBE A. and ROITMAN J. (2003) The figure of the subject in the time of crisis, in ABDOUL M. (Ed.) *Under Siege: Four African Cities*, pp. 99–126. Hatje Cantz, Ostfildern.

MITCHELL K. (2004) *Crossing the Neoliberal Line: Pacific Rim Migration and the Metropolis*. Temple University Press, Philadelphia, PA.

MITCHELL T. (Ed.) (2000) *Questions of Modernity*. University of California Press, Berkeley, CA.

NEWMAN D. (1996) The territorial politics of exurbanization, *Israeli Affairs* **3**, 61–85.

NUTTALL S. and MBEMBE A. (2005) A blasé attitude: a response to Michael Watts, *Public Culture* **17**, 193–201.

OLDS K. (2001a) *Globalization and Urban Change: Capital, Culture and Pacific Rim Mega-Projects*. Oxford University Press, Oxford.

OLDS K. (2001b) Practices for 'process geographies': a view from within and outside the periphery, *Environment and Planning D: Society and Space* **19**, 127–136.

ONG A. (1999) *Flexible Citizenship: The Cultural Logics of Transnationality*. Duke University Press, Durham, NC.

PERLMAN J. (2003) The reality of marginality, in ROY A. and ALSAYYAD N. (Eds) *Urban Informality: Transnational Perspectives from the Middle East, South Asia, and Latin America*, pp. 105–146. Lexington Press, Lanham, MD.

PORTES A., CASTELLS M. and BENTON L. (1989) *The Informal Economy*. Johns Hopkins University Press, Baltimore, MD.

PURCELL M. (2007) City-regions, neoliberal globalization and democracy: a research agenda, *International Journal of Urban and Regional Research* **31**, 197–206.

RAO V. (2006) Slum as theory: the South/Asian city and globalization, *International Journal of Urban and Regional Research* **30**, 225–232.

ROBINSON J. (2002) Global and world cities: a view from off the map, *International Journal of Urban and Regional Research* **26**, 531–554.

ROBINSON J. (2003) Postcolonialising geography: tactics and pitfalls, *Singapore Journal of Tropical Geography* **24**, 273–289.

ROBINSON J. (2006) *Ordinary Cities: Between Modernity and Development*. Routledge, London.

ROY A. (2003) *City Requiem, Calcutta: Gender and the Politics of Poverty*. University of Minnesota Press, Minneapolis, MN.

ROY A. and ALSAYYAD N. (Eds) (2003) *Urban Informality: Transnational Perspectives from the Middle East, Latin America, and South Asia*. Lexington Books, Lanham, MD.

SASSEN S. (1991) *The Global City: New York, London, Tokyo*. Princeton University Press, Princeton, NJ.

SCOTT A. J. (Ed.) (2001) *Global City-Regions: Trends, Theory, Policy*. Oxford University Press, New York, NY.

SEGAL R. and WEIZMAN E. (Eds) (2003) *A Civilian Occupation: The Politics of Israeli Architecture*. Verso, New York, NY.

SEGBERS K. (2007) *The Making of Global City Regions: Johannesburg, Mumbai/Bombay, São Paulo, and Shanghai*. Johns Hopkins University Press, Baltimore, MD.

SIMONE A. (2001) On the worlding of African cities, *African Studies Review* **44**, 15–41.

SIMONE A. (2004a) People as infrastructure: intersecting fragments in Johannesburg, *Public Culture* **16**, 407–429.

SIMONE A. (2004b) *For the City Yet to Come: Changing Life in Four African Cities*. Duke University Press, Durham, NC.

SIMONE A. (2006) Pirate towns: reworking social and symbolic infrastructures in Johannesburg and Douala, *Urban Studies* **43**, 357–370.

SINGERMANN D. and AMAR P. (Eds) (2006) *Cairo Cosmopolitan: Politics, Culture, and Urban Space in the New Middle East*. AUC Press, Cairo.

SMITH M. P. (2001) *Transnational Urbanism: Locating Globalization*. Blackwell, Cambridge.

SMITH N. (1996) *The New Urban Frontier: Gentrification and the Revanchist City*. Routledge, New York, NY.

SMITH N. (2002) New globalism, new urbanism: gentrification as global urban strategy, *Antipode* **34**, 427–450.

SOJA E. (1992) Inside exopolis: scenes from Orange County, in SORKIN M. (Ed.) *Variations on a Theme Park: The New American City and the End of Public Space*. Hill & Wang, New York, NY.

SORKIN M. (Ed.) (1992) *Variations on a Theme Park: The New American City and the End of Public Space*. Hill & Wang, New York, NY.

STREN R. (2001) Local governance and social diversity in the developing world: new challenges for globalizing city-regions, in SCOTT A. J. (Ed.) *Global City-Regions: Trends, Theory, Policy*. Oxford University Press, New York, NY.

TAYLOR P. (2000) World cities and territorial states under conditions of contemporary globalization, *Political Geography* **19**, 5–32.

WATTS M. (2005) Baudelaire over Berea, Simmel over Sandton?, *Public Culture* **17**, 181–192.

YEOH B., HUANG S. and WILLIS K. (2000) Global cities, transnational flows, and gender dimensions, *Tijdschrift voor Economische en Social Geografie* **2**, 147–158.

YIFTACHEL O. (2006) *Ethnocracy: Land and Identity Politics in Israel/Palestine*. University of Pennsylvania Press, Philadelphia, PA.

City Regions and Place Development

PATSY HEALEY

HEALEY P. City regions and place development, *Regional Studies*. The paper explores the concept of a 'city region' in the context of proposals for reconfiguring sub-national government arrangements. It considers the various arguments behind calls for a 'city region' focus, and reviews recent experiences in the Netherlands and England. This highlights that the concept of a 'city region' can be mobilized both as an organizing device and to call attention to place dynamics. There are dangers in a narrow focus on administrative and economic considerations when promoting the creation of 'city region' institutional arenas. Instead, greater attention is needed to promote more integrated, locally specific, place development agendas.

HEALEY P. 城市区域与场所发展，区域研究。在多项计划纷纷提出要重新明确国家次级政府机构安排的背景下，本文探讨了"城市区域"这一概念。文章剖析了目前"城市区域"这一学术领域所涉及到的种种观点，并且回顾了最近荷兰及英国的相关经验。文章强调，城市区域这一概念既可以看作组织化的途径同时也关注场所活力。在考虑"城市区域"这一概念在制度性领域中可能涉及的更多内容时，单纯将注意力锁定在其管理和经济意义上是值得商榷的。相反，我们应该拟定更加综合的、基于地方的场所发展议程。

大都市区域　经济竞争力　政府分权　可持续发展　社会创新　制度设计　整合的地方发展

HEALEY P. Ville-région et développement de places, *Regional Studies*. L'auteur analyse le concept de ville-région dans le contexte de propositions de reconfiguration d'arrangements gouvernementaux subnationaux. Il prend en considération les divers arguments, appelle à se concentrer sur les villes régions et passe en revue des expériences récentes menées aux Pays-Bas et en Angleterre. Il insiste sur le fait que le concept de ville-région peut être mobilisé comme dispositif d'organisation et pour rappeler l'attention sur la dynamique de places. Il est dangereux de se concentrer étroitement sur des considérations administratives et économiques lorsque l'on fait la promotion de la création d'ensembles institutionnels de villes-régions. Au contraire, il faut attacher une plus grande attention à la promotion de programmes de développement de places mieux intégrés et spécifiques sur le plan local.

HEALEY P. Stadtregionen und Raumentwicklung, *Regional Studies*. In diesem Beitrag wird das Konzept der 'Stadtregion' im Kontext von Vorschlägen zur Neugestaltung von subnationalen Regierungsformen untersucht. Ich untersuche die verschiedenen Argumente hinter der Forderung nach einem Fokus auf der 'Stadtregion' und überprüfe die jüngsten Erfahrungen aus den Niederlanden und England. Die Ergebnisse verdeutlichen, dass sich das Konzept der 'Stadtregion' sowohl als organisatorisches Instrument als auch zur Hervorhebung von örtlichen Dynamiken nutzen lässt. Bei der Förderung der Schaffung von institutionellen 'Stadtregion'-Arenen besteht die Gefahr eines zu engen Fokus auf verwaltungstechnischen und wirtschaftlichen Gesichtspunkten. Stattdessen sollte der Förderung von integrierteren und lokalspezifischen Raumentwicklungsplänen stärkere Beachtung geschenkt werden.

HEALEY P. Ciudad-regiones y desarrollo de áreas, *Regional Studies*. En este artículo analizo el concepto de 'ciudad-región' en el contexto de propuestas para reconfigurar los acuerdos gubernamentales subnacionales. Considero los diferentes argumentos con respecto al enfoque de una 'ciudad-región' y analizo las recientes experiencias en los Países Bajos e Inglaterra. Destaco que el concepto de una 'ciudad-región' puede aprovecharse como dispositivo organizativo y como elemento para destacar las dinámicas de áreas. Al fomentar la creación de escenarios institucionales de una 'ciudad-región' se corre el peligro de limitarse a las consideraciones administrativas y económicas. Más bien se debería prestar más atención para fomentar programas del desarrollo de áreas más integrados y localmente específicos.

IMAGINING CITY REGIONS

The concept of 'city region' is deeply embedded in European imagination and in spatial planning concepts (LE GALÈS, 2002). It is often assumed that a 'city region' corresponds with a 'functional reality' of integrated economic, political and social relations. This 'reality' could be grounded in a pre-industrial idea of the connection between market towns and administrative centres and their surrounding rural hinterlands. Or it could refer to integrated housing and labour markets revolving around an 'urban 'core' of an urbanized region (ORGANIZATION FOR ECONOMIC CO-OPERATION AND DEVELOPMENT (OECD), 2006b; CLARK, 2005). In recent years, the 'city region' concept has been linked to the idea that large cities are dynamic centres of economic innovation, producing 'assets' with which cities compete in global space (SCOTT, 2001; HARDING et al., 2004). Some have emphasized the 'city region' as an areal unit within which critical socio-environmental relations can be effectively contained, and, as such, a valuable focus for pursuing strategies for more environmentally sustainable forms of urban development (RAVETZ, 2000). The planning tradition in particular has traditionally looked to the 'city region' as a focus for 'comprehensive' place development strategies. These days, the idea that public policy could 'comprehensively plan' complex urban areas has long been demolished. But yet both in aspirations and in practices, those involved in 'planning systems' find themselves at the sharp end of encounters between social, environmental and economic agendas as these are played out in particular places. They are thus unavoidably engaged with 'place development' activities.

Twentieth-century regional planners and development analysts in Europe have repeatedly turned to the idea that 'functional' realities should be aligned with administrative jurisdictions, to create planning areas – city regions, metropolitan regions, functional urban areas, etc., which contain within them the critical relations upon which the future development trajectories of settlements depend. Before 20th-century urbanization, the city commune or municipality seemed to provide such correspondence. By the mid-20th century, as urban infrastructures and communications networks spread across national landscapes, urban relations exploded beyond municipal boundaries, generating all kinds of proposals to create larger administrative arenas to correspond with the perceived 'functional' city region. But attempts to tie critical economic, social, political and environmental relationships to a concept of a relationally integrated 'urban place' have become increasingly difficult, as different relational webs connect people, firms and non-human processes to all sorts of other places, often in more closely 'integrated' ways than to spatially contiguous neighbours. What then can a 'city region' be and what is its value as a planning and governance concept? Does it still have a value in promoting some kind of 'integrated' policy attention to the place qualities and place development of complex urban areas?

If city regions could be understood as 'objectively existing' phenomena, as coherent, stable, discrete, socio-spatial conjunctions and aggregations, bounding within them the major relations of all aspects of social, economic, political and economic life, then there is a case for co-aligning political jurisdictions with such functional entities. Within Europe, under the auspices of both the current mobilization of attention to European spatial development (CSD, 1999; FALUDI and WATERHOUT, 2002; FALUDI, 2003), and national concerns for reconfiguring sub-national government, there has been a recent upsurge of interest in the statistical definition of 'functional urban regions'.[1] But analyses of urban and regional development processes emphasize that the diverse relations which transect and intersect across and through urban areas have many different kinds of space–time dimensions which are rarely stable. The search for a 'city region' area which encompasses some stable 'coherence' and 'integration' relations may therefore be misguided.

In its place have come two recognitions. The first derives from an epistemology which recognizes that ideas of the city, city region, of place, are not objectively 'there', but are imagined concepts, constructed in particular times and places for specific reasons (AMIN, 2002; HEALEY, 2002; McGUIRK, 2007). This raises questions about the purposes of such constructions and the institutional work they do. The second comes from an awareness of the complexity and diversity of the socio-spatial relations through which phenomena are distributed in space and time. Any physical area has, moving through, around and over it, all kinds of relations, with diverse space–time dynamics, reach and patternings. Sometimes these interrelate and coalesce, to produce qualities, synergies (and dysfunctions) which help to create a sense of place-ness. Such qualities may become associated with a history and identity in a cultural geography. Or they may be recognized in an economic geography of 'places with assets'. Or they are linked to a political–administrative search for better coordination of public investments and programmes, or for better ways to connect the state with citizens and other stakeholders in relations which touch a 'place'. But a 'place-focus' which suits one set of relations may well bump up against the spatial patterning of another. For example, JONES and MACLEOD (2005), referring to initiatives in South West England, highlight the tension between 'localized production spaces' and 'spaces of citizenship' around which local political mobilization may occur. In other words, an integration of diverse relations in urban areas cannot be assumed to exist. Contemporary advocates of 'city region' ideas acknowledge this in comments about the 'fuzzy' boundaries around the areas they imagine (HARDING et al., 2004; NEW LOCAL GOVERNMENT NETWORK (NLGN), 2005).

Yet, some kind of 'place integration' can be cultivated by deliberate action. Creating a 'city region' as a political–administrative entity capable of promoting 'city region' place qualities might, in the long-term, have this effect (for examples, see ALBRECHTS et al., 2003; and HERRSCHEL and NEWMAN, 2005). But there is no necessary correspondence between the creation of formal jurisdictions and the production of governance capacity for place-focused development programmes. The experience of places where some kind of correspondence seems to exist, such as the Portland area in Oregon, USA (ABBOTT, 2001), or the Hanover area in Germany (ALBRECHTS et al., 2003), suggests that such a correspondence requires substantial and enduring mobilization of governance attention around a city region place development project. Mobilization of this kind involves generating attention and energy, to draw into some kind of encounter and conjunction the particular relations of significance to such a place development project. In other words, the justification for the creation of 'city regions' lies not so much in connecting political jurisdictions to objectively existing, integrated 'functional areas'. Instead, it lies in the impact which the creation of such an institutional arena and spatial conception may, over time and in some areas, come to have on the relations which weave through, around and across a physical area.

These two insights have been developed in what has come to be known as 'relational geography' (AMIN and THRIFT, 2002; AMIN, 2002; GRAHAM and HEALEY, 1999; MASSEY, 2005; HEALEY, 2004, 2007; JONES and MACLEOD, 2005; MARSTON and JONES, 2005). This emphasizes that cities were never unambiguous, integrated socio-physical objects, even in pre-industrial times. Urban life is lived through all kinds of different relational webs, which interweave across the terrain of the urban. Some webs intersect with others to produce intense synergies and complex tensions,

partly creative, partly destructive. Others barely touch each other, or clear a way through blockages in ways which displace and block the opportunities for others. The urban is always in production and always full of potentialities and tensions. All kinds of terms have been used to express different dimensions of the experience of urban life, each reflecting different imaginations and different purposes. The concept of a 'city region' is no exception. Such place concepts, in a relational geography, are 'summoned up' into imagination, fed by some resonance with an experienced reality (AMIN, 2004). When used in governance contexts such as spatial planning, they are fed back into particular relational webs, to have material effects on such realities (HEALEY, 2007). But inevitably, such concepts are selective in their focus of attention. Some relations and integrations are emphasized, while others slip out of the limelight.

The invocation of 'city regions' in a public policy context can thus be understood both as an organizing device, to focus attention and governance activity, and as a call for attention to place dynamics, to focus policy agendas and programmes. This raises three issues. Firstly, who is doing the 'summoning up' of the idea of a city region, for what purposes, and in what institutional arenas, with what legitimacy and accountability? Secondly, what relations and identities are carried within a particular conception of a 'city region', associated with what mobilization force and with what potential consequences? Thirdly, what kind of contribution could such a concept make to the form and content of place development trajectories?

This paper develops the approach outlined above through a review of the various arguments for promoting a city region as an institutional arena and a policy focus. It then briefly comments on recent experiences in constructing 'metropolitan' institutional arenas in the Netherlands and the current enthusiasm for 'city regions' in England. Both illustrate the difficulties of promoting new sub-national institutional arenas in the crowded governance landscapes of North West Europe. Finally, it returns to the questions raised above and consider the value of promoting 'institutional fixes' around 'city' and 'metropolitan' regions in relation to the promotion of place development agendas which have the capacity to link together (that is, to 'integrate') concerns for social justice, environmental well-being and economic vitality.

CITY REGIONS AND THE POLITICS OF PLACE DEVELOPMENT

There has been a vigorous promotion of ideas about city regions, urban regions, metropolitan areas, sub-regions, polycentric regions and 'functional urban areas' in Western Europe in recent years. This has been linked to a broader and diffuse project of reconfiguring formal government organization and practices (KEATING, 1997, 2006; MORGAN, 2006; BRENNER, 1999, 2004; GUALINI, 2006). Economic and administrative considerations have dominated in the debates about such initiatives. Some analysts interpret the search for sub-national reconfiguration as a move, in the context of 'globalizing' economic dynamics, beyond the nation state as the key site for negotiating relations between the spheres of the state and of economic activity. For regulation theorists, changes in the 'mode of accumulation' of the global economy generate pressures for a shift from a welfare-oriented, managerial and delivery-focused state, to an 'entrepreneurial state', focused on creating conditions for innovation and continual adaptation to changing economic contexts (JESSOP, 2000, 2002; MACLEOD, 1999). In terms of the organization of state agencies, this means devolving state power to regional and local levels, shifting more activity to economic actors, and developing horizontal relations between actors, to replace the vertical policy communities which had formed around the service delivery activities of the welfare state. In this argument, policy attention to regional development moves from a focus on redistribution of wealth from 'leading' regions to 'lagging' regions, to a focus on the autonomous (and diverse) development dynamics of all areas in an economic landscape of regional economies in competition with each other (OECD, 2006b; HARDING et al., 2004; COMBES et al., 2006). The objective is not so much to create employment opportunities for those adversely affected by industrial restructuring. Instead, it is to create wealth through cultivating innovative place-development assets. Claims are often made that 'cities' are sites of economic innovation in the context of a 'knowledge society', in which agglomeration economies and cultural synergies are assets, although there are active critical debates about such claims, not least in the pages of *Regional Studies*. MORGAN (2006) describes the claims as representing a shift from creating an 'employment dividend' to an 'economic dividend'. This 'economic competitiveness' argument serves to justify a more selective application of national government growth-promoting development investment to specific projects and areas, rather than generalized budget allocations to sub-national programmes. In this context, a 'city region' could become the critical institutional arena both for identifying and selecting projects in a new sub-national configuration of government, and for encouraging the promotion of some kind of endogenous economic development. Rather than a 'levelling up' of areas, this development conception emphasizes cities in competition with each other, both for success in creating an 'economic dividend' and for public funds to help them in this venture. As will be seen, such arguments have been influential in both the Netherlands and the UK.

These economic arguments are often buttressed by concerns about the consequences of a shift from the delivery practices of the different services within a 'welfare' nation state, to the more diffuse array of provision of welfare and infrastructure facilities and services resulting from all kinds of forms of privatization, contracting out and partnership in the provision of 'public goods'. Regulation theorists and many others often refer to this as a shift from 'government' to 'governance' (JESSOP, 1997; GUALINI, 2006). A 'city region' arena may be promoted to draw these different networks of provision together, to enable better coordination and delivery of services and infrastructures in particular places. This administrative efficiency argument may in turn be linked to the search for a better relation between citizens and state, making it easier for policy-makers to interact with and pay attention to citizens and their concerns. In this argument, a 'city region', below both the nation state and larger regional units, is rhetorically promoted as a way to give more legitimacy to public policy programmes, and thus to serve the project of 'democratic renewal' in Western European countries.

This is already a big agenda for a policy idea. But the economic and political arguments which sustain it are not uncontested or stable. In the 20th-century, initiatives to create new city region/metro region arenas have not always endured or got beyond enabling legislation (SALET et al., 2003; ALBRECHTS et al., 2001; NEUMAN and GAVINHA, 2005). To have significant effects and to endure through changes in intellectual fashions and political attention, the idea of the place of a 'city region' has to become embedded in key relations and imaginations within the place itself. It has to act as a critical identity-shaping force, mobilizing attention locally when neglected externally.[2] A 'city region' concept which has such power will then have significant effects in generating and maintaining synergies and resistances which will produce distinctive place qualities. This implies that the promotion of a 'city region' as a generalized policy idea needs to be coupled with some kind of more specific and localized 'place development' project and some idea of how this might be pursued. Such a project, of course, underlies the 'economic competitiveness' discourse, which accepts a conception of the regional differentiation of development potentials across national and European space. Cities and regions are now often presented in policy rhetoric as critical sites for the creation of development energy, of endogenous development, through the promotion of specific assets and the removal of barriers to development opportunity (CLARK, 2005; HARDING et al., 2004). Yet, this rhetoric tends to be articulated as a generalized recipe, with little specific emphasis on the particular relations and dynamics which underpin the occurrence of the 'assets' and generate the 'development opportunities' of particular localities. This criticism is forcefully made in a recent OECD study of 'Newcastle in the North East' (OECD, 2006a), and could easily have been made of other English regional and sub-regional development strategies (TEWDWR-JONES and ALLMENDINGER, 2006). The result is a 'thin' place development concept and a weak formation of enduring institutional energy to underpin a strategy. Programmes developed from and through such strategies, 'top-down regionalization' as JONES and MACLEOD (2005) call them, are likely to have some effects merely because they lever on significant national and European public funding streams. They add little value in themselves.

A further major weakness of these kinds of strategies is their pre-occupation with the economic sphere. In reconfiguring government arrangements from vertical, sectoral departments and policy communities, which separated economic, social and environmental considerations into discrete, hierarchically ordered institutional nexuses, this economic emphasis suggests a separation into government levels. City region arenas can address the relations between the state and economic actors, formerly focused at the national level (OECD, 2006b; HARDING et al., 2004), while municipalities and sub-municipal arenas can address the relations between citizens and the state. But such a separation is in striking contrast to other 'place development' ideas which have been emerging in the past two decades. Two such ideas develop a broader perspective on place qualities. Both emphasize the importance of place development agendas in which economic dimensions are integrated with environmental and social dimensions in all levels and arenas of government.

One of these is the agenda of 'sustainability' and 'sustainable development'. This takes a general perspective on how societies should develop, but is deeply concerned with how many relations play out in particular places to impact not only on relations within a locale but on wider environmental, social and economic dynamics. The concept of 'sustainable development' itself emphasizes the need to maintain economic, social and environmental considerations in some kind of constructive encounter. The city region, in this perspective, is 'summoned up' through such a lens as a critical site for identifying and managing how different relations interact, in order to reduce environmental stresses both locally and globally. This agenda emphasizes qualities of the 'liveability' of the urban environment, and its sustainability over the longer term in the face of environmental impacts and threats (SATTERTHWAITE, 1999; WILLIAMS et al., 2000; COWANS, 2006; RAVETZ, 2000; HAUGHTON and HUNTER, 1994; HAUGHTON and COUNSELL, 2004).

The 'sustainable development' movement also places considerable emphasis on involving multiple stakeholders, including residents, in strategy development, since behavioural change is a key dimension for reducing environmental stress. This discourse thus emphasizes the development of more interactive relations between citizens and the state, and between citizens, businesses and the state. Its agenda has considerable

popular momentum in Western Europe and is likely to disrupt any economic development programme which fails to give it adequate attention.

The discourses of 'economic competitiveness' and 'sustainable development' dominated urban and regional development agendas in many European countries in the 1990s, though often pursued in separate institutional nexuses.[3] However, the 'competitiveness' discourse is also challenged by a third discourse which centres around issues of social justice and cultural distinctiveness, and which hovers in the interstices of these dominant conceptions. This was partly an inheritance of the earlier welfare attention to maintaining universal standards of basic needs. It was enriched by increasing understanding of the diversity of social worlds and life trajectories, and of the importance of the imaginative and cultural dimensions of people's place attachments. As a place development concept, this discourse views place development nationally, from a concern with uneven development, and locally, from the perspective of the promotion of social well-being in places and cultivating endogenous development capacity through social as well as economic initiatives. It addresses economic and environmental relations through concepts of social innovation and well-being in cities of diversity and multiplicity (AMIN et al., 2000, 2002; MOULAERT et al., 2000, 2005; MOULAERT and NUSSBAUMER, 2005).

Different policy discourses thus embody and encourage different conceptions of the place qualities of urban areas. These various place development discourses jostle with each other as claims on the content of 'city region' concepts. They are often promoted by quite different policy communities, with only limited linkages between them. Could the insertion of a 'city region' institutional arena reconfigure governance relations and provide a site of encounter between such different discourses, and contribute to developing a more coherent, broader and more 'integrated' place development discourse? JONAS et al. (2005) suggest that the 'core cities' campaign in England has this potential (see below). Could it help to create institutional spaces for an assertive 'politics of place' which could attract attention among many of the relational nexuses which intersect and co-exist in localities, and develop enduring, localized persuasive force to shape development trajectories and place imaginations over time? Or is the mobilization of the 'city region' idea just an attempt by national elites to 'download' their difficulties in distributing development investment resources among multiple claimants?

The paper will now briefly explore the potential of the 'city region' concept from the perspective of the Netherlands and England, both countries with very open societies and economies, and with dense agglomerations of people creating many stresses and strains on the natural environment, itself subject to major future hazards as climate change gathers momentum. In both countries, the issue of the reconfiguration of sub-national government has been active in debate and public policy. In the Netherlands, there have been recent attempts to create formal metropolitan regions. Focus is especially made on the Amsterdam area, recently praised by FAINSTEIN (2000) as an exemplar of a 'just city'. In England, city regions were promoted in conjunction with the vigorous pursuit of a regional agenda and in parallel with a movement to reclaim more power and authority for local government, a 'new localism'. Both illustrate the difficulties of inserting new institutional arenas and new policy agendas in already-crowded governance contexts.

BUILDING METROPOLITAN REGION INSTITUTIONAL ARENAS IN THE NETHERLANDS

A strongly developed sense of geography has long underpinned Dutch public policy. The country has been imagined as having a strongly urbanized core, characterized in the well-established concept of the Randstad, a ring of towns and cities surrounding a 'green heart'. Here are the main centres of economic activity and trading 'mainports' (Rotterdam and Amsterdam Schiphol) connecting with the rest of the world. Around this, to the north, east and south is a landscape of towns and rural hinterlands. The development of this landscape has been managed since the mid-20th century by a co-sociation of formal levels of government (national, province and municipality), along with other major societal actors, which has produced substantial co-alignment in the policies and programmes of different sectors and levels of government.[4] There have been different emphases over time between the relative importance of dispersing development outside the Randstad core, concentrating development in the major cities, and resisting development 'sprawl' in favour of 'compact cities'. Nevertheless, considerations of economic priority, meeting social needs and aspirations to a high standard of 'liveability' and protecting and enhancing environmental resources have been drawn together in these co-alignment processes. The national spatial planning ministry played a key role in providing a policy framework which determines key investments and strategic principles for urban development. Rural development was governed by national approaches to water management and agricultural development. In both fields, national strategies and decisions were the product of intensive negotiation between levels and sectors of government, resulting in a spread of development investment resources across the country.

By the 1990s, however, this approach to the country's spatial development was coming under strain. Although the Netherlands had pioneered spatial strategies which gave a high priority to reducing the pressure on environmental resources, both locally and globally, the influence of the Europe-wide 'economic competitiveness' discourse gathered momentum. This encouraged attention to equipping the country with infrastructure investment to maintain its strength internationally as a logistics hub. It also allowed the major cities, which had been promoting their needs for a greater share of development resources due to the concentration of social problems within them, to argue that enhancing the quality of the country's major urban centres was desirable in the competition to attract global attention. By the 1990s, national spatial strategy had defined key national development projects around the 'mainports' of Rotterdam harbour and Amsterdam airport, and was encouraging the formation of formally constituted metropolitan areas centred on the 'big cities' and their surrounding municipalities. This was accompanied by a more selective approach nationally to development investment, focused on nationally important projects, accompanied by devolution of development budgets to the provincial level. Overall, the aim was to reduce and focus development expenditures. This changed the politics of negotiation over state development expenditures, from a multilevel governance activity focused on shaping national strategy and programmes, to a struggle among municipalities and provinces to get favoured projects recognized as of national importance, and among municipalities to shape provincial development investment strategies. This 'opening up' of the previous multilevel and multi-sectoral co-alignment practices was made more complex by the weakening of spatial planning at the national level in favour of ministries dealing with economic development and infrastructure matters (HAJER and ZONNEVELD, 2000).

In this context, the creation of formal metropolitan authorities around the major cities held the promise of creating a strong institutional site from which to bargain with the national ministries and to manage the tensions between adjacent municipalities over priorities for development location and investment (SALET, 2006). For many years, for example, the city of Amsterdam had worked hard to create some kind of sub-regional arena, below the level of the province, but also mobilizing inter-provincial links where the evolving 'functional linkages' (housing markets, labour markets, etc.) were spreading beyond municipal and provincial boundaries. For a while, the city council, a very influential voice at national level, promoted the idea of a metropolitan authority (ALEXANDER, 2002). The proposal for such an authority in the Amsterdam area had difficulty in maintaining support among key municipalities and was eventually defeated by Amsterdam citizens after a referendum in 1995 (HEALEY, 2007). However, the political need to find a way of building strong horizontal linkages among municipalities and between key state sectors involved in place development activity has remained, as the former vertically structured, sectoral bastions around spatial planning and rural development have weakened. In the Amsterdam area, the politics of prioritizing development investment has proceeded through the evolution of informal arenas for discussion and negotiation. In these, developing understanding of urban and regional dynamics and future potentialities has gone hand in hand with the production of spatial development concepts through which to articulate future possibilities and to locate and prioritize particular development projects. In other words, the creation of an idea of an emergent 'metropolitan region' has co-evolved with the creation of an informal institutional site for inter-municipal collaboration and conflict resolution. In organizational terms, this process provided a flexible, networked structure through which to adjust to what had become, by the 2000s, a period of considerable destabilization in the national polity and in national spatial development strategy.

In this example, the policy interest in metropolitan regions emerges as a response to shifts in the national budget priorities and a search to devolve the prioritization of all but major projects from a co-alignment at the national level to negotiations at province or sub-provincial levels. Despite the strong emphasis at national level on economic considerations, social and environmental considerations remain an important focus of attention, maintained by political parties, lobby groups and citizen concerns. The place of Amsterdam has a powerful pull on popular imagination and citizens will mobilize to defend it. This creates a grounding for 'integrated' perspectives on place development. However, as new governance practices evolved at sub-province level in the Amsterdam area, concepts of place development were continually narrowed down to the promotion of particular projects – bridges and highway connections, high speed train lines and stations, area development and redevelopment projects, and locations for major economic and housing developments. This continues the tradition in Amsterdam of place development understood as a practice of 'building the city' in physical terms. Capturing funding for a prioritized agenda of projects was at the forefront of attention, integrated area development in the background. Although some of these projects continue the Amsterdam tradition of weaving social, environmental and economic issues together in place development activities, there has been a new emphasis on creating partnerships focused on maximizing the potential of economic 'hot spots' (GUALINI and MAJOOR, 2007). One consequence has been an increasing tendency to separate out these kinds of partnerships, dominated by corporate economic interests and major national stakeholders from those to which residents and citizen groups commonly relate, which tend to be the sub-municipal Districts and neighbourhood organizations (HEALEY, 2007).

The informal metropolitan arena thus emerges as a locally developed response to changing national funding arrangements and priorities, in which prioritizing projects is a critical activity. The development of an integrated place development strategy hangs on this politics, to provide concepts and justifications both within

the various institutional sites where key place development investments are being negotiated and in subsequent lobbying for national support. The creation of a metropolitan arena is fuelled by an understanding of the complex relations of a 'network society', but an integrated place development project is not itself a mobilizing force in constructing such arenas. There are even concerns that the emphasis on public sector coordination and bidding for public funds might undermine Amsterdam's long-established focus on creating and sustaining liveable, lively and diverse urban neighbourhoods.

CITY REGIONS AND DEVOLUTION IN ENGLAND

In the mid-2000s, 'city region' suddenly became a popular idea within the national ministry charged with local government, housing and planning responsibilities in England. It was not a new concept, as it had been argued for (and rejected) as a basis for reorganizing local government back in the 1960s. Then it carried with it an idea of a city connected to its rural hinterland. Such a concept made sense in some parts of England, such as East Anglia, until recently a rural area with market towns where 'city regions' have been used as an organizing concept for spatial development policy for many years (HEALEY, 2007). Elsewhere, Britain's legacy from 19th-century industrialization is a set of overlapping urban nexuses, for which the term 'conurbation' was coined. When local government was reorganized in the 1970s, these conurbations were recognized as 'metropolitan areas' with formally created authorities, paralleling an arrangement already made for 'Greater London'. But even then, the boundaries of these authorities were, for political reasons,[5] too tightly drawn to encompass what were identified as 'functional urban areas'. By now, the complex overlapping and spatial extension of different housing markets, journey-to-work areas, and leisure opportunities makes the possibility of linking 'functionally discrete' metropolitan areas with administrative jurisdictions even more difficult, despite repeated rearrangement of municipal functions and boundaries.

But the new enthusiasm for 'city regions' is a response not so much to a search for co-aligning 'functional areas' with administrative jurisdictions', although this hope still lurks in administrative imaginations. Instead, it has arisen from a coming together of two streams of policy development, a campaign for a stronger focus on 'Core Cities' outside the London area and a campaign for stronger devolution to municipalities, under the banner of a 'new localism'.[6] Both are grounded in a critique of uneven development and the hyper-centralism of the British State. Although the discussion of uneven development is more nuanced these days, it could be said that the only long-standing spatial concept which lies below the surface in much English public policy and politics and which is embedded in popular consciousness, is that of a North–South divide. The South (and especially London and the South East; JOHN *et al.*, 2005), in this conception, is prosperous, socially complex, economically dynamic and with only a limited inheritance from the great days of Britain's industrial past. The North is economically weaker, generally bleaker (in southern eyes), industrialized and more working class. As many outside the 'South' complain, in Britain's centralized polity it is the conceptions, values and priorities of London and the South East which dominate public policy. The political struggle, within the UK as a whole and in England, has been to lever investment and development opportunities away from the South and to get more recognition for the growth potentials and diversity of development conditions in different parts of the country. This struggle underpins the long-standing attempts to reduce centralism and promote regional and local devolution. It has also been critical to the formation of a campaign by the major cities outside London and the South East, the so-called 'core cities' group, to maintain national policy attention to the needs and priorities of large urban areas, in the face of a concentration of development expenditure in the South East in the past twenty years (JONAS *et al.*, 2005; DEAS, 2006). These political concerns have made much use of the argument for the role of sub-national units – regions and cities, as key sites of economic innovation and hence significant in the overall promotion of the 'competitiveness' of the UK economy (HARDING *et al.*, 2004). The 'economic dividend' is continuously emphasized (MORGAN, 2006).

The details of the emergence of the 'city region' policy idea are well-described elsewhere (for example, NLGN, 2005). The momentum for regional devolution reached its peak in the late 1990s with a new 'New Labour' national government, committed to more autonomy for Scotland and Wales. The regional level in England, which had been administratively strengthened throughout the 1990s, was then reinforced with new Regional Development Agencies, and, in the mid-2000s, with the requirement in the revised planning system for the production of Regional Spatial Strategies. With no formal equivalent to the Dutch provinces, the national government minister in charge of regional and local government then hoped to create elected regional assemblies. The regions, however, have been formed out of administrative convenience for national government. They are large and often have within them more than one conurbation and some areas which are very rural. They thus have little functional coherence or connection to popular identities. What was actually offered in terms of the devolution of powers from national to regional government was limited and voters in the first area asked to vote on devolution were strongly negative. The regional project was left in limbo. But by this time, municipalities and other stakeholders had been mobilizing, in the

prospect that regional institutional arenas would become more important in the allocation of development investment funding, to promote projects and create alliances to push their interests. This led to arguments for more attention to sub-regions (MORPHET, 2005, 2006; COUNSELL and HAUGHTON, 2006). These could be metropolitan areas,[7] or more rural areas with several small towns. In some cases, the pressure to create sub-regions was precisely to counteract the potential that the major cities, the big players in the core cities movement, would capture all the funding available to the region.

Meanwhile, at national level, the Ministry responsible for housing, local government and planning,[8] was under pressure to cope with the severe crisis resulting from a reduction in house building, particularly for affordable housing. This crisis was at its most severe in London and the South East, where economic growth had attracted substantial immigration from elsewhere in the UK and the rest of the world. The Ministry's commitment to the 'sustainable development' agenda meant that such growth needed to be accommodated where possible on more difficult to develop brownfield sites, while popular resistance to more development without infrastructure meant that attention had to be given to major investment in 'growth areas'. The Ministry was thus caught between the investment needs of growth promotion in the South and the pressure from the 'core cities' campaign in the North. This pressure resulted in two initiatives. One was the 'Sustainable Communities Action Plan' (OFFICE OF THE DEPUTY PRIME MINISTER (ODPM), 2003) which proposed to target national urban development investment in both the longstanding 'urban regeneration' areas (mostly in urban cores across the country) and four newly defined growth areas, all in the South East. The other was the promotion of a regional concept, the 'Northern Way', which encompassed most of the core cities, and encouraged them to create city region arenas within an overarching umbrella (GONZALEZ, 2006; DEAS, 2006; COUNSELL and HAUGHTON, 2006).

As many have commented, the concepts of growth areas and of the Northern Way led towards a stronger national spatial focus for major urban development investment initiatives, but with very little specific place development content or even a significant political base. Both can be seen as concepts of momentary political convenience, having leverage in English centralized government in so far as they affected decisions about public investment priorities. Meanwhile, the national Treasury was continually exerting pressure for more attention to providing space for economic development and housing in the growth areas, justified by the national need to promote economic growth (BARKER, 2004). By early 2006, the Sustainable Communities Plan and the Northern Way were being overtaken by the momentum of the 'city region' idea, which played more into the arguments for 'economic competitiveness', and by the 'new localism' agenda, which would devolve more financial and programmatic autonomy to municipalities and associations of municipalities (CORRY and STOKER, 2002; http://www.nlgn.org.uk). Models from other European countries and from the US are frequently 'called up' in these arguments. By the end of 2006, the 'city region' concept itself was loosing momentum as political responsibilities changed at national level, and the 'new localism' agenda gathered force.[9]

The content and institutional nature of the 'city region' idea as it is currently reverberating around English sub-national political and administrative arenas is still fluid, open and contested (for example, HARDING et al., 2004; CLARK, 2005; BALLS et al., 2006). The dominant arguments emphasize the significance of 'cities' as innovative locales for economic development and 'city region' arenas as institutional sites for settling disputes between competing municipalities and focusing on projects which will have a major economic development pay off. At issue is the extent to which, as a generality, being located in a city promotes economic innovation, as well as the relation between any such linkages and formal government arrangements. However, the thrust of the economic argument for some kind of formal city region arena clearly separates the city region level from that of municipalities, and all kinds of neighbourhood political and management arrangements for the promotion of liveability and environmental sustainability. As a result, there is considerable tension between the 'new localism' campaign and the concept of a 'city region' focus (NLGN, 2005; LYONS, 2006). Even within the 'core cities' campaign, therefore, there is no clear co-alignment between 'bottom-up' calls for more integrated policy agendas, often linked to 'sustainable development' considerations, and top-down initiatives, which emphasize the economic 'dividend' (JONES and MACLEOD, 2005). Despite much rhetoric about 'integrated' policy agendas, so far there has been little sign of the development of locally specific place development strategies which bring into conjunction the social, environmental and economic dimensions of the 'place development' of 'city regions'. Such local debates tend to be crowded out by struggles over the reconfiguration of the English state, both as regards sub-national jurisdictions and general principles of distributive justice.

The 'city region' idea thus emerged as a useful policy concept to occupy an institutional space left by the perceived failure of political devolution to regions and in advance of an as-yet-unfulfilled commitment to substantial devolution to municipalities. It is mobilizing attention among political lobbyists. Sub-regional groupings formed earlier are re-badging themselves as city regions, and new alliances are appearing in the growth areas to mobilize energy in the competition for growth area funding.[10] In some areas, these funding-capture mobilizations are generating the creation of institutional arenas within which substantial attempts are being made to develop area-specific, integrated place development agendas. But the 'city region' as currently 'summoned up' in English debate is a thin and unstable policy concept, with a narrow agenda, and considerable tensions between selectivity (just a few city regions?) and universality (a new pattern of municipal government?) (HOUSE OF COMMONS (HoC), 2007). National government is no longer contemplating imposing formal city regions, indicating instead that informal alliances might be a way forward (DCLG, 2006). To quote JONAS et al. (2005):

> attempts to collapse the motives for city-regionalisation around a uniform and rational set of responses to economic competitiveness imposed from above ignores the variety of arenas of struggle around competing strategies or ideas of the city-region, conceived as a functional-territorial collective.
>
> (p. 240)

CITY REGIONS AND RECONFIGURING SUB-NATIONAL GOVERNANCE

Structurally, these experiences reinforce the argument that concepts of 'city region' and 'metropolitan region' have emerged in Europe primarily in the context of a move away from the verticality of welfare state organization towards a variety of institutional sites in which different groupings of state and non-state actors come together (BRENNER, 2004; GUALINI, 2006; KEATING, 1997; MACLEOD, 1999). But how the struggles over such reconfigurations play out in different nation states and in different parts of nation states depends on all kinds of specific contingencies. The 'city region' concept is neither a well-developed package which can be inserted into a government system to fix and reconfigure sub-national government, nor is it an empty vessel to be filled with whatever content seems locally appropriate. It is a concept that suggests both an institutional site and a spatial focus, but exactly what kind of site and what kind of 'place focus' it carries depends on all kinds of contingencies.

In both the examples reviewed above, 'city/metropolitan regions' have been promoted primarily for political–administrative and economic reasons. In England, they have not been attached to a broadly based or localized integrated place development agenda. In the Netherlands, an integrated conception of place development has a deeper history, but the work of creating an informal metropolitan region alliance in the Amsterdam area was not strongly linked to this. The 'summoning up' of the 'city region' idea emerges from these accounts as a preoccupation of policy elites – politicians, policy advisers and activists, and those involved in the various governance networks surrounding the formal arenas of the state.[11] Few outside these networks have much interest, apart from some business lobby groups. Nor is there much connection to socio-political movements linked to asserting regional identities. There are in both countries, however, significant citizen concerns about qualities of place, about 'liveability' issues and about environmental sustainability. In other words, there exist localized conceptions of place development, which are summoned up when these concerns are expressed. Sometimes, the political response to such concerns is to address these in terms of national programmes, such as safety and crime-reduction measures. But these concerns also surface routinely in the arenas of planning systems and in contestation over development proposals. It is here that a localized, multidimensional 'politics of place' is to be found, if fragmented and episodic.

The challenges such a politics generates have the potential to set pressures for some kind of integrated area development approach, which can find a way through competing social, economic and environmental agendas as these affect place qualities and experiences. In the Netherlands, municipalities and sub-municipal units provide well-developed sites through which these different agendas could come together. There are also many examples, in both urban and rural areas, of the formation of municipal alliances around managing and developing place assets. In England, municipalities are currently much weaker and much more dependent on national government. There are all kinds of 'partnerships' designed to draw different agencies and municipalities together, some with a richer and more integrated place development focus than others. But these are all strongly structured by a vertical dependency on national funding and the criteria that drive different national funding regimes. What may start as an 'integrated place development' initiative can all too easily, in such contexts, become reduced to a 'funding capture' game. Top-down regionalization initiatives tend to emphasize either one dimension of place development (especially the economic) or the search for administrative efficiencies. They have been only weakly linked to citizens' concerns about place qualities.

These experiences suggest that bottom-up regionalization initiatives, perhaps around a 'city region' concept, may emerge from local attempts to arrive at a more integrated place development approach through the creation of alliances and cooperation agreements. But their capacity may be limited unless either higher levels of government leave sufficient space for local momentum to develop or there is very powerful local mobilization. This suggests that any promotion of the idea of a 'city region' as an institutional arena needs to be left as a 'soft institutional form', possibly supported by enabling legislation, rather than introduced as an imposed formal arrangement. This seems to have been appreciated in more recent thinking in both the Amsterdam area, and in recent national proposals for English local government. Without real and enduring devolution to local governments in England, as the LYONS (2006) report and its various predecessors over the years have emphasized,[12] building local governance capacity to develop and pursue place development agendas which can resolve the conflicts and tensions between competing conceptions of place qualities is very difficult.[13]

In such contexts, the relations and identities emphasized in the current promotion of 'city region' initiatives, in Europe at least, are primarily those of government agencies. They relate to struggles over 'funding capture'. The language of local identity and of integrated, strategy-focused place development may be used in these struggles, but with little connection to either a deep understanding of the ongoing dynamics of the complex intersecting and co-existing of multiple relations in particular places, or to the potential development of 'place politics' in the wider society. This is particularly so in England. The Netherlands experience suggests that more local autonomy, adequate municipal funding and a more positive identity of citizens with governments, both national and local, may generate the capacity for broadly based and integrated place development strategies. But even in the Amsterdam area, current changes in national development funding tend to cultivate a project-driven, public sector politics rather than building connections with the economy and civil society. This suggests that a critical missing ingredient in the debates over government reconfiguration and institutional design is an active debate about what locally specific, endogenously grounded but exogenously positioned, place development strategies might look like.

The policy discourses of 'economic competitiveness', 'sustainable development' and 'social innovation' all point to the importance of coherent place development strategies as a valuable mobilizing and coordinating force in developing more horizontal governance forms, less driven by national state agendas, and more open to influences from economic and civil society relational nexuses. But in current European debates there is often too much generalized rhetoric and too little endogenous development. In this context, the 'city region' idea may be useful, both as a concept to focus attention on an array of social, economic and environmental relations, and as an institutional possibility. The danger of the idea is that it becomes a generalized solution, to be inserted into a reorganization of sub-national government or a requirement in funding rules. This is unlikely to produce the local mobilization and embedding which could energize and focus a vigorous, locally specific, multi-facetted politics of place. Where there is significant decentralization of power and resources to local governments, there are real incentives to mobilize locally, creating place development alliances, rather than channelling local concerns into vertical relations dependent on national funding flows and regulatory power.

This argument implies that the promotion of 'city regions' should avoid being presented as a political and/or jurisdictional fix. Instead, it may be more helpful to promote integrated place development agendas, informed by an open-minded conception of the diversity and complexity of the social, economic and environmental relations which interweave through an area and generate its place qualities. An open-minded conception means paying attention to the complex relations which connect one place with another, and could lead to the development of all kinds of alliances and partnerships. Through such initiatives, institutional arenas, whether informal or formal, are co-produced with place-specific development content. Rather than promoting 'city regions' as an 'institutional fix', it is perhaps more helpful in the current Western European context, to use the idea of a 'city region' as a focusing device, to help in the wider project of turning attention away from narrow policy agendas, towards nurturing and cultivating the positive synergies of co-existence in shared spaces. Such a refocusing is much needed, to help release an open-minded, multi-facetted 'politics of place' to counterbalance hyper-centralism, narrow sectoral agendas and introverted localism. The 'city region' concept is not so useful as a political–administrative institutional 'insert' designed to 'fix' deep-seated anomalies in the sub-national constitution of nation states.

Acknowledgements – The author thanks Sara Gonzalez for discussions and for keeping her up to date with the fast-moving English debates, and to the Editors and referees of this special issue for helpful comments on earlier drafts.

NOTES

1. See especially the work commissioned by the European Spatial Planning Observatory Network (ESPON) (http://www.espon.eu).
2. This point is made clearly in the interim report of the Lyons (2006) inquiry into the future of local government in England.
3. See the influence of the ESDP (CSD, 1999) and through this, on planning policy communities, in several nation states, including the UK, in the later 1990s/early 2000s. In this way, those advocating the 'economic competitiveness' discourse referred to 'planning' as a drag on innovative energy, wrapping up the 'sustainable development' and other discourses into a simple concept of the way 'land use regulation' impedes development energy.
4. The account here draws on a range of materials used in Healey (2007).
5. In the 1970s, the large urban authorities tended to be in Labour control and areas around in Tory control. Under a national Tory administration, boundaries were drawn so as to minimize leakage of Labour voters into Tory areas.
6. In parallel, in the context of developing the regional level of the planning system, there has also been encouragement to develop a 'sub-regional' focus when drawing up regional planning guidance and strategies (Bianconi et al., 2006).
7. Because 'metropolitan counties' were created in the 1970s and then abolished, this term has not been used in recent debates.
8. This Ministry has been subject to frequent changes in name and in responsibilities in recent years. It is currently (since June 2006), the Department for Communities and Local Government.
9. A much-heralded 'White Paper' in October 2006 discusses 'city region' arrangements, but as possibilities to emerge from a strengthened local government (Department for Communities and Local Government (DCLG), 2006).
10. This is evident in the news items of the weekly magazine *Planning*.
11. Motte (2006) comes to a similar conclusion with respect to the French experience.
12. See http://www.lyonsinquiry.org.uk/. There was a major review of local government in the 1960s, which led to changes in the 1970s, with further reviews and changes in the 1980s and 1990s.
13. Many criticize the capacity of municipalities, arguing that they are too introverted and competitive with each other to see 'the wider picture', and that the quality of staff and politicians is poor. This criticism has been voiced in England since the 1930s. It is partly a self-fulfilling prophecy, as Lyons (2006) points out. Limited autonomy and strong dependency on national funding and practice rules limits the development of local capacity. It also reflects a fear at the national level of local authorities which pursue agendas that are different from that of the national government.

REFERENCES

Abbott C. (2001) *Greater Portland: Urban Life and Landscape in the Pacific Northwest*. University of Pennsylvania Press, Philadelphia, PA.

Albrechts L., Alden J. and Rosa Pires A. D. (Eds) (2001) *The Changing Institutional Landscape of Planning*. Ashgate, Aldershot.

Albrechts L., Healey P. and Kunzmann K. (2003) Strategic spatial planning and regional governance in Europe, *Journal of the American Planning Association* **69**, 113–129.

Alexander E. R. (2002) Metropolitan regional planning in Amsterdam: a case study, *Town Planning Review* **73**, 17–40.

Amin A. (2002) Spatialities of globalisation, *Environment and Planning A* **34**, 385–399.

Amin A. (2004) Regions unbound: towards a new politics of place, *Geografisker Annaler* **86B**, 33–44.

Amin A., Cameron A. and Hudson R. (2002) *Placing the Social Economy*. Routledge, London.

Amin A., Massey D. and Thrift N. (2000) *Cities for the Many Not the Few*. Policy, Bristol.

Amin A. and Thrift N. (2002) *Cities: Reimagining the Urban*. Polity/Blackwell, Oxford.

BALLS E., HEALEY J. and LESLIE C. (2006) *Evolution and Devolution in England: How Regions Strengthen Our Towns and Cities*. New Local Government Network, London.

BARKER K. (2004) *Delivering Stability: Securing Our Future Housing Needs: Barker Review of Housing Supply: Final Report*. Stationary Office, London.

BIANCONI M., GALLENT N. and GREATBACH I. (2006) The changing geography of subregional planning in England, *Environment and Planning C: Government and Policy* **24**, 317–330.

BRENNER N. (1999) Globalisation as reterritorialisation: the re-scaling of urban governance in the European Union, *Urban Studies* **36**, 431–452.

BRENNER N. (2004) Urban governance and the production of new state spaces in Western Europe 1960–2000, *Review of International Political Economy* **11**, 447–488.

CLARK G. (2005) Cities, regions and metropolitan development agencies, *Local Economy* **20**, 404–411.

COMBES P. P., DURANTON G., OVERMAN H. G. and VENABLE A. J. (2006) *Economic Linkages Across Space*. Office of the Deputy Prime Minister (ODPM), London.

COMMITTEE FOR SPATIAL DEVELOPMENT (CSD) (1999) *The European Spatial Development Perspective*. European Commission, Luxembourg.

CORRY D. and STOKER G. (2002) *New Localism: Refashioning the Centre–Local Relationship*. New Local Government Network, London.

COUNSELL D. and HAUGHTON G. (2006) Advancing together in Yorkshire and Humberside?, in TEWDWR-JONES M. and ALLMENDINGER P. (Eds) *Territory, Identity and Spatial Planning: Spatial Governance in a Fragmented Nation*, pp. 106–122. Routledge, London.

COWANS J. (2006) *Cities and Regions of Sustainable Communities – New Strategies*. Town and Country Planning Association, London.

DEAS I. (2006) The contested creation of new state spaces: contrasting conceptions of regional strategy building in North West England, in TEWDWR-JONES M. and ALLMENDINGER P. (Eds) *Territory, Identity and Spatial Planning: Spatial Governance in a Fragmented Nation*, pp. 83–105. Routledge, London.

DEPARTMENT FOR COMMUNITIES AND LOCAL GOVERNMENT (DCLG) (2006) *Strong and Prosperous Communities: The Local Government White Paper*. DCLG/Stationary Office, London.

FAINSTEIN S. (2000) New directions in planning theory, *Urban Affairs Review* **34**, 451–476.

FALUDI A. (2003) Special issue on the application of the European Spatial Development Perspective (Introduction and Conclusion by A. Faludi), *Town Planning Review* **74**, 1–12, 121–140.

FALUDI A. and WATERHOUT B. (Eds) (2002) *The Making of the European Spatial Development Perspective*. Routledge, London.

GONZALEZ S. (2006) *The Northern Way: A Celebration or a Victim of the New City-Regional Government Policy?* Working Paper No. 28. ESRC/DCLG Postgraduate Research Programme, Leeds.

GRAHAM S. and HEALEY P. (1999) Relational concepts in time and space: issues for planning theory and practice, *European Planning Studies* **7**, 623–646.

GUALINI E. (2006) The rescaling of governance in Europe: new spatial and institutional rationales, *European Planning Studies* **14**, 881–904.

GUALINI E. and MAJOOR S. (2007) Innovative practices in large urban development projects: conflicting frames in the quest for 'new urbanity', *Planning Theory and Practice* **8**, 297–318.

HAJER M. and ZONNEVELD W. (2000) Spatial planning in the network society – rethinking the principles of planning in the Netherlands, *European Planning Studies* **8**, 337–355.

HARDING A., MARVIN S. and SPRIGINGS N. (2004) *Releasing the National Economic Potential of Provincial City-Regions: The Rationale for an Implications of a 'Northern Way' Growth Strategy: Report for the ODPM*. SURF, Salford.

HAUGHTON G. and COUNSELL D. (2004) *Regions, Spatial Strategies and Sustainable Development*. Routledge, London.

HAUGHTON G. and HUNTER C. (1994) *Sustainable Cities*. Routledge, London.

HEALEY P. (2002) On creating the 'city' as a collective resource, *Urban Studies* **39**, 1777–1792.

HEALEY P. (2004) The treatment of space and place in the new strategic spatial planning in Europe, *International Journal of Urban and Regional Research* **28**, 45–67.

HEALEY P. (2007) *Urban Complexity and Spatial Strategies: Towards a Relational Planning for Our Times*. Routledge, London.

HERRSCHEL T. and NEWMAN P. (Eds) (2005) *Global Competition and City Regional Governance in Europe*. Ashgate, Aldershot.

HOUSE OF COMMONS/DEPARTMENT OF COMMUNITIES AND LOCAL GOVERNMENT COMMITTEE (HoC) (2007) *Is There a Future for Regional Government?* Fourth Report of Session 2006–07 (HC 352-1). Stationary Office, London.

JESSOP B. (1997) Capitalism and its future; remarks on regulation, government and governance, *Review of International Political Economy* **4**, 561–581.

JESSOP B. (2000) The crisis of the national spatio-temporal fix and the tendential ecological dominance of globalising capitalism, *International Journal of Urban and Regional Research* **24**, 323–360.

JESSOP B. (2002) Institutional re(turns) and the strategic–relational approach, *Environment and Planning A* **33**, 1213–1235.

JOHN P., TICKELL A. and MUSSON S. (2005) Governing the mega-region: governance and networks across London and the South East of England, *New Political Economy* **10**, 91–106.

JONAS A. E. G., GIBBS D. C. and WHILE A. (2005) Uneven development, sustainability and city-regionalism contested: English city-regions in the European context, in SAGAN I. and HALKIER H. (Eds) *Regionalism Contested: Institution, Society and Territorial Governance*, pp. 223–246. Ashgate, Aldershot.

JONES M. and MACLEOD G. (2005) Regional spaces, spaces of regionalisation: territory, insurgent politics and the English Question, in SAGAN I. and HALKIER H. (Eds) *Regionalism Contested: Institution, Society and Governance*, pp. 93–122. Ashgate, Aldershot.

KEATING M. (1997) The invention of regions: political restructuring and territorial government in Western Europe, *Environment and Planning C: Government and Policy* **15**, 383–398.

KEATING M. (2006) Nationality, devolution and policy development in the United Kingdom, in TEWDWR-JONES M. and ALLMENDINGER P. (Eds) *Territory, Identity and Spatial Planning: Spatial Governance in a Fragmented Nation*, pp. 22–34. Routledge, London.

LE GALÈS P. (2002) *European Cities: Social Conflicts and Governance*. Oxford University Press, Oxford.

LYONS M. (2006) *National Prosperity, Local Choice and Civic Engagement: A New Partnership between Central and Local Government for the 21st Century*. Stationary Office, London.

MACLEOD G. (1999) Place, politics and 'scale dependence': exploring the structuration of euro-regionalism, *European Urban and Regional Studies* **6**, 231–254.

MARSTON S. A. and JONES III J. P. (2005) Human geography without scale, *Transactions of the Institute of British Geographers* **30**, 416–432.

MASSEY D. (2005) *For Space*. Sage, London.

McGUIRK P. (2007) The political construction of the city-region: notes from Sydney, *International Journal of Urban and Regional Research* **31**, 179–187.

MORGAN K. (2006) Devolution and development: territorial justice and the north–south divide, *Publius* **36**, 189–206.

MORPHET J. (2005) The rise of the sub-region, *Town and Country Planning* **74**, 268–270.

MORPHET J. (2006) Global localism: interpreting and implementing new localism in the UK, in TEWDWR-JONES M. and ALLMENDINGER P. (Eds) *Territory, Identity and Spatial Planning: Spatial Governance in a Fragmented Nation*, pp. 305–319. Routledge, London.

MOULAERT F. with DELLADETSIMA P., DELVAINQUIERE J. C., DEMAZIERE C., RODRIGUEZ A., VICARI S. and MARTINEZ M. (2000) *Globalisation and Integrated Area Development in European Cities*. Oxford University Press, Oxford.

MOULAERT F., MARTINELLI F., SWYNGEDOUW E. and GONZALEZ S. (2005) Towards alternative model(s) of local innovation, *Urban Studies* **42**, 1969–1990.

MOULAERT F. and NUSSBAUMER J. (2005) The social region: beyond the territorial dynamics of the learning economy, *European Urban and Regional Studies* **12**, 45–64.

MOTTE A. (2006) *La notion de planification strategic spatialisee en Europe (1995–2005)* [Strategic Spatial Planning in Europe]. PUCA, Paris.

NEUMAN M. and GAVINHA J. (2005) The planning dialectic of continuity and change: the evolution of metropolitan planning in Madrid, *European Planning Studies* **13**, 985–1012.

NEW LOCAL GOVERNMENT NETWORK (NLGN) (2005) *Seeing the Light? Next Steps for City Regions*. NLGN, London.

OFFICE OF THE DEPUTY PRIME MINISTER (ODPM) (2003) *Sustainable Communities: Building for the Future*. ODPM, London.

ORGANIZATION FOR ECONOMIC CO-OPERATION AND DEVELOPMENT (OECD) (2006a) *Newcastle in the North East*. OECD, Paris.

ORGANIZATION FOR ECONOMIC CO-OPERATION AND DEVELOPMENT (OECD) (2006b) *Competitive Cities in a Global Economy – Horizontal Synthesis Report*. OECD, Paris.

RAVETZ J. (2000) *City Region 2020: Integrated Planning for a Sustainable Environment*. Earthscan, London.

SALET W. (2006) Rescaling territorial governance in the Randstad Holland: the responsiveness of spatial and institutional strategies to changing socio-economic interactions, *European Planning Studies* **14**, 959–978.

SALET W., THORNLEY A. and KREUKELS A. (Eds) (2003) *Metropolitan Governance and Spatial Planning: Comparative Studies of European City-Regions*. E&FN Spon, London.

SATTERTHWAITE D. (Ed.) (1999) *The Earthscan Reader in Sustainable Cities*. Earthscan, London.

SCOTT A. J. (Ed.) (2001) *Global City-Regions: Trends, Theory, Policy*. Oxford University Press, Oxford.

TEWDWR-JONES M. and ALLMENDINGER P. (Eds) (2006) *Territory, Identity and Spatial Planning: Spatial Governance in a Fragmented Nation*. Routledge, London.

WILLIAMS K., BURTON E. and JENKS M. (2000) *Achieving Sustainable Urban Form*. E&FN Spon, London.

City-Regions: New Geographies of Uneven Development and Inequality

DAVID ETHERINGTON and MARTIN JONES

ETHERINGTON D. and JONES M. City-regions: new geographies of uneven development and inequality, *Regional Studies*. Recent years have witnessed a burgeoning literature on the 'new regionalism'. Protagonists have made persuasive arguments about regions as successful models of economic and social development. This paper argues that the championing of 'city-regions' provides an opportunity for taking these debates further. It draws on research taking place on the Sheffield City-Region, UK, and particularly discusses the interrelationships between competitiveness, work–welfare regimes – those policies and strategies dealing with labour market governance and welfare state restructuring – labour market inequalities and low pay. The paper suggests that city-regions reinforce, and have the potential to increase, rather than resolve, uneven development and socio-spatial inequalities.

ETHERINGTON D. and JONES M. 城市区域：不平衡发展和不公平的新地理学, *Regional Studies*. 最近几年关于'新地区主义'的文献开始迅速发展起来。提倡者们对区域作为经济和社会发展的成功模型提出了极具说服力的论据。作者们认为'城市区域'的斗争提供了进一步辩论的机会。本文利用对设菲尔德城市区域的研究，尤其讨论了竞争，工作–福利制度，这些关于劳动力市场管理和福利调整–劳动力市场不平等的政策和策略和低薪的相互关系。结果表明城市区域加强了不平衡发展和社会–空间不平等，并具有增大而不是解决它们的潜力。

新地区主义 权力下放 城市区域 劳动力市场 不平等 低薪

ETHERINGTON D. et JONES M. Les Cités-Régions: de nouvelles géographies du déséquilibre et de l'inégalité, *Regional Studies*. Pendant les dernières années, on a témoigné de la croissance d'une documentation sur le 'nouveau régionalisme'. Les partisans ont prôné la région comme modèle du développement économique et social. Cet article cherche à affirmer que se faire le champion des 'cités-régions' donne la possibilité d'approfondir ce débat. En puisant dans les recherches faites à propos de la cité-région de Sheffield, on discute en particulier de la corrélation entre la compétitivité, les actions travail-assistance sociale – à savoir, les politiques et stratégies qui traitent de la maîtrise du marché du travail et de la restructuration de la protection sociale – les inégalités sur le marché du travail et les petits salaires. L'article laisse supposer que les cités-régions renforcent, et ont le potentiel d'augmenter plutôt que de résoudre, le déséquilibre et les inégalités socio-géographiques.

ETHERINGTON D. und JONES M. Stadtregionen: Neue Geografien von ungleichmäßiger Entwicklung und Ungleichheit, *Regional Studies*. In den letzten Jahren ist eine aufkeimende Literatur über den 'neuen Regionalismus' entstanden. Ihre Autoren haben Regionen mit überzeugenden Argumenten als erfolgreiche Modelle der wirtschaftlichen und sozialen Entwicklung dargestellt. Wir argumentieren, dass die Förderung von 'Stadtregionen' eine Chance bietet, um diese Debatten einen Schritt weiter zu führen. Für unseren Beitrag nutzen wir Forschungsarbeiten in der Stadtregion von Sheffield und erörtern insbesondere die wechselseitigen Beziehungen zwischen Wettbewerbsfähigkeit, Arbeits- und Sozialplänen (also den Politiken und Strategien zur Lenkung des Arbeitsmarkts und zur Umstrukturierung des Sozialstaats), Ungleichheit auf dem Arbeitsmarkt und Niedriglöhnen. Wir argumentieren, dass Stadtregionen eine ungleichmäßige Entwicklung und sozioräumliche Ungleichheit verstärken und potenziell noch erhöhen, statt sie abzubauen.

ETHERINGTON D. y JONES M. Ciudad-regiones: nuevas geografías, desarrollo desequilibrado y desigualdades, *Regional Studies*. En los últimos años hemos observado una literatura floreciente sobre el 'nuevo regionalismo'. Los autores han defendido las regiones con argumentos persuasivos de modelos prósperos del desarrollo económico y social. Aquí defendemos que al apoyar las 'ciudad-regiones' se brinda la oportunidad de ampliar estos debates aún más. Basamos nuestros datos en estudios llevados a cabo en la ciudad-región de Sheffield y abordamos en particular las interrelaciones entre competitividad, las políticas sobre trabajo y bienestar (es decir, las políticas y estrategias para la gobernanza del mercado laboral y la reestructuración del estado del bienestar), las desigualdades del mercado laboral y los salarios bajos. En este artículo sugerimos que las ciudad-regiones refuerzan, y potencialmente aumentan, el desequilibrio del desarrollo y las desigualdades socio espaciales en vez de evitarlo.

INTRODUCTION

Once again, cities are the focus of attention. In the late 1990s, the Centre for Urban and Regional Development Studies (CURDS) was commissioned by the Office of the Deputy Prime Minister (ODPM) Core Cities Group to examine the interaction of cities and regions and to explore how they could stimulate economic growth within the regions (CURDS, 1999). The report discussed the concept of the 'city-region' and its possibilities and constraints for reducing endemic spatial inequalities within the UK.[1] In state discourse, city-regions are, of course, not new. As Western European experience over the past half century has demonstrated, this 'metropolitan concept' normally follows in the wake of failed attempts to build stable 'regional units' of state intervention (DICKINSON, 1967). We have been here before, and will probably come here again. Following the findings of the CURDS study, and in parallel with other research, the idea of city-region *competitiveness* was developed further by an ODPM Working Group emphasizing certain specific policy areas, in particular skills, knowledge, innovation, enterprise, and competition as the drivers of growth (ODPM, 2003; also CENTRE FOR SUSTAINABLE URBAN AND REGIONAL FUTURES (SURF), 2003).

The city-region idea has gained much currency and is now in the vanguard of potential solutions to reducing uneven development and its manifestation as the North–South divide. In 2004, for instance, the 'Northern Way' was encouraged by the ODPM comprising the three northern Regional Development Agencies (RDAs) – One North East, Yorkshire Forward and North West RDA – with the aim of 'bridging the £29 billion output gap' and to restructure the Northern economy on a more competitive footing (GONZALEZ, 2006; GOODCHILD and HICKMAN, 2006). Indeed, competitiveness is the dominant theme and underlying principle on which the 'Northern Way Growth Strategy' was based. Citing the Spending Review:[2]

> The best way to overcome regional disparities in productivity and employment rates is to allow each nation, region and locality the freedom and flexibility and

funding to exploit their indigenous sources of growth.
> (NORTHERN WAY, 2004, p. 1)

Within this pursuit of reducing regional and urban disparities, the Northern Way identified eight city-regions in the North – Liverpool, Central Lancashire, Manchester, Sheffield, Leeds, Hull and Humber Ports, Tees Valley, and Tyne and Wear – as the basis for fulfilling its strategic growth objectives, championed by H. M. Treasury as part of the *Devolving Decision Making* agenda:

> Cities represent the spatial manifestation of economic activity – large, urban agglomerations in which business choose to locate in order to benefit from proximity to other business, positive spillovers and external economies of scale. ... [C]ities can contribute to competitive regions, stimulating growth and employment, promoting excellence in surrounding areas and joining up separate business hubs to expand existing markets and create new ones. ... [T]his document extends the analysis and understanding of the economic role of *cities and regions in lifting regional and national growth, and tackling disparities between places.*
> (H. M. TREASURY et al., 2006, p. 1; emphases added)

This agenda is currently being pursued by (the Department of) Communities and Local Government (DCLG) (DCLG, 2006a, b, 2007; H. M. TREASURY et al., 2007) as part of a *new local state framework*, which emphasizes a balanced competitiveness agenda of bringing lagging cities/regions to a common baseline without disturbing the strategic and dominant position of leading cities/regions. The framework for this is to be set by City Development Companies – city-wide economic development institutions formed to drive economic growth and regeneration in the English city-regions. Whether all this reorientation of urban and regional policy, which might be tentatively called the 'hollowing out' of regional economic governance (upwards to pan-regionalism, downwards to cities, and outwards to more relational city-regions), will produce positive dividends is a pressing question for regional studies and is the subject of debate in this journal (cf. GOODCHILD and HICKMAN, 2006; GOODWIN et al., 2005; KITSON et al., 2004; MALECKI, 2004; PARR, 2005; TUROK, 2004) and elsewhere (HALL and PAIN, 2006; HARRISON, 2007; TEWDWR-JONES and

ALLMENDINGER, 2006; TEWDWR-JONES and McNEILL, 2000). Critical here are those enquiries questioning the benefits, distributional consequences, and pivotal inter-linkages of growth strategies with the wider socio-economic environment, which are never adequately specified in accounts promoting city-regions. Moreover, the mobilization of city-regions has the potential to have adverse and damaging impacts in terms of social and labour market inequalities (cf. H. M. TREASURY et al., 2006, p. 4), and the present paper explores how this new scale of governance and regulation can *reinforce rather than resolve* the problems of uneven development and socio-spatial inequalities.

Sheffield is used as a case study to discuss all this. Sheffield represents a particularly interesting example of a British city struggling with the policy discourses of city-regional competitiveness because its employment and occupational structure has been transformed over the past 20 years from a high-paid employment economy with a plentiful supply of skilled jobs in the steel and engineering industries to a de-industrialized economy where many of the new jobs created in the service sector tend to be low paid (on these trends in general, see DANSON, 2005). Despite this, and like many other rustbelt city-regions in Britain, Sheffield (and its broader Yorkshire and Humberside region – part of the Northern Way) is frequently presented as a laboratory for nurturing a sustainable skills and knowledge-based economy (cf. BOOTH, 2005; CROUCH and HILL, 2004; LEE, 2002; ROBSON et al., 2000; SHEFFIELD ONE, 2005; YORKSHIRE-FORWARD, 2003). Interestingly, Sheffield is ranked 17th in the economic performance table on English city-regions and seventh in the employment performance table (H. M. TREASURY et al., 2006, pp. 26, 30). However, this hides the qualitative micro-economic and social geographies of this complex city-region and specifically glosses over issues such as the quality and sustainability of the employment base and inequality more broadly (on these points, see also JONAS and WARD, 2007b; and SOUTH YORKSHIRE PARTNERSHIP, 2005).

The remainder of this paper develops this argument through a series of interlocking layers.[3] The next section situates the arguments within current new regionalist academic discussion. This is followed by an analysis of the development of the Sheffield City-Region, its strategies, and here it will be outlined how Sheffield's economy and labour market is represented within policy documents, including those produced by regional scale institutions. The paper then attempts to draw out the nature of social inequality and poverty within the Sheffield City-Region. It firstly examines the construction of a city-region narrative on the knowledge-based economy and the benefits therein, before, secondly, probing on the politics of poverty and uneven development, and, thirdly, how this city-region is reinforcing processes and patterns of labour market

inequalities and social exclusion. The paper concludes with an appraisal of the findings for a variety of debates.

NEW REGIONALISMS, CITY-REGIONS, UNEVEN DEVELOPMENT

Recent years have certainly witnessed a burgeoning literature on the 'new regionalism' in the social and political sciences (BOUDREAU, 2003; BRENNER et al., 2003; KEATING, 1998, 2001; KEATING et al., 2003; ROSSI, 2004; SÖDERBAUM, 2004; STORPER, 1997; VÄYRYNEN, 2003). Protagonists, both at academic (e.g. SCOTT, 1998, 2001) and political (e.g. H. M. TREASURY et al., 2003; ODPM, 2003, 2004) levels, have made important arguments on the existence of regions, and city-regions more recently, as successful models of economic development in an increasingly post-national age. Given the increasing context of economic globalization and the so-called 'borderless' and relational nature of transactions across the contemporary world, the new regionalism captures a belief that site and place-specific scales of intervention can firstly anchor and secondly nurture nodes of dense economic, social and political activity (cf. STORPER, 1997; COOKE and MORGAN, 1998).

This position has been delicately summarized in this journal by SCOTT and STORPER (2003). For Scott and Storper, globalization is challenging the scalar macro-economic planning and development integrity of the nation state. By focusing on heterodox and endogenous ways of doing economic development, 'government agencies, civic associations, private–public partnerships, or a host of other possible institutional arrangements, depending on local traditions and political sensibilities' armed with supply-side innovation strategies are considered appropriate for mobilizing and promoting a 'regional economic commons' to capitalize on the increasingly localized agglomeration and the intense clustering of economic activity. Given this persuasive argument, it is not hard to see why city-regions, i.e. metropolitan-scaled clusters of socio-economic importance (SCOTT et al., 2001), are being presented as selective 'windows of locational opportunity' for capturing and developing an specialized reordering and rescaling of economic activity (SCOTT and STORPER, 2003, p. 587). In short, city-regions are coming to function as the basic motors of the global economy – a proposition that points as a corollary to the further important notion that globalization and city-region development are but two facets of a single integrated reality (SCOTT, 2001; SCOTT et al., 2001).

Those seeking to engage with these claims have been suggesting for a while now a need to consider several issues. First, there are those authors pointing to the continued significance of national state power in underpinning regional and city-regional competitiveness strategies, and particularly their dynamics and future trajectories (HARRISON, 2006; HUDSON, 1999, 2005, 2006; LOVERING, 1999; MUSSON *et al.*, 2005). In turn, attention has been paid to the links between the state and the political economy of scale, and the ways in which regions have limited capacities to act and are embedded in a politics of territory and crisis management more broadly (BRENNER, 2004; JONES and MACLEOD, 1999; JONES, 2001; LARNER and WALTERS, 2002; MACLEOD, 2001). Second, others have been concerned with defining and delimiting regions, and analysing the ways in which they emerge, become institutionalized, and sometimes even disappear (MACLEOD, 2001; MACLEOD and JONES, 2001; PAASI, 2002, 2004). This has, thirdly, precipitated literatures more interested in issues of identity, senses of place, and regions as spaces of territorial belonging (BUDD, 2005; JONES and MACLEOD, 2004; MACLEOD, 1998). In short, this academic critique has questioned the geographical generalizations and reifications produced by a global city-region thesis as the paradigm shift for economic growth.

Fourthly, and at a lower level of abstraction, a group of authors have been concerned with stressing the importance of connections between the economic geographies of cities and the development of regions and regional systems (DEAS and WARD, 2000, 2002; HERRESCHEL and NEWMAN, 2002; LEIBOVITZ, 2003; PASTOR *et al.*, 2000). As noted above, this latter topic is currently being hotly debated in the UK with political lobbying for explicit city-regions as solutions to economic and democratic deficits (H. M. TREASURY *et al.*, 2006; NEW LOCAL GOVERNMENT NETWORK (NLGN), 2005) (see also below). Fifthly, and related to this, economic geographers have been interested in exploring the connections between firms and regions, which has surprisingly been played down in debates on economic governance and softer approaches to regional studies – much to the annoyance of authors such as MARKUSEN (1999). Notable here is the work of authors interested in systems of learning and innovation, how these make regions and city-regions work, and also how structures of spatial regulation and governance can nurture this to provide (or not provide) the atmosphere for such developments (COOKE, 2003; MACKINNON *et al.*, 2002; MARTIN and SUNLEY, 2003; MASKELL, 2001). Collectively, this body of critique has allowed the authors to focus on economic linkages and from this to tease out the internal dynamics within regions and city-regions.

This paper is situated within all this and specifically engages with an emerging sixth literature within regional studies – one which critiques the new regionalism from an often neglected *socio-economic stance*. Important here has been the work of MACLEOD (2000), DONALD (2001), CHRISTOPHERSON (2003), TUROK and EDGE (1999) and Ward and Jonas (JONAS and WARD, 2002, 2007a; WARD and JONAS, 2004) on the conflicts between securing economic

competitiveness for city-regions and managing the everyday politics of collective consumption and social reproduction in these mobilized spaces. Ward and Jonas argue that new regionalist literatures are myopic because they focus heavily on supply-side aspects of global-regional economic development and city-regional capacities are accordingly treated as functional to the needs of this model of neoliberal growth and change. This significantly dodges issues of inequality, redistribution, conflict, counterstrategies, and politics more broadly. They shift one's attention away from the spectacle of globalization and the reordering of the political–economic space – as read through those literatures cited above – towards more micro-scaled city-regional socio-economic geographies. In short, for JONAS and WARD (2007a):

> there has been an under-emphasis in the city-region literature on how new territorial forms are constructed politically and reproduced through everyday acts and struggles around consumption and social reproduction. An especially notable lacuna is serious treatment of the role of the state and an associated politics of distribution constructed around various sites, spaces and scales across the city-region. In some respects, this silence on matters of politics and collective social agency arises from a tendency to reify the city-region itself as an agent of wealth creation and distribution. This comes at the expense of knowledge about the people, interests, and socio-political agents who populate and work in city-regions.
>
> (p. 170)

These authors make a call for several research agendas under the heading 'geographies of collective provision' (WARD and JONAS, 2004) and 'ordinary geographies' (JONAS and WARD, 2007a) – with both seeking to capture the 'lived' and 'living city'. These are: the links between economic, social and political governance, labour control, service provision, welfare policies, democracy, the politics of the urban environment, and sustainability. Engaging with this, these authors argue, will allow for a more rounded and holistic view of sub-national state territorialities (JONAS and WARD, 2002; WARD and JONAS, 2004; also JONAS, 1996).

This approach is extremely important in that it acknowledges the much neglected links between city-regions and the politics and outcomes of uneven development (also COX, 2004; KRUEGER and SAVAGE, 2007; MCCANN, 2007; MCGUIRK, 2007). City-regions as 'new state spaces' (or perhaps, more accurately, described as *reconstructions* of existing forms of metropolitan governance) embody alliances and social forces engaged in strategy formation responding to processes of economic restructuring, social inequalities, as well as promoting competitive advantage. However, as BRENNER (2003) observes, there are limitations and deep contradictory outcomes to this:

> For in their current, market-led forms, metropolitan institutions likewise tend to intensify intra-national sociospatial

inequality, uneven development and interspatial competition, and thus to undermine the territorial conditions for sustainable economic development. Moreover, despite their explicit attention to problems of interscalar coordination and meta-governance, metropolitan political institutions cannot, in themselves, resolve the pervasive governance failures, regulatory deficits and legitimation problems that ensue as public funds are spread out ever more thinly among a wide number of subnational entrepreneurial initiatives.

(p. 317)

At a political and policy level, commenting on the 'rapid ascent of the city-regions agenda', this observation is supported by GONZALEZ et al. (2006):

> The main risk in the particular interpretation of the city-region agenda ... is its displacement of issues of uneven development and regional disparities by concentrating only on places that are doing well. This has at least three problematic consequences. First, the emphasis will be mainly on the urban core of the city-regions at the expense of secondary cities, smaller towns and remoter rural areas. Second, it will downplay the importance of the national scale as a frame where regional disparities are still (re)produced. Third, a reified view of scales is being used in this debate, one which assigns different functions to different scales.

(p. 317)

Pushing a socio-economic stance and sensitive to the consequences of this state-promoted uneven development, our approach to critical regional studies draws attention to city-regional entrepreneurialism, supply-side policies in the form of welfare-to-work and employability programmes, and the restructuring of labour control and reproduction through skills and training initiatives. This dominance of 'workfare' – where benefits are conditional of unemployed people participating in employment and training schemes – tends to be locked into managing decline and creating the conditions for the creation of surplus value, rather than preparing labour for new and sustainable employment opportunities. The effect of these policies, as highlighted in the research of SUNLEY et al. (2006), is to make labour markets more competitive through enhanced flexibility vis-à-vis minimal regulations and in doing so can reinforce their contingent nature. Workfare, because of its regulatory regime and frequent compulsion, removes any (supposedly) barriers for employers obtaining a ready supply of labour. Social groups who enter welfare-to-work and training programmes tend to be vulnerable and disadvantaged. The 'work first' principle tends to give prominence to the first job offer and the assumption that work will be sustained and there will be some sort of upward mobility. Workfare in turn increases competition, or 'workfare churning', as a result of substitution as subsidized employment is used to replace 'real' jobs. The direction of the unemployed to low-paid work creates a 'crowding' effect on the labour market, which puts even more downward pressures on wages in certain sectors (for perspectives on these issues, see PECK and THEODORE, 2000). To paraphrase FINE (2001), there is a continuing imperative of value theory in advanced capitalism.

To summarize the contention, then, city-regional strategies tend to pay scant attention to the distributional consequences of competitive policies – there is little focus on the nature and extent of poverty and social inequality, the need to establish poverty reduction targets, and any assessment of how policies are likely to reduce poverty rates. The discourses and representation by 'hegemonic interests' of city-region spaces in relation to how problems are analysed and policy solutions offered are of crucial importance to shaping policy agendas. As JESSOP (1997) has argued:

> The entrepreneurial city or region has been constructed through the intersection of diverse economic, political and socio cultural narratives which seek to give meaning to current problems by construing them in terms of past failures and future possibilities.

(p. 30)

The authors are also particularly concerned with addressing the call made by HARDING (2007) for research to address the 'changing *material circumstances* of city-regions', in contrast to accounts 'reading off' city-regionalisms from a 'global neoliberal project'. The next section accordingly explores in more detail how some of these dominant economic narratives and representations are being produced in the Sheffield City-Region, before moving on to analyse their impacts and effects.

BUILDING THE SHEFFIELD CITY-REGION NARRATIVE: 'NEW URBAN RENAISSANCE' AND THE KNOWLEDGE-BASED ECONOMY

The national context

> *After decades of post-industrial malaise, Britain's cities are finally turning the corner.* Although some major cities still lag behind their European counterparts, our urban base has put the nadir of the 1980s behind it. Inner-city residency is now climbing, *wages are rising*, and there is a tangible sense of civic pride on the back of successful sporting events and cultural redevelopments. ... But while physical infrastructure is important, *human capital is the key to creating vibrant cities.*
>
> (MILIBAND and HUNT, 2004, p. 23; emphases added)

On the back of the so-called 'new urban renaissance' – a policy discourse that presents city-regions as exciting places to work, rest, and play – Britain is believed to be escaping the social and economic problems of the 1980s and 1990s. Accordingly, the 21st century is the era of the 'new urbanism' with 'creative city-regions' based on a new model of social and economic development that refashions the built environment and, most importantly in the context of this paper, nurtures a 'knowledge-based economy'. On one level, the knowledge-based economy is characterized by rising employment in financial services, high-technology and the information and communication technology (ICT) sector, media and the broader cultural economy, and the continued rise in self-employment (THUROW, 1999). On another level, the knowledge-based economy is about a new kind of labour market where deeply entrenched unemployment becomes a policy problem of the past, those *temporarily* involved in the bottom-end of the labour market are actively involved in training and welfare-to-work policies to increase employability and transferable skills, and a high proportion of the remaining workforce is engaged in knowledge-intensive industries and products as listed above (for reviews, see JESSOP, 2002a). In short, the 'nadir' of the past few decades is being left behind and up-and-coming city-regions based on knowledge-based workers are the places to be (HUNT, 2005a, b). As MACLEOD and WARD (2002, p. 153) observe, this spatial-fix is often presented as nothing short of 'a new Eden for the informational age', though accounts rarely consider the corrosive impacts of neoliberal accumulation strategies and hegemonic projects on the social, economic and political fabric of city-regions.

Regional articulations: strategic directions for city-regions

As noted above, the Northern Way, comprising a loosely based coalition or network of government and quasi-government agencies, was established in 2004 and charged with reducing the £30 billion output gap between the North and South of England. Its role has been to establish a strategic economic development programme for the North as well as act as a pressure organization to influence public investment across the regions. Its establishment coincided with – and indeed was influenced by – the government's city-region agenda and in 2005 provided the framework for identifying and establishing eight city-regions (including Sheffield) in the North. Each city-region is responsible for producing City Region Development Programmes (CRDP) and reflects a shift in focus away from reducing the North–South divide to the role of cities as engines and locations of economic growth and vitality (cf. GOODCHILD and HICKMAN, 2006).

GONZALEZ's (2006) evaluation of the Northern Way found that as an organization it was a 'weak concept' and in many respects it was unrealistic to develop a loosely based partnership or coalition that would effectively bring together territorially, as well as economically and politically, such diverse interests. However, through its emphasis on competitive cities discourses, the Northern Way has successfully diverted attention *away* from any debate about redistribution and regional disparities. For example:

the strong focus on economic growth and competitiveness is complemented by a light touch on the environment and passing concern for issues of social cohesion and inclusion ... although the Northern Way does acknowledge the territorial imbalances between London and the South East and the North of England it does not seem to address the existing disparities within the North or the potential disparities that the Northern Way might cause.

(GONZALEZ, 2006, pp. 23, 24)

Almost perversely the analysis provided by the various policy agendas coming out of the Northern Way and city-region programmes seems to conceptualize the North as something as an economic millstone around the country's neck, which can only be 'released' if it got its act together or 'pulled its socks up'. Thus, the Northern Way epitomises a move away from a redistributive logic between the South and the North by partially turning the regional divide around, arguing that the underperformance of the North is 'holding back the UK's international competitiveness and is inequitable' (GONZALEZ, 2006, p. 11).

Alongside this, in February 2006, the Department of Work and Pensions (DWP) introduced *City Strategies* to deliver an improvement in the working-age employment rate, particularly for disadvantaged groups such as benefit claimants, lone parents, disabled people and those with health conditions, older people, and people from minority ethnic groups. The City Strategy focuses on the more deprived urban centres and invites the key stakeholders from the public, private and voluntary sectors to come together into a concerted local programme – a 'consortium' – to improve the way support for individual jobless people is coordinated and delivered on the ground. Already a number of city-regions (or quasi-city-regions) including Sheffield have received Pathfinder Status and this is the clearest expression of the way the state is attempting to rescale labour market policy and consolidate the supply-side agenda within city-regions.

Discourses and representations of Sheffield's labour market – talking up the 'new revival'

The Sheffield City-Region is currently in the making and encompasses South Yorkshire and North East Derbyshire, thus uniquely cutting across two RDA boundaries (Yorkshire Forward and East Midlands). Building on the critiques of the new regionalism noted above, this act questions the 'natural' status of a political space created by central-government diktat and political fiat. Also, and connecting further with the lines of academic enquiry noted above, when probing the internal dynamics of this, the Sheffield City-Region comprises two Sub Regional Partnerships (South Yorkshire Partnership and Alliance Sub Regional Strategic Partnership). In addition to the two RDAs and two Sub Regional Partnerships, there are eight local authorities and the Peak Planning Board. Within these, there are additional numerous strategies and local strategic partnerships/neighbourhood partnerships based around Single Regeneration Programmes. In short, 'governance complexity' is taking place based on different rounds of 'filling in' (GOODWIN et al., 2005) the sub-national state apparatus for the business of doing economic development and striving to deliver economic growth.

The City Region Development Programme (CRDP) reflects the overall growth orientations as set down by the Northern Way. Four priority interventions are outlined (SOUTH YORKSHIRE PARTNERSHIP/ALLIANCE SUB REGIONAL STRATEGIC PARTNERSHIP, 2005, p. 14):

- Developing knowledge and research on an internationally competitive scale.
- Developing a comprehensive connectivity strategy.
- Providing the skills required by an internationally competitive economy.
- Creating an environment to encourage investment and higher quality of life.

The CRDP states that there are barriers to growth, economic activity rates are 'patchy', and that levels of mobility:

> depend upon a package that addresses each of the specific barriers in deprived communities – including public transport, childcare and 'bridging learning to Learners'.
> (SOUTH YORKSHIRE PARTNERSHIP/ALLIANCE SUB REGIONAL STRATEGIC PARTNERSHIP, 2005, p. 18)

Plugging the skills mismatch is also seen as a high priority. The CRDP also recognizes that 'renewed targeting at the most deprived communities is required to better connect them to the larger pool of jobs and services across the city region' (SOUTH YORKSHIRE PARTNERSHIP/ALLIANCE SUB REGIONAL STRATEGIC PARTNERSHIP, p. 24). As discussed below – and connecting with those academic debates above stressing the connections between power, crisis management, and the politics of scale – the ability of Sheffield's city-regional policy-makers to address all this is proving very difficult given the limited levers and drivers available to shape and steer economic activity in a meaningful manner.

With respect to labour market opportunities, the Regional Development Agency (Yorkshire Forward) has already begun to 'talk up' the prospects of the regional economy. To give one example of this, it is claimed that:

> Yorkshire & Humber has a robust, diverse and bullish economy. ... Yorkshire's power is it's people, our 2.5 million strong workforce leads the country in sectors as varied as advanced engineering, food production, bioscience and digital technologies. Unemployment is at a 30 year low and the same as the national average.
> (YORKSHIRE-FORWARD, 2005, p. 1; emphases added)

Elsewhere, there is an upbeat tone about how the Sheffield City-Region and its knowledge-based economy should be seen and narrated, which reinforces the strategies of Yorkshire-Forward. An implicit 'inter-textuality' (FAIRCLOUGH, 2001) could be seen to be at work, whereby through repeated statements, discourses on the economy develop an almost scientific truth status with respect to the benefits of neoliberal accumulation strategies, which is in turn used to justify local state intervention. The Sheffield City Strategy 2002–2005, for instance, asserts that:

> As late as 1999 it was legitimate to pose the question – 'can Sheffield re-discover the inventiveness which previously made it a world wide brand, or is the City locked in a downward spiral in which talented people and organisations will progressively migrate elsewhere?' By 2002 there was convincing evidence that such questions are now irrelevant – the City has turned the decisive corner and is now 'on the up'.
> (SHEFFIELD FIRST, 2003, p. 10; emphases added)

Beyond glossy images and photographs taken with soft-focus-enhancing qualities, the 'convincing evidence' on 'turning the decisive corner' is never really presented. Whilst this promotion of the city is in some ways understandable given the need, from the perspective of Sheffield First Partnership (SFP), to represent an 'image' which will attract inward investment, this appears to be at the expense of an understanding, and indeed an analysis, of the daily lives and experiences of people living in poverty. For example, the Sheffield First Partnership Social Inclusion Strategy, launched in 2002, barely acknowledged the existence and persistence of poverty. Linked to this, there has been a lack of an attempt to seek to understand the dynamics of 'worklessness' in the Sheffield City-Region and how it relates to social exclusion. For example, the Open Forum for Economic Regeneration (OFFER), a community-based coalition that has representation on the Local Strategic Partnership (LSP), commented:

> The City Regional Development Plan still doesn't appear to be making the connections with community needs particularly around issues like worklessness and in some cases seems to be asking the Government for things which have already been approved, e.g. support to establish the new Adult Skills & Work Board.
> (interview, OFFER Officer, 2005)

As discussed below, both 'worklessness' and low pay are crucial ingredients of the landscape of social inequality in the Sheffield City-Region.

POLITICS OF POVERTY AND UNEVEN DEVELOPMENT IN THE SHEFFIELD CITY-REGION

Unemployment, worklessness and poverty in the Sheffield City-Region

Between 1981 and the mid-1990s, thousands of jobs were lost in the Sheffield/South Yorkshire economy – those in employment declined by a staggering 12.4% between 1981 and 1991 and a further 5.4% between 1991 and 1996 (DABINETT, 2004). Furthermore, during this period employment replacement occurred but tended to be based in retail, hotels and construction. In stark contrast to the era of steel and manufacturing – with highly paid, highly skilled jobs for life – new labour market opportunities have invariably been precarious and based on part-time, low-paid, insecure contracts. And during the past 20 years, employment growth has not necessarily been accompanied by a relative increase in prosperity. The mid-term review of the South Yorkshire Objective 1 Programme, for instance, stated that:

> while GDP [gross domestic product] has increased in South Yorkshire and now stands at 76.03% of the EU [European Union] average, the gap between the sub-region and the UK as a whole has barely altered. The South Yorkshire economy continues to struggle with issues of productivity, the stock of registered businesses, and the level of Gross Value Added in manufacturing. Productivity levels remain below that of the region in regards to the top ten South Yorkshire Employers.
>
> (LEEDS METROPOLITAN UNIVERSITY/SHEFFIELD HALLAM UNIVERSITY, 2003, p. 17)

The jobs or employment gap, which was identified as a central problem in the South Yorkshire submission for Objective 1 status in 1999, has been highlighted more recently in the Sheffield draft Employment Strategy prepared by the influential labour market think-tank the Centre for Economic and Social Inclusion (CESI). In this it is suggested that:

> One of the key Public Service Agreements (PSAs) for the Department of Work and Pensions (DWP) is to narrow the gap between the UK employment rate and those local authorities with low employment rates. The DWP report 'Full Employment in every Region' identified Sheffield as requiring 13,000 more local people to be in employment to reach the UK average. Our figures show that to reach the current UK employment rate of 74.9%, Sheffield needs to assist 17,000 unemployed residents into jobs ... if the current trend in the employment rate in Sheffield were to continue, this jobs gap would increase. Sheffield would need to assist an additional 3,300 people into employment per annum over the next five years in order to meet this target.
>
> (CESI, 2005, p. 19)

The CESI Report states that there are 83 000 people 'outside the labour market' as they are claiming incapacity benefit or income support, or not claiming at all with a total of nearly 100 000 people within the city-region claiming incapacity benefits (IB) (SOUTH YORKSHIRE PARTNERSHIP, 2006b). The reasons for an increase in incapacity benefit claims relates to the nature of the labour market. During the 1970s when skilled men were out of work, a lower proportion withdrew from the labour force. When the labour market became more competitive, with rising unemployment and less unskilled jobs being created, this group found that they could get higher benefits by claiming IB. Transfer to IB was officially sanctioned by the Employment Service at that time as a strategy for reducing the claimant count and, therefore, viewed as a form of hidden or disguised unemployment (cf. KING, 1995, WEBSTER, 2006). Today, inactivity is four times higher than in the 1970s and reflects quite dramatic changes in the nature of demand for certain types of skills and the type of jobs being created. As shown in Table 1, there are significant numbers of claimants in the city-region with the majority who are what can be termed 'long-term unemployed'.

Whilst there seems to be some consensus that worklessness and 'dependency' upon long-term benefits is a cause of poverty, there are fewer acceptances from official government channels about the connection between level of benefits (what people actually receive in cash) and poverty. Yet Table 1 provides some indication of the numbers (and families) that are likely or vulnerable to experiencing financial problems. As the Child Poverty Action Group (CPAG) states:

> Despite the Government's concern about the generosity of benefits acting as a deterrent to work, high levels of poverty among disabled people indicate that they do not provide an adequate financial safety net. It is hardly surprising that IB (currently a meagre £78.50 a week) is failing to safeguard disabled people from living in poverty. Although it is an 'earnings' replacement benefit, rates are between 16 per cent and 30 per cent of average earnings. While the long term rate of IB is more generous than JSA [Jobseekers Allowance], this is an indication of the inadequacies of JSA, not the generosity of IB.
>
> (PRESTON, 2006, p. 101)

A Welfare Rights Worker in the Sheffield City-Region pointed out that claimants received Jobseekers Allowance (JSA) benefit increases of £0.55 a week in April 2005, giving a total of £56.20 per week:

> The figures show the stark reality for people living on JSA. Far from the popular myth that unemployed people are living the high life they are now £30.30 pence worse off than if benefits had increased with average earnings.
>
> (interview, Welfare Rights Worker, 2006)

A survey of poverty in an inner-city area of Sheffield revealed the number of households relying on very low incomes. As one Neighbourhood Worker observed:

Table 1. *Baseline data for target categories in South Yorkshire*

Group	Sheffield	Rotherham	Doncaster	Barnsley
Incapacity Benefit (including Disability Living Allowance (DLA) and Income Support (IS))	23 400 residents (8% of the working-age population)	15 150 residents (9.8% of the working-age population)	17 965 residents (10% of the working-age population)	18 500 residents (13.9% if the working-age population)
Lone parents claiming income support	6880, or 2.3% of the city's working-age population	3000, or 1.9% of the working-age population	4190, or 2.4% of the working-age population	2500, or 1.9% of the working-age population
Partners of benefit claimants	8500, mainly women (10% of those adults who are outside of the labour market)	n.a.	n.a.	n.a.
Black and minority ethnic (BME) communities	Gap between the employment rate for white and all BME communities is 22%	Gap between the employment rate for white and all BME communities is 24.2%	n.a.	n.a.
Disadvantaged wards	Twelve wards where the employment rate is significantly below the city average reflecting the geographical polarization of the city	Incapacity Benefit (IB) and Severe Disablement Allowance (SDA) claim rates for Rotherham's disadvantaged wards far exceed the borough average with the worst performing standing at 17.2% of the working-age population	Significant disparities within and between communities in Doncaster, the highest concentrations of IB claimants in some is twice the borough average	Ten wards where claim rates exceed the local authority average

Note: n.a., Not available.
Source: SHEFFIELD CITY COUNCIL (2006, p. 6).

We found that in the sample household survey 16% of households had incomes below £5,200 and 48% below £10,400. Furthermore of those on less than £10,400 28% are in owner occupation so you could say that low income owner occupation is a crucial issue, particularly in relation to how they manage housing costs.

(interview, Neighbourhood Worker, 2006)

However, an increasing component of poverty also relates to low-paid employment, which has become a more prominent feature of employment restructuring in old industrial regions, such as Sheffield, in recent years. The paper now turns to examine this.

Low pay and poor work in the Sheffield City-Region

Low pay and poor work are closely connected; people in low-paid employment (particularly in part-time work) tend not to have access to training and other 'benefits' such as trade union representation, pension schemes, and sick pay, and the reality is that there are limited opportunities of upskilling and career/employment progression as routes out of low pay (MCGOVERN *et al.*, 2004). Using the low-pay threshold within the £6–7 per hour range as defined by HOWARTH and KENWAY (2004) across Britain's city-regions, there are some 6.5–7.5 million UK workers in the low-paid bracket. The largest single sector where low-paid jobs exist is the retail and wholesale trade, although there

are significant numbers in the public sector. In terms of the proportion of jobs in low-paid employment, the hospitality industry (i.e. hotels and restaurants) has half its employees in low-paid employment.

South Yorkshire still lags behind the national average in relation to wages and many new jobs created within the region tend to be low paid (Tables 2a and 2b). Using the New Earnings Survey (NES), YEANDLE *et al.* (2004) report a £250 per week threshold income. From the above discussion, the low-pay bracket could be considered in the range £250–350 per week for full-time employment. At £7 per hour, this would equate to around 30% of men in full-time employment within the Sheffield economy. Tables 2a and 2b also reveal the extent of job polarization as a feature of employment restructuring, with significant gaps occurring between the top and bottom 10% of earners.[4]

Part-time jobs are a major feature of employment growth during the 1990s and beyond. As shown in Table 3, over 12% of total employment in Sheffield comprises part-time work with a major proportion of these jobs performed by women.

On a related theme, vacancy data are often used to underscore labour market health and vitality. CESI undertook a survey of Jobcentre vacancies and found that a vast majority involved elementary and sales and customer services occupations, which are traditionally low paid (CESI, 2005, p. 43). Although some of the

Table 2a. Distribution of weekly earnings: men in full-time employment

Area	Percentage earnings under:			10% earned:	
	£250	£350	£460	Less than (£)	More than (£)
Barnsley	17	40	69	220.50	668.90
Doncaster	18	49	73	222.30	594.00
Rotherham	12	43	68	230.90	642.80
Sheffield	15	42	63	225.00	715.00
South Yorkshire	15	43	67	225.30	656.60
England	12	35	56	240.00	852.60

Source: Adapted from YEANDLE *et al.* (2004).

Table 2b. Distribution of weekly earnings: women in full-time employment

Area	Percentage earnings under:			10% earned:	
	£250	£350	£460	Less than (£)	More than (£)
Barnsley	12	40	68	182.20	577.80
Doncaster	11	35	62	184.30	572.90
Rotherham	12	43	71	182.30	590.90
Sheffield	8	30	58	198.30	591.50
South Yorkshire	10	35	62	191.20	656.60
England	8	27	55	196.20	623.80

Source: Adapted from YEANDLE *et al.* (2004).

higher paid jobs are advertised in other agencies and through the media, these findings do reflect some observed patterns of labour market development in Sheffield.

Employment restructuring has reinforced occupational segregation, as women are concentrated in particular sectors and types of employment. Women's

Table 3. Economic activity/inactivity in Sheffield

	Total	Men	Women
n	374 148	185 734	188 414
Economically active total (%)	–	69.3	57.0
Employee part-time (%)	12.4	3.7	21.0
Employee full-time (%)	37.0	47.2	27.0
Self-employed part-time with employees (%)	0.3	0.3	0.4
Self-employed full-time with employees (%)	1.9	3.1	0.7
Self-employed part-time without employees (%)	1.1	1.1	1.0
Self-employed full-time without employees (%)	2.9	5.1	0.8
Unemployed (%)	4.2	5.8	2.6
Full-time student (%)	3.3	3.1	3.4
Economically inactive total (%)	36.9	30.7	**43.0**
Retired (%)	13.5	11.4	15.7
Student (%)	8.1	8.5	7.7
Looking after home family (%)	5.9	1.1	10.7
Permanently sick/disabled (%)	6.2	6.9	5.4
Other (%)	3.1	2.7	3.6

Source: SHEFFIELD CITY COUNCIL (2001).

vulnerability to low pay and poverty in Sheffield has been documented in recent research (SHEFFIELD CITY COUNCIL, 2003; ETHERINGTON, 2005) as being related to care and family responsibilities, combined with the lack and high cost of childcare provision. These barriers affect career choices and earnings for women. The gendered nature of low pay in Sheffield is largely a result of women taking up part-time employment as the only route into the labour market.

The picture becomes more complicated when analysing work and pay by ethnicity. For example, certain black and minority ethnic groups have a propensity to be concentrated in economic sectors where low pay is prevalent. In South Yorkshire, more than half of the Chinese and Bangladeshi men work in the transport, hotels and restaurants sectors. Public sector employment, where many new jobs tend to be part time and low paid, has drawn in large numbers of black and minority ethnic groups including over 50% of Irish, Black Caribbean and Bangladeshi women who work in public administration, education and health. Also, significant numbers of men from Bangladesh and Pakistan are in part-time employment (28% and 17%, respectively) compared with 6% for White British males (YEANDLE, 2004, pp. 25–28).

An important consideration of how poverty and low-paid work are linked relates to the fact that many people who move into 'entry-level' jobs carry debts with them (FLETCHER, 2007). As one individual commented:

Table 4. Learners achieving National Vocational Qualification (NVQ) Level 2 by age 19 years in 2004 and 2005

	2004	2005
England (%)	67	70
Yorkshire and Humberside (%)	64	67
North Yorkshire (%)	85	87
West Yorkshire (%)	60	64
South Yorkshire (%)	58	60

Source: SOUTH YORKSHIRE PARTNERSHIP (2006a, p. 86).

> I became poorer by going back to work. I took a six month contract; when it finished, it took a year to sort out my benefits, leading to rent and council tax arrears and a court appearance. I lost my right to free school meals.
> (participant in the 'Every Child Matters' event, 2006)[5]

Another welfare rights worker pointed out that there are many people who do not claim Working Tax Credits and that the extra income obtained by moving into employment (even though some people are not necessarily financially better off) can be offset by child-care costs:

> In spite of the subsidies child care costs are too high for many one parent families and families on low incomes. In fact the quality and quantity of childcare provision in poorer communities is a lot to be desired. Provision is fragmented but it is not just cost – in some areas accessing child care can be extremely difficult.
> (interview, Welfare Rights Worker, 2006)

Training and upskilling

A high proportion of adults in South Yorkshire possess poor basic skills and there are low levels of attainment in National Vocational Qualification (NVQ) Levels 2 and 3. The CESI report noted above found that a high percentage of young people entering the New Deal programmes lacked NVQ qualifications. Combined with a lack of employment experience, their chances in the labour market are extremely limited (CESI, 2005, p. 24).

This fact is underlined by the trend towards a high proportion of young people reaching compulsory school leaving age without Level 2 skills, which are required to prepare them for the labour market. For South Yorkshire, this is 55% and 60% for those attaining Level 2 skills by the age of 19 years in 2004 and 2005, respectively (Table 4). Geographies of qualification attainment are illustrated in Table 4, with South Yorkshire being 10% under the national average.

The predominance of low skills is illustrated by Table 5, where there is a high rate of people in the labour market with no qualifications. However, the nature and value of NVQs as a vocational qualification that facilitates further progression in the labour market is questionable. This is because NVQs tend to replicate labour market weaknesses due to their focus on in-work behaviour and the fact that they tend to be employer-led in terms of their design, delivery, and 'regulation'. The implications of this are that future skill needs and requirements of particular employees are not built into the NVQ system (GRUGULIS, 2003). Similar arguments hold for standards and accreditation systems for firms, such as Investors in People, which do not possess any levers to influence or regulate rogue employer behaviour significantly (HOQUE, 2003).

People classed as economically inactive are particularly vulnerable in the labour market because most can be classed as unskilled – with 65% possessing no qualifications whatsoever (SOUTH YORKSHIRE PARTNERSHIP, 2006a, p. 92). ETHERINGTON (2005), based on earlier research on the South Yorkshire economy by EKOS (2002), highlighted the divergence in those receiving training with only a small proportion of those in lower-status occupations receiving on-the-job training compared with managerial and professional occupations. Updated analysis for the South Yorkshire Partnership suggests that South Yorkshire is above the national average in terms of employer-funded training – 58% between 2004 and 2005. This figure is based on a relatively small sample, but it suggests that given the scale of the skills 'crisis' in the local economy, this is an inadequate performance. This finding is perhaps unsurprising, but it has a major impact upon mobility in the labour market. Many policies relating to 'employability' are based on the basic assumption that work is a route out of social

Table 5. Qualifications of people aged 16–74 years in South Yorkshire in 2001

	No qualifications (%)	Level 1	Level 2	Level 3	Levels 4/5	Unknown
England	29	16.6	19.4	8.3	19.9	6.9
Yorkshire and Humberside	33	17.1	18.0	7.7	16.4	7.6
South Yorkshire	36	17.5	17.2	7.5	14.5	7.4
Barnsley	41	18.0	16.7	5.4	11.1	7.8
Doncaster	38	18.6	18.5	5.4	11.8	7.5
Rotherham	37	19.2	18.8	5.5	11.5	8.2
Sheffield	32	15.9	16.0	10.4	18.8	6.9

Source: SOUTH YORKSHIRE PARTNERSHIP (2006a, p. 91).

exclusion and that once in the labour market work will be the foundation for further progression and advancement. In the Sheffield City-Region such opportunities will of course arise, but for many and perhaps the majority there are high chances of being 'trapped' in low-paid employment (FLETCHER, 2007).

THE CITY REGION AND ECONOMIC COMPETITIVENESS: REINFORCING SOCIAL EXCLUSION?

The Sheffield City-Region (and its various 'strategies'), as has been argued above, needs to be viewed within the wider political economy context of state restructuring. In the words of JESSOP (2002b), his speculations on the future of the capitalist state:

> The economic policy emphasis now falls on innovation and competitiveness, rather than on full employment and planning. Second, social policy is being subordinated to economic policy, so that labour markets become more flexible and downward pressure is placed on the social wage that is now considered as a cost of production rather than a means of distribution and social cohesion. In general the aim is to get people from welfare to work, rather than resort to allegedly unsustainable welfare expenditures, and, in addition, to create enterprising subjects and to overturn a culture of dependency. Third the importance of the national scale of policy making and implementation is being seriously challenged, as local, regional, and supranational levels of government and social partnership gain new powers. *This is reflected in the concern to create postnational 'solutions' to current economic, political, social and environmental problems*, rather than primarily relying upon national institutions and networks.
>
> (pp. 459–460; emphases added)

The agenda under discussion could be seen as an attempt to displace the economic management of cities to city-regional networked entrepreneurial governance. This sentiment is evident in UK state strategies:

> To achieve the Government's economic and social objectives therefore, all cities must lift their economic performance through enhanced employment and productivity growth while seeking to promote economic and social inclusion. As cities are diverse and face different challenges, effective partnership and leadership at regional and local level, with enhanced freedoms and flexibilities to address local problems, will be important. As many economic challenges cut across administrative boundaries, greater collaboration between local authorities, and with regional agencies, will reap economic rewards.
>
> (H. M. TREASURY et al., 2006, p. 58)

As JESSOP (2002a) suggests, though, balancing these objectives is invariably contradictory as this strategic focus underpins a more market and private-sector approach to economic regeneration and tends to downplay or ignore the connections between the economic and the social or even the potential unequal outcomes of policies (also GOUGH et al., 2006, p. 25). Welfare-to-work programmes, as mentioned above, are instrumental in reinforcing labour market exclusion. For example, welfare-to-work policies and the New Deal specifically have mobilizing effects on the 'reserve army of labour', making the labour market apparently more competitive, but in doing so place downward pressures on pay (GROVER, 2003). More broadly, as GRAY (2004) argues in an analysis of welfare-to-work in Europe, the operation of the New Deal and 'activation' policies needs to be analysed as closely linked to labour market deregulation and a reduction in trade union bargaining rights. Both these policies also contribute towards the reproduction of low-paid labour markets, with a considerable proportion of unemployed people tending to go into low-paid minimum wage employment. And although the 'work-first' aspect of the welfare-to-work programmes has been understandably the focus of attention, there are subtle ways in which Personal Advisor Counselling and work-focused interviews have played a vital role in adapting people to local labour markets and shaping their expectations thereafter.

Grounding all this in the Sheffield City-Region, HOOGVELDT and FRANCE (2000) initially undertook a 'client' survey tracking the experiences of the unemployed involved and not involved (termed *the disengaged* in the New Deal programme). They found in their evaluation of the New Deal Pathfinder in Sheffield that the objectives of the New Deal were not only to make the participants 'employable', but also to adjust young peoples' expectations about career paths and employment routes. Many people, for example, found that service employment was the only type of work they could obtain and these aspirations also seem to be influenced by the Advisors. This finding accords with later research on the North East for Jobcentre Plus (DOBBS et al., 2003), which found through focus groups involving the unemployed that expectations of a possible wage well above the minimum wage was frowned on by Advisors.

Another interesting finding from Hoogveldt and France's study is the attitudes of the disengaged. They found that many had previously worked in higher paid and skilled work than new entrants to the labour market, and considered that the New Deal could not offer them anything. In more recent research, FLETCHER (2007) has explored these issues further in evaluating the Working Neighbourhoods Pilots, which are area-based regenerations experiments aimed at targeted concentrations of the workless in twelve localities across Great Britain (one being the Manor Estate, Sheffield). Commenting on how active labour market policy is currently operating within the Sheffield City-Region, Fletcher suggests that:

policy makers should be wary of placing undue emphasis on area-based approaches. First, many people living in the pilot areas are not unemployed or economically inactive and most of those without work live outside such area. This is known as the 'ecological fallacy'. Second, *the underlying causes are primarily of a structural nature and are, therefore, external to the local communities where their effects are most acute.* This means that the Working Neighbourhoods Pilot, whatever its achievements, is incapable of challenging the root causes of worklessness. Moreover, in focusing on cultural explanations of unemployment it might contribute to the pathologisation of such problems.

(p. 79; emphases added)

These sentiments could be seen to connect with critical new regionalist concerns expressed above on relations of power between different scales of the state and also questions around the restricted 'capacities to act' of localities placed at the periphery of prevailing accumulation strategies (see especially HUDSON, 2006; and JONES, 2001). Fletcher's arguments are also evident through the present authors' fieldwork undertaken in 2005–06, where a voluntary sector officer involved in the establishment of the Working Neighbourhood Pilot in Sheffield observed that in the household survey most people who were economically inactive expressed views of not wanting to work because of their perceptions of the type of work they could obtain, and also of not wanting to get involved with the New Deal. This was further echoed by the views of other community activists and voluntary sector workers who point to their lack of confidence in welfare-to-work programmes delivering sustainable jobs and that participation in the New Deal is not a positive experience. The implications of this finding are potentially far reaching when considering other employment/non-employment routes, which the disengaged will take, including the 'black' economy and casual employment.

Likewise, research on the New Deal for Lone Parents in Sheffield undertaken by CASEBOURNE (2003) underlines some of the points made above about the gendered nature of low pay, but also illustrates the way policies can act to guide lone parents into jobs that do not pay them a living wage. Paid work alone, despite the introduction of minimum wages, is not enough to lift all lone parents out of poverty successfully, given the ongoing segmentation of labour markets (SCOOP AID, 2001). A regeneration seminar held in January 2007 also highlighted, amongst other things, the uneven impacts of regeneration across gender divides, and according to the Executive Director of Sheffield Council's Neighbourhoods and Community Care Directorate:

Issues of who holds the power are key here, as is the difference between sitting on a board and making a meaningful contribution. ... Today, we can start to think about how we can incorporate a gender aware approach into regeneration work across the city to achieve better outcomes for

women and men we are working to benefit.

(SHEFFIELD CITY COUNCIL, 2007, p. 5)

Despite this, current national-level changes to the welfare-to-work regime, as part of the Freud Review on 'options for the future of welfare to work', have a particular city-regional focus and necessity by virtue of the urban geographies of unemployment (GREEN and OWEN, 2006). There are two significant changes to the governance of welfare-to-work strategies, which have important implications for the Sheffield City-Region. The first of these is the Pathways to Work pilots, which are being rolled out across South Yorkshire to engage those on incapacity benefit. Pathways to Work have been introduced in Rotherham, Barnsley, Doncaster, and Sheffield in 2006. The programme is aimed at increasing the employment rate by supporting new entrants to Incapacity Benefit (IB) to return-to-work, whilst existing claimants can volunteer to join the programme. An important aspect of Pathways is the role of health services through the Condition Management Programme, which helps people manage their disability or health condition in the course of their participation in the various Pathways schemes. All this involves mandatory interviews, specialist personal advisors, and also return-to-work credits. Initial assessment of Pathways suggests that the government is increasingly bringing more 'economically inactive' into work-first-based programmes. It has been noted that the system may raise false expectations, particularly when the evidence suggests that many people do not succeed in obtaining jobs or that many jobs on offer are low paid, which reinforces those trends outlined above (PRESTON, 2006).

Second, changes have occurred with respect to the management of welfare-to-work, namely its delivery and contracts therein. Although it is too early to assess privatization trends and contracting out, it is possible to chart changes to Jobcentre Plus – the local state manifestation of the merged services for the unemployed and benefit claimants. Firstly, cuts have been exercised across the employment option of the New Deal, which were explained as a result of declining JSA claimants. This has had negative implications for those claiming benefits and those being able to be lifted into available work. Secondly, further cuts to staffing levels have been put in place, comprising a shift in resources to more front-line services. One local Advice Agency commented:

There is an issue about the lack of information reaching people and around the reduction in staff at the DWP, where things will get worse before they get better. There is also a massive issue around the Welfare Reform Bill. Government Departments do not talk to each other and they hide behind the Data Protection Act. The need to fill in multiple forms puts people off. As an Advice Centre, core funding is always an issue that we talk about, because we have more and more demands placed upon our time. We are well aware that we reach only a fraction of the people who need help in this city.

(individual participant in the 'Every Child Matters' event, 2006)

The core element of Jobcentre Plus organizational changes involves a dislocation between benefit claimants and advice services because of the introduction of the Call Centre system (Customer Management System) where claimants have to use and pay for an 0845 number for the initial contact. According to Welfare Rights Workers there has been a reduction in the quality of service to claimants with delayed decisions, incorrect advice being common:

> For many claimants even after the telephone process has been completed, there is a further delay before they are interviewed at the Jobcentre Plus office. Time intervals in excess of 8 weeks between initial contact and receiving benefit are very common.
>
> (interview, Welfare Rights Worker, 2006)

Given also that benefit (or the threat of) sanctions are still common, combined with considerable shortfalls in rights services to people who are seeking representation this, only serves to highlight the vulnerability and further impoverishment of benefit claimants.

The Sheffield Welfare Action Network (SWAN) has voiced concerns over all these moves:

> Just as privatisation of the NHS [National Health Service] was once 'unthinkable' and so far out of mainstream political thinking and is no proceeding apace: now welfare reform is to undergo the same process. Policies that would have been fiercely resisted by opposition parties if carried out by the Thatcher Govt [government] are now routinely passed by parliament. There would appear to be a consensus across the main political parties that drastic welfare reform is needed. Combined with the draconian Welfare Reform Bill its clear now that we are seeing the biggest structural changes in welfare since the 1940s; indeed, there are now clear similarities between the Freud Review proposals and President Clinton's seminal 1996 welfare reforms which have been such a disaster for the poor in the U.S.
>
> (SHEFFIELD WELFARE ACTION NETWORK, 2007, p. 1)

In short, within this intensifying welfare-to-work urban regime, it is very difficult to envisage if and how the SOUTH YORKSHIRE PARTNERSHIP/ALLIANCE SUB REGIONAL STRATEGIC PARTNERSHIP (2005, p. 14) can provide the basis for developing knowledge and research on an internationally competitive scale; providing the skills required by an internationally competitive economy; and creating an environment to encourage investment and higher quality of life.

CONCLUSION

In order to intervene effectively to improve sub-national economic performance and to improve the prospects of people in deprived areas, it is important to be clear about the causes of spatial disparities, the interaction of the characteristics of people and places, and the extent to which they are driven by market or government failures. To lift economic performance at sub-national levels, and to tackle spatial disparities, it will be necessary to tackle any market or government failures in the underlying drivers of productivity and growth which impact differently across places. Differential impacts from market or government failures may result from differences between places and may be exacerbated by concentrations of people with particular characteristics. However, tacking spatial differences by tackling market or government failures may support convergence in welfare between people with similar skills and levels of employability.

(H. M. TREASURY et al., 2007, pp. 20–21)

The present paper has sought to undertake two connected lines of critique, the first being the UK government's approach to economic competitiveness and social cohesion through city-regions, and the second being an engagement with new regionalist literatures in the social and political sciences. This has sought to be both a critique *and* a constructive engagement.

On the latter, the authors have specifically tried to take this forward by addressing the city-regions agenda advocated by Ward and Jonas (WARD and JONAS, 2004; JONAS and WARD, 2007a) on 'geographies of collective provision'. For these authors, an approach was deemed necessary to uncover how struggle, conflict, uneven development and inequalities were occurring in contemporary capitalism as a 'politics of space'.

This connects to the former and by focusing on the Sheffield City-Region the present paper has attempted to develop this through links between the interventions of 'active' labour market policies and knowledge-based economy informed skills strategies, and their potential influences on the local labour market for producing inequalities and sustaining low-paid employment. There is little evidence that upskilling to achieve upward mobility of the kind inferred in recent government documentation on city-regions (DCLG, 2006; H. M. TREASURY et al., 2006, 2007) and in turn constructing the sustainable basis for a 'global city-region' based on localized agglomeration (SCOTT, 2001) occurs to any significant degree within the Sheffield City-Region labour market. It has been argued herein that there is also a substantial skills gap to accompany the employment gap within the Sheffield economy, which current strategies appear to be unable to plug.

Yes, the causes of the problem are deeply economic and supply-side initiatives can make a difference in the right context, but they are also deeply political; they relate to the shortcoming of the neoliberal model of city-regional competitiveness, its 'everyone's a winner' discourse (BRISTOW, 2005), and multiple rounds of market failure, government failure, government-induced market failure, and market-induced government failure. The socio-spatial pathology approach being explicitly advocated by the H. M. Treasury quotation above — taken from the *Review of Sub-National Economic Development and Regeneration* — is probably considered to be the price worth paying to protect the 'golden goose' of London and the South East. The key to UK (and Sheffield) success in an expanding global economy will be the ability to innovate and apply technology, and to control an increasingly intellectual property portfolio. This requires an economy able to produce, absorb, and reproduce highly skilled people, which policies in the Sheffield City-Region appear to be unable to provide in a sustainable manner. In these policy-relevant times, those interested in regional studies, and the authors include themselves in this category, need to work hard to consider alternative policy scenarios, and the authors would encourage future research on the consequences of the scenarios outlined here for: the future of labour markets without a growing and sustainable stock of 'good' jobs; social exclusion geographies stemming from this; and those local people and place characteristics uttered above with respect to unevenly developing cultures of (un)employability.

Acknowledgements — Earlier versions of this paper were presented at the Regional Studies Annual Conference (2006), the Association of American Geographers Conference (2007), and the Institute for Advanced Studies Conference, 'Regions and Regionalism In and Beyond Europe' (2007). The authors would like to thank participants at these, the anonymous references, and the Editor of *Regional Studies* for insightful comments on the paper. David Etherington would like to thank the Open University for financial support; Martin Jones would like to acknowledge The Leverhulme Trust for research funding through a Philip Leverhulme Prize. The usual disclaimers apply.

NOTES

1. The notion of 'city-region' is interpreted in this paper as 'the area over which key economic markets, such as labour markets as measured by travel to work areas, housing markets and retail markets, operate' (H. M. TREASURY *et al.*, 2006, p. 8). The city-region is thus the 'economic footprint' of the city; a 'fuzzy' concept that indicates a stretched-out or relational space that does not always correspond to administrative city boundaries (ROBSON *et al.*, 2006). City-regions have been referred to elsewhere as metropolitan regions (cf. BRENNER, 2004; HARDING, 2007; JONAS and WARD, 2007a, b; and McGUIRK, 2007).

2. In the UK, 'Spending Reviews' set Departmental Expenditure Limits and, through Public Service Agreements (PSA), define the key improvements that the public can expect from these resources (ADAMS, 2002). They are instruments for enabling centralized control and also creating spaces of regional/local expectation, set within constrained limits. Based on outputs, as opposed to inputs, it could be argued that this 'scalar compact' is a constrained form of devolution (cf. H. M. TREASURY *et al.*, 2006).

3. The research encompasses a variety of qualitative research strategies: semi-structured face-to-face interviews with a wide range of political and policy actors, welfare-rights organizations and training providers; focus groups with benefit recipients; and content analysis of policy documents, and narrative policy analysis more broadly. This was undertaken between 2002 and 2006.

4. For a wider analysis of the UK labour market on this issue, see GREEN and OWEN (2006).

5. The Every Child Matters Event was organized by the End Child Poverty Coalition, held in Sheffield in April 2006 (END CHILD POVERTY, 2006). This voiced experiences of, exposed challenges for, and also suggested solutions around ending child poverty in Sheffield and the UK more broadly. Transcripts of the event have been made available for this research.

REFERENCES

ADAMS J. (2002) PSAs and devolution: target setting across the UK, *New Economy* **9**, 31–35.

BOOTH P. (2005) Partnerships and networks: the governance of urban regeneration in Britain, *Journal of Housing and the Built Environment* **20**, 257–269.

BOUDREAU J. (2003) Politics of territorialization: regionalism, localism and other isms . . . the case of Montreal, *Journal of Urban Affairs* **2**, 179–199.

BRENNER N. (2003) Metropolitan institutional reform and the rescaling of state space in contemporary Western Europe, *European Urban and Regional Studies* **10**, 297–324.

BRENNER N. (2004) *New State Spaces*. Oxford University Press, Oxford.

BRENNER N., JESSOP B., JONES M. and MACLEOD G. (2003) Introduction: State space in question, in BRENNER N., JESSOP B., JONES M. and MACLEOD G. (Eds) *State/Space: A Reader*, pp. 1–26. Blackwell, Oxford.

BRISTOW G. (2005) Everyone's a winner: problematising the discourse of regional competitiveness, *Journal of Economic Geography* **5**, 285–304.

BUDD L. (2005) Emotional labour and the regional question, *International Journal of Work Organisation and Emotion* **1**, 105–119.

CASEBOURNE J. (2003) *Work Poverty and Welfare Reform — Welfare to Work Programmes for Lone Parents in Depressed Local Labour Markets*. Centre for Social and Economic Inclusion, London.

CENTRE FOR ECONOMIC AND SOCIAL INCLUSION (CESI) (2005) *More Jobs, More Skills — The Future for Sheffield's Labour Market*. CESI, London.

CENTRE FOR SUSTAINABLE URBAN AND REGIONAL FUTURES (SURF) (2003) City thinking: transformation in principles and practice. Unpublished Paper. SURF, University of Salford, Salford.

CENTRE FOR URBAN AND REGIONAL DEVELOPMENT STUDIES (CURDS) (1999) *Core Cities: Key Centres for Regeneration.* CURDS, Newcastle.

CHRISTOPHERSON S. (2003) The limits to 'new regionalism': (ee)learning from the media industries, *Geoforum* **34**, 413–415.

COOKE P. (2003) *Knowledge Economies: Clusters, Learning and Cooperative Advantage.* Routledge, London.

COOKE P. and MORGAN K. (1998) *Associational Economies.* Oxford University Press, Oxford.

COX K. (2004) The politics of local and regional development: the difference the state makes and the US/British contrast, in WOOD A. and VALLER D. (Eds) *Governing Local and Regional Economics Institutions Politics and Economic Development,* pp. 247–275. Ashgate, Aldershot.

CROUCH C. and HILL S. (2004) Regeneration in Sheffield: from council dominance to partnership, in CROUCH C., LE GALÈS P., TRIGILIA C. and VORLZKOW H. (Eds) *Changing Governance of Local Economies: Responses to European Local Production Systems,* pp. 180–196. Oxford University Press, Oxford.

DABINETT G. (2004) *Uneven Spatial Development and Regeneration Outcomes in the UK: Reversing Decline in the Northern City of Sheffield?* Mimeograph, Sheffield University, Sheffield.

DANSON M. (2005) Old industrial regions and employability, *Urban Studies* **42**, 285–300.

DEAS I. and WARD K. (2000) From the 'new localism, to the 'new regionalism'? The implications of regional development agencies for city-regional relations, *Political Geography* **19**, 273–292.

DEAS I. and WARD K. (2002) Metropolitan manoeuvres: making Greater Manchester, in PECK J. and WARD K. (Eds) *City of Revolution: Restructuring Manchester,* pp. 116–132. Manchester University Press, Manchester.

DEPARTMENT OF COMMUNITIES AND LOCAL GOVERNMENT (DCLG) (2006a) *Strong and Prosperous Communities: The Local Government White Paper Cmn 6939-1.* DCLG, London.

DEPARTMENT OF COMMUNITIES AND LOCAL GOVERNMENT (DCLG) (2006b) *The Role of City Development Companies in English Cities and City-Regions: A Consultation.* DCLG, London.

DEPARTMENT OF COMMUNITIES AND LOCAL GOVERNMENT (DCLG) (2007) *The Role of City Development Companies in English Cities and City-Regions: Summary of Responses to the Consultation Paper Published by Communities and Local Government.* DCLG, London.

DICKINSON R. E. (1967) *The City Region in Western Europe.* Routledge & Kegan Paul, London.

DOBBS L., FISHER T., GERMANEY L., MOORE C. and O'DONNELL A. (2003) *Job Centre Plus North East Region Customer Consultation, Final Report.* Centre for Public Policy, Northumbria University, Newcastle.

DONALD B. (2001) Economic competitiveness and quality of life in city regions: compatible concepts, *Canadian Journal of Urban Research* **10**, 259–274.

EKOS (2002) *Progress in South Yorkshire 2002 – Technical Report.* Learning Skills Council, Sheffield.

END CHILD POVERTY (2006) *Unequal Choices: Voices of Experience Exposing Challenges and Suggesting Solutions to Ending Child Poverty in the UK.* Joseph Rowntree Foundation, London.

ETHERINGTON D. (2005) Poverty, low pay and worklessness in Sheffield: proposals for change. Paper presented at the Employment Advisory Board, Sheffield First for Learning and Work, Sheffield, UK.

FAIRCLOUGH N. (2001) *New Labour, New Language?* Routledge, London.

FINE B. (2001) The continuing imperative of value theory, *Capital and Class* **75**, 41–52.

FLETCHER D. R. (2007) A culture of worklessness? Historical insights from the Manor and Park area of Sheffield, *Policy and Politics* **35**, 65–85.

GONZALEZ S. (2006) *The Northern Way: A Celebration or a Victim of the New City-Regional Government Policy?* ESRC/DCLG Postgraduate Research Programme Working Paper No. 28. ESRC, Swindon.

GONZALEZ S., TOMANEY J. and WARD N. (2006) Faith in the city-region?, *Town and Country Planning* **November**, 315–317.

GOODCHILD B. and HICKMAN P. (2006) Towards a regional strategy for the North of England? An assessment of the 'Northern Way', *Regional Studies* **40**, 121–133.

GOODWIN M., JONES M. and JONES R. (2005) Devolution, constitutional change and economic development: explaining and understanding the new institutional geographies of the British state, *Regional Studies* **39**, 421–436.

GOUGH J., EISENSCHITZ A. and McCULLOCH A. (2006) *Spaces of Social Exclusion.* Routledge, London.

GRAY A. (2004) *Unsocial Europe: Social Protection or Flexploitation?* Pluto, London.

GREEN A. and OWEN D. (2006) *The Geography of Poor Skills and Access to Work.* Joseph Rowntree Foundation, York.

GROVER C. (2003) New Labour, welfare reform and the reserve army of labour, *Capital and Class* **79**, 17–23.

GRUGULIS I. (2003) The contribution of national vocational qualifications to the growth of skills in the UK, *British Journal of Industrial Relations* **41**, 457–475.

H. M. TREASURY, DEPARTMENT OF BUSINESS ENTERPRISE AND REGULATORY REFORM, and COMMUNITY AND LOCAL GOVERNMENT (2007) *Review of Sub-National Economic Development and Regeneration.* H. M. Treasury, London.

H. M. TREASURY, DTI and ODPM (2003) *A Modern Regional Policy for the United Kingdom.* Stationery Office, London.

H. M. TREASURY, DTI and ODPM (2006) *Devolving Decision Making: 3 – Meeting the Regional Economic Challenge: The Importance of Cities to Regional Growth.* Stationery Office, London.

HALL P. and PAIN K. (Eds) (2006) *The Polycentric Metropolis – Learning from Mega-City Regions in Europe.* Earthscan, London.

HARDING A. (2007) Taking city regions seriously? Response to debate on 'city-regions: new geographies of governance, democracy and social reproduction', *International Journal of Urban and Regional Research* **31**, 443–458.

HARRISON J. (2006) Re-reading the new regionalism: a sympathetic critique, *Space and Polity* **10**, 21–46.

HARRISON J. (2007) From competitive regions to competitive city-regions: a new orthodoxy, but some old mistakes, *Journal of Economic Geography* **7**, 311–332.

HERRESCHEL T. and NEWMAN P. (2002) *Governance of Europe's City Regions: Planning, Policy and Politics.* Routledge, London.

HOOGVELDT A. and FRANCE A. (2000) New Deal: the experience and views of clients in one pathfinder city (Sheffield), *Local Economy* **15**, 112–127.

HOQUE K. (2003) All in all, it's just another plaque on the wall: the incidence and impact of the Investors in People standard, *Journal of Management Studies* **40**, 543–571.

HOWARTH C. and KENWAY P. (2004) *Why Worry Anymore About the Low Paid.* New Policy Institute, London.

HUDSON R. (1999) The learning economy, the learning firm and the learning region: a sympathetic critique, *European Urban and Regional Studies* **6**, 59–72.

HUDSON R. (2005) Region and place: devolved regional government and regional economic success?, *Progress in Human Geography* **29**, 618–625.

HUDSON R. (2006) Regional devolution and regional economic success: enabling myths and illusions about power, *Geografiska Annaler* **88B**, 159–171.

HUNT T. (2005a) *Building Jerusalem: The Rise and Fall of the Victorian City.* Phoenix, London.

HUNT T. (2005b) Foreword, in *Seeing the Light? New Steps for City Regions.* New Local Government Network (NLGN), London.

JESSOP B. (1997) A neo-Gramscian approach to the regulation of urban regimes, in LAURIA M. (Ed.) *Reconstructing Urban Regime Theory.* Sage, London.

JESSOP B. (2002a) *The Future of the Capitalist State.* Polity, Cambridge.

JESSOP B. (2002b) Liberalism, neoliberalism and urban governance: a state theoretical perspective, *Antipode* **34**, 452–473.

JONAS A. (1996) Local labour control regimes: uneven development and the social regulation of production, *Regional Studies* **30**, 323–338.

JONAS A. and WARD K. (2002) A world of regionalisms: towards a US–UK urban and regional policy framework comparison, *Journal of Urban Affairs* **24**, 377–402.

JONAS A. and WARD K. (2007a) Introduction to a debate on city-regions: new geographies of governance, democracy and social reproduction, *International Journal of Urban and Regional Research* **31**, 169–178.

JONAS A. and WARD K. (2007b) There's more than one way to be 'serious, about city-regions', *International Journal of Urban and Regional Research* **31**, 647–656.

JONES M. (2001) The rise of the regional state in economic governance: 'partnerships for prosperity' or new scales of state power?, *Environment and Planning A* **33**, 1188–1211.

JONES M. and MACLEOD G. (1999) Towards a regional renaissance? Reconfiguring and rescaling England's economic governance, *Transactions of the Institute of British* Geographers **24**, 295–313.

JONES M. and MACLEOD G. (2004) Regional spaces, spaces of regionalism: territory, insurgent politics and the English question, *Transactions of the Institute of British Geographers* **29**, 433–452.

KEATING M. (1998) *The New Regionalism in Western Europe: Territorial Restructuring and Political Change.* Edward Elgar, Cheltenham.

KEATING M. (2001) *Nations Against the State: The New Politics of Nationalism in Quebec, Catalonia and Scotland.* Palgrave, London.

KEATING M., LOUGHLIN J. and DESCOUWER K. (2003) *Culture, Institutions and Economic Development.* Edward Elgar, Cheltenham.

KING D. (1995) *Actively Seeking Work? The Politics of Unemployment and Welfare Policy in the United States and Great Britain.* University of Chicago Press, Chicago, IL.

KITSON M., MARTIN R. and TYLER P. (2004) Regional competitiveness: an elusive yet key concept, *Regional Studies* **38**, 991–1000.

KRUEGER R. and SAVAGE L. (2007) City-regions and social reproduction: a 'place, for sustainable development?, *International Journal of Urban and Regional Research* **31**, 215–223.

LARNER W. and WALTERS W. (2002) The political rationality of 'new regionalism': towards a genealogy of the region, *Theory and Society* **31**, 391–432.

LEE S. (2002) Yorkshire (and the Humber), in TOMANEY J. and MAWSON J. (Eds) *England: The State of the Regions.* Policy Press, Bristol.

LEEDS METROPOLITAN UNIVERSITY/SHEFFIELD HALLAM UNIVERSITY (2003) *Objective 1 Mid Term Evaluation.* Policy Research Institute, Leeds.

LEIBOVITZ J. (2003) Institutional barriers to associative city-region governance: the politics of institution-building and economic governance in 'Canada's Technology Triangle', *Urban Studies* **40**, 2613–2642.

LOVERING J. (1999) Theory led by policy: the inadequacies of the 'new regionalism' (illustrated from the case of Wales), *International Journal of Urban and Regional Research* **23**, 379–395.

MACKINNON D., CUMBERS A. and CHAPMAN K. (2002) Learning, innovation and regional development: a critical appraisal of recent debates, *Progress in Human Geography* **26**, 293–311.

MACLEOD G. (1998) In what sense a region? Place hybridity, symbolic shape, and institutional formation in (post-)modern Scotland, *Political Geography* **17**, 833–863.

MACLEOD G. (2000) The learning region in an age of austerity: capitalizing on knowledge, entrepreneurialism, and reflexive capitalism, *Geoforum* **31**, 219–236.

MACLEOD G. (2001) New regionalism reconsidered: globalization and the remaking of political economic space, *International Journal of Urban and Regional Research* **25**, 804–829.

MACLEOD G. and JONES M. (2001) Renewing the geography of regions, *Environment and Planning D: Society and Space* **19**, 669–695.

MACLEOD G. and WARD K. (2002) Spaces of utopia and dystopia: landscaping the contemporary city, *Geografiska Annaler: Series B, Human Geography* **84**, 153–170.

MALECKI E. (2004) Jockeying for position: what it means and why it matters to regional development policy when places compete, *Regional Studies* **38**, 1101–1120.

MARKUSEN A. (1999) Fuzzy concepts, scanty evidence and policy distance: the case for rigour and policy relevance in critical regional studies, *Regional Studies* **33**, 869–886.

MARTIN R. and SUNLEY P. (2003) Deconstructing clusters: chaotic concept or policy panacea?, *Journal of Economic Geography* **3**, 5–35.

MASKELL P. (2001) Towards a knowledge-based theory of the geographical cluster, *Industrial and Corporate Change* **10**, 921–943.

McCANN E. J. (2007) Inequality and politics in the creative city-region: questions of livability and state strategy, *International Journal of Urban and Regional Research* **31**, 188–196.

McGOVERN P., SMEATON D. and HILL S. (2004) Bad jobs in Britain, *Work and Occupation* **31**, 225–249.

McGUIRK P. (2007) The political construction of the city-region: notes from Sydney, *International Journal of Urban and Regional Research* **31**, 179–187.

MILIBAND D. and HUNT T. (2004) Learn from Victorians, *The Guardian*, Comment & Analysis **8 September**, 23.

MUSSON S., TICKELL A. and JOHN P. (2005) A decade of decentralisation? Assessing the role of Government Offices for the English regions, *Environment and Planning A* **37**, 1395–1412.

NEW LOCAL GOVERNMENT NETWORK (NLGN) (2005) *Seeing the Light: Next Steps for City Regions.* NLGN, London.

NORTHERN WAY (2004) *Moving Forward: The Northern Way First Growth Strategy Report: Summary.* Northern Way Steering Group, Newcastle.

OFFICE OF THE DEPUTY PRIME MINISTER (ODPM) (2003) *Cities, Regions and Competitiveness.* ODPM, London.

OFFICE OF THE DEPUTY PRIME MINISTER (ODPM) (2004) *Competitive European Cities: Where do the Core Cities Stand?* ODPM, London.

PAASI A. (2002) Place and region: regional worlds and regional words, *Progress in Human Geography* **26**, 802–811.

PAASI A. (2004) Place and region: looking through the prism of scale, *Progress in Human Geography* **28**, 536–546.

PARR J. B. (2005) Perspectives on the city-region, *Regional Studies* **39**, 555–566.

PASTOR M., DREIER P., GRIGSBY III J. E. and LÓPEZ-GARZA M. (2000) *Regions that Work: How Cities and Suburbs can Grow Together.* University of Minnesota Press, Minneapolis, MN.

PECK J. and THEODORE N. (2000) Work first: welfare-to-work and the regulation of contingent labour markets, *Cambridge Journal of Economics* **24**, 119–138.

PRESTON G. (Ed.) (2006) *A Route Out of Poverty? Disabled People, Work and Welfare Reform.* Child Poverty Action Group (CPAG), London.

ROBSON B., BARR B., LYMPEROPOULOU K., REES J. and COOMBES M. (2006) *A Framework for City-Regions.* Working Paper No. 1: Mapping City-Regions. Office of the Deputy Prime Minister (ODPM), London.

ROBSON B., PECK J. and HOLDEN A. (2000) *Regional Agencies and Area-Based Regeneration.* Policy Press, Bristol.

ROSSI U. (2004) New regionalism contested: some remarks in light of the case of the Mezzogiorno in Italy, *International Journal of Urban and Regional Research* **28**, 466–476.

SCOOP AID (2001) *Recommendations for a Lone Parenting Targeting Strategy.* Scoop Aid, Sheffield.

SCOTT A. (1998) *Regions and the World Economy: The Coming Shape of Global Production, Competition, and Political Order.* Oxford University Press, Oxford.

SCOTT A. (2001) Globalization and the rise of city-regions, *European Planning Studies* **9**, 813–826.

SCOTT A., AGNEW J., SOJA E. and STORPER M. (Eds) (2001) *Global City-Regions: Trends, Theory, Policy.* Oxford University Press, Oxford.

SCOTT A. and STORPER M. (2003) Regions, globalization, development, *Regional Studies* **37**, 579–593.

SHEFFIELD CITY COUNCIL (2001) *Census Topic Reports.* Sheffield City Council, Sheffield.

SHEFFIELD CITY COUNCIL (2003) *Women living in poverty.* Report to the Sheffield First for Inclusion Partnership Board, 2 October 2003. Corporate Policy Unit, Sheffield.

SHEFFIELD CITY COUNCIL (2006) *Extension of the Sheffield New Deal for Towns, Cities and Regions Business Case and Expression of Interest for DWP City Strategy on Behalf of the Prospective Consortium for Sheffield, Barnsley, Doncaster and Rotherham.* Sheffield City Council Employment Unit, Sheffield.

SHEFFIELD CITY COUNCIL (2007) *Gender in Regeneration Seminar Report, 11th January 2007.* Sheffield City Council/Oxfam UK Poverty Programme, Sheffield.

SHEFFIELD FIRST (2003) *Sheffield City Strategy 2002–2005.* Sheffield First Partnership, Sheffield.

SHEFFIELD ONE (2005) *Annual Review 2004/2005.* Sheffield One, Sheffield.

SHEFFIELD WELFARE ACTION NETWORK (2007) *Welfare Reform: The 'Unthinkable, May Be About To Happen'.* Press Release, 20 March 2007. Sheffield Welfare Action Network (SWAN), Sheffield.

SÖDERBAUM F. (2004) *The Political Economy of Regionalism: The Case of South Africa.* Palgrave, Basingstoke.

SOUTH YORKSHIRE PARTNERSHIP (2005) *South Yorkshire Investment Plan.* South Yorkshire Partnership, Barnsley.

SOUTH YORKSHIRE PARTNERSHIP (2006a) *Progress in South Yorkshire.* South Yorkshire Partnership: Barnsley.

SOUTH YORKSHIRE PARTNERSHIP (2006b) *Sheffield City Region Development Programme, A Submission to the Northern Way, September 2006.* South Yorkshire Partnership: Barnsley.

SOUTH YORKSHIRE PARTNERSHIP/ALLIANCE SUB REGIONAL STRATEGIC PARTNERSHIP (2005) *City Region Development Programme.* Northern Way, Newcastle.

STORPER M. (1997) *The Regional World: Territorial Development in a Global Economy.* Guilford, New York, NY.

SUNLEY P., MARTIN R. and NATIVEL C. (2006) *Putting Workfare in Place: Local Labour Markets and the New Deal.* Blackwell, Oxford.

TEWDWR-JONES M. and ALLMENDINGER P. (Eds) (2006) *Territory, Identity and Spatial Planning: Spatial Fragmentation in a Fragmented Nation*. Routledge, London.

TEWDWR-JONES M. and MCNEILL D. (2000) The politics of city-region planning and governance, *European Urban and Regional Studies* **7**, 119–134.

THUROW L. C. (1999) *Building Wealth: The New Rules for Individuals, Companies and Nations in a Knowledge-Based Economy*. HarperCollins, New York, NY.

TUROK I. (2004) Cities, regions and competitiveness, *Regional Studies* **38**, 1069–1083.

TUROK I. and EDGE N. (1999) *The Jobs Gap in Britain's Cities: Employment Loss and Labour Market Consequences*. Policy Press, Bristol.

VÄYRYNEN R. (2003) Regionalism: old and new, *International Studies Review* **5**, 25–51.

WARD K. and JONAS A. (2004) Competitive city-regionalism as a politics of space: a critical reinterpretation of the new regionalism, *Environment and Planning A* **36**, 2119–2139.

WEBSTER D. (2006) Welfare reform: facing up to the geography of worklessness, *Local Economy* **21**, 107–116.

YEANDLE S., BUCKNER L., GORE R. and POWELL R. (2004) *Gender Profile of South Yorkshire's Labour Market 2002*. Objective 1 Directorate, Wath-upon-Dearne.

YORKSHIRE-FORWARD (2003) *Regional Economic Strategy 2003–2012*. Yorkshire-Forward, Leeds.

YORKSHIRE-FORWARD (2005) *Why Yorkshire?* Yorkshire-Forward, Leeds.

Limits to the Mega-City Region: Conflicting Local and Regional Needs

IVAN TUROK

TUROK I. Limits to the mega-city region: conflicting local and regional needs, *Regional Studies*. There has been a revival of interest in the city region in recent spatial planning and development policy. The economic arguments have been most prominent, while the environmental and social dimensions have been neglected. This paper analyses the tension within large or 'mega'-city regions between local needs and regional interests, using the United Kingdom's Thames Gateway initiative as an example. It has gained support as a plan to concentrate the supply of new housing in an area east of London in response to wider growth pressures and housing constraints. Yet, the priority locally is economic and social development for existing residents rather than more housing for incomers. The paper explores the contrast between the regional housing agenda and the needs of established local communities for jobs, skills, and improved services. It shows how the pursuit of narrow regional objectives may complicate the task of local regeneration. There are important lessons for city region theory and practice in not constraining the role envisaged for secondary cities and towns in relation to the core city.

TUROK I. 对巨型城市区域的制约：地方及区域需求的冲突，区域研究。在目前的空间规划与发展政策理论领域，城市区域又重新成为了学术讨论的焦点。经济再度成为讨论的主题而忽视了与环境、社会相关的问题。本文以英国泰晤士门户区为例分析了大、巨型城市区域中地方需求与区域兴趣之间的张力。为了应对大范围增长压力以及房屋需求制约，一项针对东伦敦地区而提出的新房供应计划已获支持。然而地方首要的需求并非为新居民提供更多住房，而是在于促进现有居民的经济及社会发展。文章探讨了区域住房议程与当地社区对于工作、技能、提升服务水准需求之间的矛盾。研究指出，为了实现具体的区域目标，地方更新任务变得愈加复杂。这也为在城市区域理论及实践中不限制预定二级市镇之于核心城市的作用提供了重要借鉴。

城市区域　　经济发展　　空间规划　　住房

TUROK I. Les limites de la mégacité-région: le conflit entre les besoins locaux et régionaux, *Regional Studies*. Récemment, l'aménagement du territoire a fait preuve d'un regain d'intérêt pour la cité-région. Le raisonnement économique a joué un rôle de premier plan, tandis que l'on n'a fait attention aux perspectives ni sociale, ni environnementale. A partir d'une étude de cas, à savoir la Thames Gateway, cet article cherche à analyser le conflit au sein des grandes ou des 'mégas' cités-régions entre les besoins locaux et les intérêts régionaux. Cette initiative trouve du soutien comme schéma directeur qui cherche à concentrer l'offre de nouveaux logements dans une zone à l'est de Londres en réponse à la demande de croissance et aux restrictions à la construction de logements. Toujours est-il que la priorité sur le plan local s'avère le développement économique et social pour les habitants existants plutôt que la construction de logements pour les nouveaux venus. L'article examine le contraste entre le programme régional quant au logement et la demande d'emploi, d'habilités et de meilleurs services des communautés locales. On montre comment la poursuite des objectifs régionaux limités peut compliquer la tâche de la régénération locale. Il y a d'importantes leçons à tirer pour les cité-régions en théorie et en pratique dans la mesure où il ne faut pas limiter le rôle prévu des grandes villes et des villes secondaires par rapport à la ville principale.

TUROK I. Grenzen der Megastadtregion: der Konflikt zwischen lokalen und regionalen Bedürfnissen, *Regional Studies*. In letzter Zeit hat sich in der Politik zur Raumplanung und -entwicklung das Interesse für die Stadtregion wieder belebt. Die wichtigste Rolle hierbei spielten die wirtschaftlichen Argumente, während die Umwelt- und sozialen Dimensionen vernachlässigt wurden. In diesem Beitrag wird die Spannung zwischen lokalen Bedürfnissen und regionalen Interessen innerhalb großer bzw. 'Mega'-Stadtregionen anhand des Beispiels der Thames-Gateway-Initiative in Großbritannien analysiert. Diese Initiative fand Unterstützung als Plan zur Konzentration des Wohnungsbaus in einem Gebiet östlich von London, mit dem auf den Druck für breiteres Wachstum und die Einschränkungen im Bereich des Wohnungsbaus reagiert wurde. Zugleich liegt jedoch die Priorität vor Ort statt im Bau zusätzlicher Wohnungen für hinzuziehende Anwohner in der wirtschaftlichen und sozialen Weiterentwicklung der vorhandenen Anwohner. In diesem Beitrag wird der Kontrast zwischen den regionalen Wohnungsbauplänen und den Bedürfnissen der vorhandenen Gemeinschaften vor Ort in den Bereichen Arbeitsplätze, Ausbildung und verbesserte Dienstleistungen untersucht. Es wird gezeigt, dass sich durch das Verfolgen enger regionaler Ziele die Aufgabe der lokalen Regeneration verkomplizieren kann. Hieraus ergibt sich als wichtige Lehre für die Theorie und Praxis der Stadtregion, dass die für die sekundären Städte in Bezug auf die zentrale Stadt vorgesehene Rolle nicht zu eng gestaltet werden darf.

TUROK I. Límites a la región mega-ciudad: el conflicto entre necesidades locales y regionales, *Regional Studies*. En la reciente política de planificación y desarrollo espacial se ha observado una reactivación de intereses en la región metropolitana. Los argumentos económicos han sido más destacados mientras que las dimensiones medioambientales y sociales han sido ignoradas. En este artículo analizo la tensión en las grandes o mega regiones metropolitanas entre las necesidades locales y los intereses regionales usando como ejemplo la iniciativa británica en el estuario del Támesis. El plan ha obtenido un amplio apoyo para concentrar la construcción de nuevas viviendas en un área al este de Londres como respuesta a las presiones generales de crecimiento y las limitaciones de viviendas. Sin embargo, la prioridad a nivel local es el desarrollo económico y social para los residentes actuales más que construir más viviendas para recién llegados. En este artículo analizo el contraste entre la agenda regional de viviendas y las necesidades de las comunidades establecidas locales sobre trabajo, habilidades y mejora de servicios. Se demuestra que buscar objetivos regionales más estrechos puede complicar la tarea de la regeneración local. Estos factores son importantes lecciones para la teoría y práctica de la región metropolitana de modo que no debe limitarse el rol previsto para las ciudades y localidades secundarias con relación a la ciudad central.

INTRODUCTION

Interest in the city region in United Kingdom planning and development policy has been rekindled after some three decades in abeyance (EDDINGTON, 2006; H. M. TREASURY, 2006, 2007, 2008; PARKINSON *et al.*, 2006). A series of reports from academics and think tanks have coincided with wider political and economic developments to revive city-region thinking in spatial decision-making (NEW LOCAL GOVERNMENT NETWORK (NLGN), 2005; HARDING *et al.*, 2006; JONES *et al.*, 2006; MARSHALL and FINCH, 2006). One of the concept's apparent policy attractions today is that it seems to be just as relevant to the goal of economic regeneration in the North and West of Britain as to the challenges of growth management in the South East (HARDING *et al.*, 2006; H. M. TREASURY, 2006).

The city region is commonly defined as a city or group of cities within a wider territory that have a close, interdependent relationship (PARR, 2005; DAVOUDI, 2008; RODRIGUEZ-POSE, 2008). Different places perform distinct and complementary functions, and they therefore interact through commuting, trade, information or other flows. A useful shorthand description of this functional geography or market area is the economic 'footprint' of the city. It is widely argued that if policies towards spatial planning, infrastructure, and service delivery are devolved to the city-region level and coordinated across relevant local authority jurisdictions, they may improve the efficiency of labour and housing markets, streamline transport systems, and generate economic spin-offs through increased productivity, knowledge spillovers, and innovation (SCOTT, 2001;

HALL and PAIN, 2006; H. M. TREASURY, 2006, 2008; EDDINGTON, 2006). In other words, city regions are held to offer considerable potential for integrated development strategies for places that are functionally coherent rather than arbitrarily defined.

Putting a city-region policy framework into place in the UK is proving to be more complex than originally envisaged. The process to date has been ad hoc, uneven and incremental, with continuing uncertainties about city-region powers, resources, and accountability mechanisms (HOUSE OF COMMONS COMMUNITIES AND LOCAL GOVERNMENT COMMITTEE (HCCLGC), 2007). A novel feature is a heavy reliance on 'thin' institutions and voluntary arrangements for coordination, in contrast to a dedicated tier of government or other formal structures at the city-region level, as occurred, for example, during the 1970s with the creation of the metropolitan county councils in England and the regional councils in Scotland (DEPARTMENT FOR COMMUNITIES AND LOCAL GOVERNMENT (DCLG), 2006a; HARDING *et al.*, 2006; H. M. TREASURY, 2007). This approach reflects a desire to avoid the costs of organizational restructuring and to include a wider range of influential stakeholders, within and outside government, in decision-making. Another emerging feature of current practice is that investment is to be targeted on localities with the greatest economic 'potential', which is reminiscent of growth pole arguments. In the face of local resistance, new housing is also to be developed in particular parts of the region rather than spread around (HCCLGC, 2007; DCLG, 2008). Claims are still made that city-region policies can promote the regeneration of run-down areas and reduce social and spatial disparities within and between regions (DCLG, 2008; H. M. TREASURY, 2007, 2008).

Many of the issues and implications arising from the pursuit of city-region ideas are only just emerging, as is clear from several of the other papers in this special issue. Although it has often been presented as a policy panacea for balanced and sustained regional development, the city region seems unlikely to provide a simple means of reconciling diverse economic, environmental, and social objectives (KEATING, 1998; BUCK et al., 2005; RODRIGUEZ-POSE, 2008). For example, economic growth pressures may demand a larger labour pool for the core agglomeration, longer-distance commuting for the enlarged workforce, and more business travel and trade between centres, all implying greater mobility, higher carbon emissions, and more congestion, especially if the private car continues to dominate travel patterns (WHEELER, 2009). The distinctive character and socio-economic needs of individual localities may also get neglected with a shift in perspective to the city-region level and greater emphasis placed on economies of scale and region-wide connectivity (HEALEY, 2009). In short, depending on how they are pursued, city-region policies could potentially reinforce spatial inequalities and unsustainable development processes, rather than mitigate these tendencies (JONAS and WARD, 2007; NEUMAN and HULL, 2009).

The purpose of this paper is to assess the idea that there may be some drawbacks associated with a city-region approach, particularly if the perspective is narrow or one-dimensional. These consequences may be particularly clear in places that were not previously covered by this scale of planning framework. It is instructive to consider the Thames Gateway initiative in the South East of England through a city-region lens because it illustrates important features of city-region thinking. Thames Gateway is an ambitious plan to accelerate the supply of new housing because of shortages in and around London as a result of its recent economic dynamism and population growth. High house prices in the South East have been inflationary and undermined Britain's economic performance (BARKER, 2004). In the past, government regional housing targets were distributed among localities within the region. However, local opposition to development across much of the South East means that the new plan seeks to concentrate new housing into an urban corridor stretching 40 miles eastwards from London, along with three other 'growth areas' (Fig. 1) (OFFICE OF THE DEPUTY PRIME MINISTER (ODPM), 2003a, 2005). The scale of the Thames Gateway initiative means it is of considerable national significance in the UK. It was also recently described as Europe's largest regeneration programme (NATIONAL AUDIT OFFICE (NAO), 2007). Discussion of the Thames Gateway to date has tended to focus on two issues: (1) the complex governance arrangements;

and (2) difficulties in financing all the new infrastructure required (JOHN et al., 2005; RACO, 2005; URBAN TASK FORCE (UTF), 2005; GORDON, 2006; OXFORD BROOKES UNIVERSITY, 2006; HOUSE OF COMMONS COMMITTEE OF PUBLIC ACCOUNTS (HCCPA), 2007; NAO, 2007; CATNEY et al., 2008). The principal concern of the present paper is with the substantive policies, namely the nature of proposed development and its likely impact on the area.

The analysis focuses in on the city of Medway, one of the largest urban areas in the greater South East located about 30 miles east of London and with a population of 250 000 (Fig. 2). It is strategically positioned as one of six priority locations for development during the first phase of the Thames Gateway (DCLG, 2007). Local socio-economic and environmental conditions are poor by the standards of the South East, and Medway has been somewhat bypassed by rising regional prosperity over the last decade (MEDWAY COUNCIL, 2006a; PARKINSON et al., 2006). Consequently, it is an important place in which to consider the impact of the Thames Gateway initiative.

This paper illustrates how city-region ideas can influence local development priorities and projects, and what the effects are on the ground in specific places and communities. In particular, it seeks to examine how a rather simple city-region concept based on limited sensitivity to local circumstances can amplify tensions between local needs and regional growth interests. The evidence assembled for this analysis includes extensive secondary economic and demographic data and a wide range of policy documents and reports, supplemented by extended interviews conducted by the author with twenty senior decision-makers at local and regional levels (see Appendix 1 for details).

The paper is organized as follows. The first section discusses the meaning of the city-region concept and the reasons for its appeal to policy-makers. The second and third sections analyse the contemporary economic and social situation in Medway and the challenges faced. The fourth section considers the history of the Thames Gateway initiative in its regional context. The fifth section explores how the basic objectives are being applied in Medway and how regional growth pressures can shape local development priorities and complicate the challenges facing the existing community. The conclusion draws out some wider implications for city-region debates and explains why the arguments about Medway may apply to other secondary cities and towns in city regions elsewhere, particularly where their economic role and locational advantages are circumscribed.

RECENT INTEREST IN THE CITY REGION

There are at least four reasons for the burgeoning recent policy interest in the city-region concept. One is the declining significance of the administrative and built-up boundaries of cities as a result of falling transport costs, rising mobility, and the dispersal of households and business activity (SALET et al., 2003; PARR, 2005; HALL and PAIN, 2006; HARDING et al., 2006). Consequently, the spatial reach or sphere of influence of core cities has been expanding, development pressures on the surrounding countryside have been increasing, and policy-making has been obliged to reflect the reality of growing cross-boundary flows and interactions, both physical and economic. All sorts of anomalies and mismatches are likely if policies and services are not aligned across administrative boundaries to take account of functional geographies and market realities – such as journeys to work, retail catchments, and leisure and entertainment patterns. The gradual extension of the urban field and the desire to incorporate or cooperate with adjacent jurisdictions also reflects the continual search for greater efficiencies in the provision of many public and private services (DCLG, 2006a; HEALEY, 2009). This has to be balanced against the need for a close relationship between service providers and users, especially for personal and household services that are inherently local.

A second influence is the recognition that central government is too remote and unwieldy for the effective planning and delivery of certain functions (DCLG, 2006a; ORGANISATION FOR ECONOMIC CO-OPERATION AND DEVELOPMENT (OECD), 2006; H. M. TREASURY, 2007; RODRIGUEZ-POSE, 2008). Decentralized institutions are more responsive to local and regional circumstances and better placed to set priorities in line with local needs and development potential (HCCLGC, 2007; DCLG, 2008). The city region is particularly important for the coordination and integration of strategic land-use, transport, and other bulk infrastructure decisions because of the intensity of everyday flows at this scale and the disruptive effects of inconsistent or contradictory decisions (EDDINGTON, 2006; WHEELER, 2009). Economic growth may be held back if a city region is not functioning well because of traffic congestion, bottlenecks in housing supply, or basic infrastructure deficiencies, such as inadequate water or power supply, or insufficient capacity for waste disposal. European spatial planning ideas and initiatives have also been influential, with similar themes of policy integration and coherent territorial organization reflected in the notion of the 'polycentric urban region' (DAVOUDI, 2003; TUROK and BAILEY, 2004; FALUDI, 2006; HALL and PAIN, 2006). This is usually defined as a particular type of city region without a dominant city. There is more emphasis on balanced development across dispersed urban centres rather than on concentrated growth in the core city. Spatial policy may deliberately encourage investment in secondary centres in order to spread income and employment from the leading city and create viable counterweights or 'sustainable settlements' elsewhere.

The third and perhaps most important current reason for pursuing the city-region model is that it reinforces the economic advantages of agglomeration, including business access to a deep labour pool, diverse suppliers, specialized services, and good external connections (TUROK, 2004; H. M. TREASURY, 2006, 2008; RICE et al., 2006). Firms can 'mix and match' their inputs and alter their workforce more easily in response to changing technology and business needs (BUCK et al., 2005). This flexibility lowers costs, raises productivity, and improves economic resilience. Knowledge-intensive activities may benefit from proximity to universities and the greater circulation of information and ideas, generating superior learning and innovation (BRACZYK et al., 1998; AUDRETSCH and FELDMAN, 2004; H. M. TREASURY, 2006; JONES et al., 2006). Policies made at city-region level should be able to incorporate a fuller range of strategic economic assets beneficial to competitiveness than local policies, and be better placed to promote institutional collaboration, sharing of resources, and labour market matching (DCLG, 2006a; H. M. TREASURY, 2006). This is a popular argument in the expansive 'super-region' or 'mega-city region' of the greater South East, as well as in some other metropolitan regions in Europe and further afield (HALL and PAIN, 2006; GORDON, 2006; SCOTT, 2001; SALET et al., 2003; SALET, 2006). It reflects a view that large city regions or 'super-agglomerations' are emerging all over the world as the engines of the contemporary global economy in what may amount to a new phase in capitalist territorial development (SCOTT and STORPER, 2003; see also HALL and PAIN, 2006).

Finally, the city-region agenda could fill the lacuna left by the government's stalled regional devolution project in the North and West of England (PARR, 2005; GONZALEZ et al., 2006; HARDING, 2006; HCCLGC, 2007; HEALEY, 2009). The city region is sufficiently flexible to cover many different kinds of places with a variable outer boundary depending on the defining criteria and thresholds applied (HARDING et al., 2006). In principle, it appeals to the interests of cities as well as surrounding towns and rural areas, encouraging investment in improved transport links between such settlements, enabling places to tap into growth occurring in neighbouring areas and 'borrow' the advantages of agglomeration by combining resources and avoiding duplication. It has also been linked to the urban regeneration agenda through the need to set clearer objectives and priorities for public investment and to connect deprived communities with economic opportunities elsewhere (DCLG, 2008). The emphasis on selectivity and functional specialization means that places have to think through their distinct qualities, economic roles, and relationships with other towns and cities. This conforms with the prevailing approach to tackling regional inequalities in focusing on indigenous growth and self-sufficiency, rather than diverting investment from prosperous regions and other forms of resource transfer (FOTHERGILL, 2005). The renewed interest in city regions is therefore consistent with what has been widely described as the 'new regionalism' (KEATING, 1998; PIKE *et al.*, 2006).

Although it is not a tightly defined concept and is open to different interpretations, many of the arguments for city regions tend to imply that higher levels of internal connectivity within the city region are beneficial, and that the bigger the city region the better, especially for economic competitiveness. This helps to explain the popularity of terms such as 'global city region', 'mega regions' and 'polycentric mega-city region' (SCOTT, 2001; HALL and PAIN, 2006; HALL, 2009). The justification for city regions in the UK has arguably been rather narrow and the policy agenda somewhat restricted in scope, being dominated by concerns about economic growth and efficient public spending (DAVOUDI, 2008; HEALEY, 2009; see also HCCLGC, 2007; and H. M. TREASURY, 2008). The environmental aspects have generally been neglected, along with the consequences for localities that are disadvantaged or bypassed for whatever reason in a more open, competitive regional context, where public resources are allocated more selectively. There are also unresolved questions in the discussion of city regions about the appropriate relationship between regional and local decision-making, and risks that regional priorities will override local concerns in enlarging the scale of territorial planning. This was one of the issues that the sub-national review of economic development and regeneration sought to address, although without a simple resolution (H. M. TREASURY, 2007).

Before turning to the case study, four basic themes or questions can be drawn out of this discussion to provide a framework to guide the empirical analysis. First, how strongly connected is the particular city or town to the wider functional area? The linkages may take different forms (commuting, trade, information, etc.), but for a secondary city or town to be planned as part of a city region, one would expect reasonably strong flows or interactions with the core city. Second, what is the nature of the relationship between the secondary city and the core city? Is it a fairly balanced relationship with mutual dependence between places, or an unequal situation with the core city benefiting disproportionately from the quantity and quality of investment, employment and incomes? Third, how do social conditions in the secondary city compare with the wider city region, in terms of the welfare of the local population, level of education, social infrastructure and amenities, social fabric, civic pride and identity, summed up as 'social cohesion'? Finally, what are the environmental implications of the secondary city being part of the wider city region, in terms of the nature and quality of transport connections, level of congestion and carbon emissions, and the 'quality of place' – its functional coherence, built environment,

and physical infrastructure? Taken together, these questions get to the heart of how effectively a particular city is integrated into a wider city region.

THE MEDWAY CONTEXT: A POROUS ECONOMY

Situated at the heart of the Thames Gateway, Medway is made up mainly of a continuous built-up area comprising the five historic towns of Chatham, Rochester, Gillingham, Rainham, and Strood that have coalesced over the years (Fig. 3). Medway Council is a unitary (single-tier) authority and was created in 1998 by the amalgamation of two lower-tier councils (Rochester and Gillingham). For many years the local economy was quite self-contained and dominated by the Royal Naval Dockyard at Chatham and other port-related industries. The Dockyard's closure in 1984 and concurrent deindustrialization destroyed many manual jobs and left a legacy of derelict and contaminated land. Subsequent recovery has been slow and patchy, resulting in very low household incomes and productivity compared with regional and national averages (Table 1).

The local economy also differs from the wider region with fewer jobs in high-value industries. There are 20% fewer jobs in finance, information technology, and other business services than in the South East region as officially defined (that is, excluding London and the East of England) and 17% more jobs in public administration and health (see Appendix Table A1). Only 35% of Medway residents are employed in professional, managerial, and technical occupations compared with 47% in the wider region (see Appendix Table A2). Medway's social composition is unusual for the South East, reflecting its industrial history and position in the regional housing market.

Economic weakness has forced many residents to look elsewhere for work, including London. Through out-commuting the employment rate has recovered from the nadir of the 1980s and is not as far below the regional average as might been have expected

Table 1. Economic indicators

	Medway	South East	Britain
Gross value added per head, 2002	10 326	16 758	15 614
Average household income, 2001/2002 (£)	19 500	24 740	21 170
Gross hourly pay for full-time men, 2007 (£)[a]	11.93	13.02	12.14
Gross hourly pay for full-time women, 2007 (£)[a]	9.69	10.86	10.48

Notes: [a]Earnings data are workplace-based.
South East is the official region (that is, excluding London).
Sources: Office for National Statistics (ONS) via the National On-line Manpower Information System (NOMIS); and MEDWAY COUNCIL (2006b).

Table 2. *Labour market indicators, 2006/2007*

	Medway (%)	South East (%)	Britain (%)
Employment rate	76.5	78.3	74.2
Unemployment	5.5	4.4	5.3
Key benefit claimants	13.3	9.7	14.2
Economically inactive wanting a job	7.3	5.4	5.5

Sources: Office for National Statistics (ONS), Annual Population Survey (April 2006–March 2007); and Department for Work and Pensions (DWP) benefit claimants.

(Table 2). Nevertheless, there are sizeable numbers on welfare benefits and many inactive people who want to work, suggesting disguised unemployment (Table 2). Youth unemployment is particularly high, perhaps because young people are less inclined to commute or lack relevant skills.

A useful way of characterizing Medway's recent evolution is towards a more porous or 'leaky' economy. The evidence presented below suggests that resources (financial and human) flow into and out of the area with weaker local circulation and less propensity to 'stick' than in other settlements of comparable size. This affects the quality of local amenities and infrastructure, including the public realm and transport system. It means that Medway has less functional integrity, and therefore attractiveness, as a place to live, work, study, and socialize than many other cities. This is highly relevant to the discussion below about the impact of policy efforts to insert it more deliberately into the city region through the Thames Gateway proposals for substantial additional housing in the area.

For example, the ratio of total employment to the working-age population (the 'jobs density') is only 0.68. In other words, there are about two jobs available for every three adults of working age. The figure for the official South East (excluding London) is 0.88, suggesting a sizeable jobs deficit in Medway. Appendix Table A3 shows that the jobs density for other places that are loosely comparable in terms of size and distance from London varies between 0.71 and 1.17. It is not a perfect comparison because the statistics are based on administrative boundaries, which are tighter in some places than in others. Yet, it does seem that Medway has a bigger shortfall in employment than other cities in the region.

Medway 'exports' more than two out of five (41%) working residents. Nearly 48 000 people commute elsewhere to work compared with fewer than 19 000 who commute into Medway (see Appendix Table A4). The average distance Medway residents travel to work is 17.5 kilometres compared with 14.9 kilometres in the whole region, 15.6 kilometres in Brighton, 14.1 kilometres in Milton Keynes, 11.4 kilometres in Portsmouth, and 10.9 kilometres in Southampton. This implied link between a lack of jobs and long-distance commuting is supported by a recent study of South

East commuting: 'a lack of job opportunities close to the place of residence was a strong feature of longer commutes' (TITHERIDGE and HALL, 2006, p. 74). According to key informants in the present study, commuters incur a heavy personal cost in travel time and fatigue, weakening the community, as discussed below. Long commutes also exacerbate transport congestion, energy consumption, and carbon emissions (LUCAS, 1998).

Commuting patterns are strongly influenced by occupation. More than half (53%) of local residents who commute to London are professionals, managers, and employers compared with only 29% of people who both live and work in Medway (see Appendix Table A4). This is not unusual because highly skilled, well-paid workers normally commute further on average than people in other occupations (HARDING *et al.*, 2006; TITHERIDGE and HALL, 2006). Conversely, only 12% of commuters to London are in routine and semi-routine occupations compared with 33% of people who live and work locally. The skewed composition of out-commuting is also reflected in in-commuting (see Appendix Table A5).

The need to commute elsewhere is matched by a propensity for residents to consume elsewhere too. There seems little doubt among key informants that local retail and leisure facilities are inferior to many other places: 'Many of Medway's centres suffer from a negative image' (MEDWAY COUNCIL, 2006a, p. 16). This is both a symptom and a cause of household spending outside the area, including at Britain's largest regional shopping mall Bluewater near Dartford, as well as at Thurrock Lakeside just over the Dartford Crossing. Considerable spending on entertainment, recreation, and related services also occurs in London.

Cities of Medway's size normally function as regional service centres with a sizeable professional and financial sector and high-order social and cultural facilities. Proximity to London, poor internal connectivity, and a truncated hinterland resulting from a coastal location hamper Medway's ability to operate as a dynamic hub of activity attracting and spawning different consumer and business services. Instead, it seems more like five independent dormitory towns adjacent to each other and largely bypassed by the consumer boom and general high street revival of the last fifteen years.

Medway has features that have always attracted visitors, including the second oldest cathedral in England, a Norman castle (both Rochester), the historic Dockyard and a Charles Dickens connection. Yet, most are day visitors on coaches because of the limited hotels, restaurants, and related facilities. The River Medway also accommodates several large marinas with many pleasure boats and yachts, but most are owned by people living elsewhere who take advantage of the cheap berths and spend little time or money onshore. The lack of quality services to detain people for longer means that Medway has a relatively small share of jobs in tourism, despite its rich history and rec-reational assets (see Appendix Table A1).

Until recently there was no local university, raising concerns that Medway was losing out from learning opportunities for school leavers and the economic stimulus and status that other places derive from universities (OECD, 2007). With external funding, the universities of Greenwich and Kent established a joint satellite campus in Chatham. Yet, only one in eight of the first 2500 students came from Medway itself. Most of the others were commuting from London on a daily basis, against the prevailing traffic flow. Efforts to improve ancillary social and sports facilities may encourage more students from elsewhere to come and live locally and more local school leavers to go to university. A local Member of Parliament suggested that a more prestigious university might have a bigger impact in this respect (HCCPA, 2007).

Medway's porous economy is reflected in its physical structure. The five towns lack a focal point for the transport network that could have become a viable city centre. Instead, there are four separate high streets, three municipal centres, and five railway stations. External connectivity has improved over time, but this may have made the economy more permeable rather than increased inward investment. Given its strategic location between London and the Channel ports, one might have expected greater buoyancy. Unhelpful external perceptions, the long distance to an international airport, and poor workforce skills (see below) seem to have discouraged investment. Other towns in Kent are benefiting more from the high-speed Channel Tunnel Rail Link (CTRL), particularly Ashford and Ebbsfleet as the sites of new stations (HALL and PAIN, 2006). A strong regeneration case could have been made for routing the CTRL through Medway. This was a significant missed opportunity.

MEDWAY'S SOCIAL CONTEXT: CHALLENGES OF COHESION

There are other towns in the greater South East with porous economies and out-commuting. However, they tend to be desirable residential locations with high-quality housing that function as dormitory areas for London. Competition to live there is reflected in high house prices and high incomes. Industrial and commercial development is restricted to protect the environmental amenity. People choosing to live there accept the need to commute elsewhere to work and can afford to do so. Such places have been functionally integrated into the wider city region for longer and with more success.

Medway is a different kind of place. Apart from lower incomes (Table 1), house prices are only 68% of the regional average: 'This is a stark reflection on Medway's poor image, connectivity and economic performance'

(MEDWAY COUNCIL, 2006b, p. 7). Much of the social housing stock is in poor condition and requires renewal or replacement. Human capital is also relatively low. Only 18.3% of adults have a degree or Higher National Diploma (HND) (National Vocational Qualification (NVQ) 4 and above) compared with 30.5% in the official South East (see Appendix Table A6). One in eight have no qualifications at all. Traditional industries preferred apprenticeships rather than formal education, which meant that 'learning' and 'earning' were not strongly linked in local working-class culture.

Economic difficulties have created a range of linked social problems more typical of Northern industrial cities (TUROK et al., 2006). Many interviewees described a certain malaise within the community, including loss of civic pride, depressed expectations, and a weak social fabric with many households vulnerable to domestic disputes, family breakdown, and educational disaffection among children. Extensive commuting deprives Medway of community vitality and self-organization through commuters' inability or unwillingness to contribute to school parent associations, youth projects, charities, and other civic activities. Youth services are generally under-funded, including learning and cultural facilities, leisure and sports amenities, and detached youth workers. Responding to incidents of antisocial behaviour is a higher priority than constructive work with young people.

Medway's health record is also poor (MEDWAY COUNCIL, 2006b). High teenage pregnancy is associated with low expectations and poor prospects for working-class girls. Primary care is dominated by stand-alone general practitioners, whose recruitment is complicated by London's shadow effect, as is the case with teachers and some other professionals. Medway lacks community-based services offering integrated healthcare, family advice, children's services, community nurses, and anti-smoking programmes.

THE THAMES GATEWAY INITIATIVE

Medway is the largest of several towns along the Thames Estuary facing similar challenges of deprivation, decay, and damaged reputations (NAO, 2007). The sub-region was not a regeneration priority for many years because conditions were worse in Inner London. The first government recognition of the problem was in 1967 when the South East Economic Planning Council identified the area as requiring attention in their Strategic Plan (CHURCH and FROST, 1995; LUCAS, 1998). The subsequent version of the Plan confirmed South Essex as one of five planned growth areas in the South East.

These plans had little real impact and the origins of the actual Thames Gateway initiative can be traced to early 1980s local authority lobbying in North Kent in the face of industrial job losses and out-migration, together with perceptions of neglect by the rest of Kent (CHURCH and FROST, 1995; HULL, 1998). The London Planning Advisory Committee drew a connection between the depressed conditions East of London and the buoyant West. They raised the possibility of altering the balance, partly to alleviate congestion and overheating in the West. This was pursued by the London and South East Regional Planning Conference (SERPLAN) in its 1987 guidance to the government. SERPLAN proposed an East Thames Corridor (ETC) as a focus for development, including major regeneration sites requiring reclamation and improved infrastructure. It said the ETC would also need a stronger identity to attract private investment.

In the early 1990s government became more interested in the potential of the ETC to redress the regional economic imbalance (HULL, 1998; LUCAS, 1998). Studies were commissioned that confirmed significant development opportunities, subject to public investment in transport and land improvement. Under Michael Heseltine the idea gained a high profile, indeed it became central to his political ambitions (RYDIN, 1998). He re-branded it 'Thames Gateway' – a key strategic link between the UK and Europe, reinforcing London's position as a World City (CHURCH and FROST, 1995; NAO, 2007). However, the case was not compelling at a time of economic slowdown, and the Treasury refused the support needed for a major regeneration programme (RYDIN, 1998). Creating an economic counter-magnet to the West of London required a degree of coordinated public sector action that was unfashionable at the time. The ethos of the government was about enabling market forces rather than steering them in particular directions.

Instead, the mid-1990s was characterized by a series of separate, mostly low-key projects in the Thames Gateway. It was decided to work in partnership with the local authorities, rather than set up a special urban development corporation (UDC) and risk repeating the conflict created in the London Docklands and elsewhere during the previous decade. The national land-renewal agency English Partnerships began to invest in site assembly and remediation in Medway and elsewhere. Several transport schemes acquired a higher priority as a team of civil servants tried to skew resources towards the Thames Gateway. Parts of the corridor were given assisted area status and became eligible for regional aid and European structural funds. Several Thames Gateway localities also bid successfully for projects under the Single Regeneration Budget. 'At that point, the focus was very much upon economic regeneration and the creation of employment for some of the most impoverished communities in the south east' (HARDING et al., 2006, p. 55).

Meanwhile, housing pressures were building up in the South East, partly because of London's resurgence coupled with vigorous opposition to new development. Advisers began to suggest that the Thames Gateway 'offers the only part of the Region where land needs – primarily for housing – can be met without major, expensive, delaying and politically damaging controversy' (CROOKSTON, 1994, p. 11). CHURCH and FROST (1995) referred to the Thames Gateway as 'a safety valve for the next boom in the South East' (p. 208). This perspective was clearly giving priority to regional housing interests above the local regeneration needs that had been articulated previously. To deliver large-scale housing required substantial government investment in transport, land reclamation, and other infrastructure. Concerted efforts were also required to enhance the image and appeal of the area if it was to attract private investors, developers, and above all households from elsewhere in the South East.

As regional growth constraints increased into the new millennium, the demands for stronger government action mounted. The Barker Review was particularly influential in making the case for a step change in housing supply (BARKER, 2004). The 2003 Sustainable Communities Plan was the immediate response, reflecting the need 'to accommodate the economic success of London and the wider South East and ensure that the international competitiveness of the region is sustained' (ODPM, 2003a, p. 46). The Thames Gateway was one of four 'growth areas' identified for 200 000 extra homes above existing plans by 2016 (Fig. 1). Indicating high-level government support, the Thames Gateway was allocated almost three-quarters of the initial five-year £610 million funding for site assembly, remediation, and infrastructure because it was better prepared to absorb the additional housing capacity, having been a priority area for longer. A target of 120 000 new homes was set by 2016, 40 000 above the existing regional planning figure. The term 'sustainable community' was introduced to indicate the aspiration, in principle at least, to create well-serviced, energy-efficient, thriving places rather than sprawling dormitory settlements (ODPM, 2003a, 2003b, 2005).

The Thames Gateway was officially described as a 'huge opportunity' for five reasons: its sheer scale, proximity to London, good transport links to the continent, many brownfield sites, and lastly the opportunity to regenerate existing deprived communities (ODPM, 2003a, p. 52). A subsequent report confirmed that the Thames Gateway 'represents outstanding potential to expand housing supply close to London' (ODPM, 2003b, p. 9). These reports also indicated some ambitious job targets, but no justification was offered and no indication given of how they might be achieved. There was an acknowledgement in one report that 'We need to take account of the impact on existing communities' (ODPM, 2003b, p. 5), but again no elaboration at all of what this meant in practice. In response to subsequent evidence of accelerating population growth in London, fuelled partly by international migration, the government raised the housing target again in 2006 by 40 000 to a total of 160 000 homes

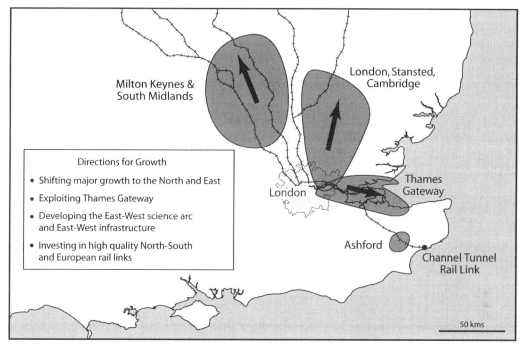

Directions for Growth

- Shifting major growth to the North and East
- Exploiting Thames Gateway
- Developing the East-West science arc and East-West infrastructure
- Investing in high quality North-South and European rail links

Fig. 1. Growth areas in the South East
Source: OFFICE OF THE DEPUTY PRIME MINISTER (ODPM) (2003b)

by 2016 (DCLG, 2006b). In a keynote speech to the Thames Gateway Forum, the Minister Ruth Kelly reiterated the emphasis: 'Our aim is to build homes, not houses. Create communities, not conurbations' (KELLY, 2006).

Such statements support COCHRANE's (2007) contention that 'What is being promised is the creation of new "communities", rather than the organic development of existing communities' (p. 54). Subsequent, the National Audit Office (NAO) and House of Commons Committee of Public Accounts (HCCPA) inquiries were highly critical of the Thames Gateway's vague targets and weak procedures. On the issue of who would benefit, the HCCPA (2007) concluded that:

> There is a risk that the economic benefits of regeneration will not reach existing residents [. . . and] that improved public services, infrastructure and housing will be concentrated in new developments.
>
> (pp. 6–7)

Local authorities generally welcomed the Thames Gateway initiative as 'an opportunity to direct much needed resources to their areas' (RACO, 2005, p. 150). They felt in no position to challenge the government's basic priorities for what was 'now primarily a housing-based programme' (HARDING et al., 2006, p. 56), believing that the investment would have a

catalytic effect in their areas. In Medway, there was remarkably little debate in the local media or elsewhere about the strategy being pursued, reflecting the low level of civic engagement and perhaps a sense of desperation to see investment of any kind. A variety of local special-purpose vehicles with varying powers were introduced across the Thames Gateway to help deliver the scale of change expected, including the complex tasks of brownfield land assembly, site preparation, and infrastructure provision. Unlike the earlier UDCs, they were required to work in partnership with local authorities (NAO, 2007). In Medway the government agreed to the council having a larger role in delivery because they had some prior experience and endorsed the strategy.

To summarize this section, the priorities for the Thames Gateway shifted during the 1990s from its intrinsic regeneration needs towards its potential to deliver a wider regional agenda. At first the interest was in economic development and relieving growth pressures West of London. The focus subsequently changed to alleviating housing shortages throughout the greater South East. It was this housing role that gave the Thames Gateway initiative momentum by unlocking substantial government investment and high-level Cabinet backing. It was also recognized that environmental improvements would be needed to attract incoming households with a choice of where to

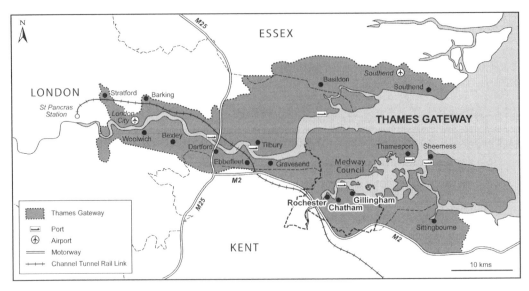

Fig. 2. Extent of Thames Gateway

live. Use of ambiguous terms such as 'regeneration' and 'sustainable communities' helped to disguise some of the tensions and differences of purpose behind the initiative.

THE IMPLICATIONS FOR MEDWAY

The Sustainable Communities Plan stated that at least 10 000 new homes would be built in Medway by 2016 (ODPM, 2003b). This was subsequently raised to 16 000, with the population expected to increase by no less than 50 000 (20% growth). The scale of vacant and derelict land made Medway an attractive location for the government. Its capacity to accommodate substantial new housing on brownfield sites was far more important than its social needs in securing special attention. The council was granted £95 million to lay the foundations for accelerated redevelopment. A series of regeneration projects was proposed under the umbrella of the Medway Waterfront Renaissance Strategy. A dedicated delivery unit called Medway Renaissance was established to plan and coordinate these schemes. Government support also stirred renewed interest in the area from private investors and property developers. A major urban regeneration specialist (St Modwen Properties Plc) was subsequently selected as Medway's 'investment partner' in a joint venture to deliver much of the redevelopment and lever in £1 billion of private funding on the basis of shared costs and profits.

The main physical projects are mapped in Fig. 3 and summarized in Fig. 4. They are at various stages of master planning, site acquisition, land preparation, and building construction. Much of the first few years has been devoted to preparing development frameworks and planning briefs, so some of the details are still uncertain. Nevertheless, the emphasis on new housing is immediately apparent. Commercial uses also feature, particularly retail and leisure. The special government grant was conditional on the delivery of new homes. With house-builders interested in buying vacant sites, the council as planning authority found it difficult to safeguard land for employment uses, especially as this is of lower value than housing. The large sites at Rochester Riverside, Strood Riverside, Chatham Dockyard, and Gillingham (Akzo Nobel) were major employment locations not long ago, but they are all now becoming mostly housing. Housing is the main use that produces the returns required to fund or at least to offset the up-front costs of clearance works, remediation, flood protection, and piling.

There is some recognition that land is required for employment uses, but resources have not been committed to this and the council has been unwilling to release any lower amenity greenfield sites on the city fringe that the private sector might develop for this purpose. Table 3 shows the dominance of housing in future investment expectations, with economic development well down the list, below culture and on a par with environment and sports and leisure. Medway has supported light industrial estates in the past – Gillingham Business Park and City Estate on the north bank – and provided flexible units for small enterprises. However, there has been little of this activity recently. A range of speculative office buildings were constructed in Chatham in the 1990s in an effort to attract corporate headquarters and financial services, with mixed results.

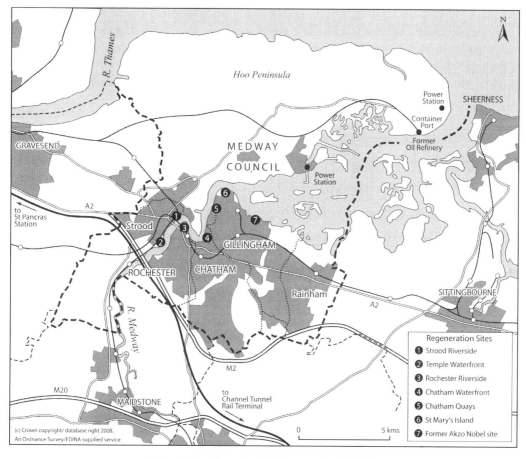

Fig. 3. Main settlements and development sites in Medway

The economic impact of the new housing is crucial to judgements about the benefits of the Thames Gateway to Medway. There will be many temporary jobs in construction, although the nature of this industry means that few will probably go to local workers unless special training and recruitment deals are negotiated with contractors (HCCPA, 2007). The permanent jobs generated by the new household spending on services should be more significant. The scale will depend on household composition, and there will be difficult trade-offs in this respect. The biggest impact should come from attracting people from elsewhere with high disposable incomes, but they may be the most difficult to attract because of the area's reputation (BENNETT and MORRIS, 2006). There will be pressure from government to accommodate lower-income households from London in order to alleviate its housing needs (HCCPA, 2007). There will also be local pressure to make a share of the new housing accessible to Medway residents.

The local employment multiplier should increase over time if perceptions change, the population expands, and local services improve. These jobs will tend to reproduce the existing employment structure through more public services and relatively low-value personal and consumer services. They will not add greatly to higher-value or externally traded activity. A larger resident workforce will also mean more competition for emerging vacancies. All things considered, there is no guarantee that the job prospects of existing residents will improve. Experience elsewhere casts doubt on the benefits of housing-led regeneration for employment and deprivation: 'addressing poor housing will not lead to a lasting improvement in deprived areas if problems of worklessness and under-performing local economies are not also dealt with' (PRIME MINISTER'S STRATEGY UNIT (PMSU), 2005, p. 17; see also LUPTON, 2003; and KINTREA, 2007). The sub-national review of regeneration and the subsequent regeneration framework endorsed a much stronger focus on economic development (H. M. TREASURY, 2007; DCLG, 2008).

- Rochester Riverside

This 30-hectare site is one of the flagship projects of the Thames Gateway. The site has been cleared and a planning application for 2000 homes, two hotels, shops, restaurants, pubs and cafes was submitted in 2005 and approved in 2006. There will also be a river walk and some health and community space

- Chatham Centre and Waterfront

A development brief has been prepared to expand and modernize the current Pentagon shopping centre to become a new commercial, cultural, and civic centre. Three other neighbouring sites will be redeveloped: Waterfront, Brook, and Station Gateway. Some 3500 new homes are expected. A new bus interchange will be created as well as a river walk and a regional cultural venue on the riverfront

- Strood Riverside

This 10-hectare site has been acquired and a development brief prepared for 550 homes at high density. Watermill Wharf will provide space for social enterprise and be a feature point of Strood riverfront and river walk

- Chatham Quays

A planning application for mixed uses including 300 homes has been approved, with an S106 Agreement under negotiation

- Dickens World in Chatham

A themed visitor attraction and multi-screen cinema was opened in 2007. It aims to attract 300 000–400 000 visitors per year

- St Mary's Island in Chatham

There are plans to develop 900 homes in addition to the 900 already built

- Temple Waterfront

A development brief has been prepared for mixed uses including 500 homes

- Strood and Gillingham town centres

A development framework and action plan are being prepared for some 650 new homes along with the growth of the evening economy, leisure, and retail uses through improvements to the environment, road network, and car parking

- Former Akzo Nobel site in Gillingham

A development brief was adopted in 2004 for a mixed-use scheme including 800 homes on 8 hectares. Planning consent has subsequently been granted

- Former Chattenden Barracks

The Ministry of Defence has approved the sale of part of this site for some 5000 new homes and related community facilities (DEPARTMENT FOR COMMUNITIES AND LOCAL GOVERNMENT (DCLG), 2007)

- Universities at Chatham

New and refurbished buildings for teaching, support services, and student accommodation to create a more complete university campus in Chatham

- Innovation Centre

An Innovation Centre in partnership with BAE Systems, local universities, and others to accommodate high-technology manufacturing, spin-out companies, and specialized business services

Fig. 4. Medway Renaissance projects in the pipeline
Source: Compiled by the author from a variety of sources, including MEDWAY COUNCIL (2006a)

Most of the new projects are concentrated along the waterfront and in Chatham Maritime. The impact could remain localized and leave other areas behind, without stimulating a wider revitalization of the city or improving its functional coherence. There may be pressure from the developers (and some sections of the council) to create places that are clearly distinct from established neighbourhoods in order to attract higher-income households. A recent housing development on St Mary's Island provides grounds for this concern, as does the gated community at New Road in Rochester. Much depends on the council's attitude towards secluded development and its commitment to integrate new schemes into the existing urban fabric. The task is complicated by the finite resources available and the major investment required to upgrade established neighbourhoods and high streets. There is also pressure from government to deliver the new housing as quickly as possible (HCCPA, 2007; NAO,

2007). But obtaining synergies from the separate projects and avoiding a piecemeal approach will be vital to capture wider benefits for Medway.

Integration of new and old is a social and economic as well as a physical process. It is likely to require a series of practical mechanisms to link emerging opportunities to existing residents. Some involve developing skills, confidence, and recruitment channels for people to compete for jobs. Others involve capacity-building and procurement arrangements for local firms to obtain business contracts. Improved community infrastructure and services are important to tackle underlying social concerns. And greater consultation with existing communities is needed to respond to their fears and aspirations. Table 3 suggests that a reasonable level of investment in learning and skills is expected. However, the resources anticipated for social and community regeneration are perfunctory.

Table 3. Estimated investment required to deliver Medway's regeneration framework, 2006–2016

Theme	Level of investment (£, millions)
Housing	835
Transport	250
Culture	250
Learning and skills	185
Infrastructure	150
Health	140
Environment	89
Economy	85
Sports and leisure	80
Town centres	70
Tourism and heritage	45
Social and community regeneration	18

Source: MEDWAY COUNCIL (2006a).

CONCLUSION

The city region has become an influential idea in spatial planning and development policy. It gives explicit recognition to the interactions between localities within a region and encourages strategic decisions to be made at an appropriate spatial scale. Coordination or integration is an important principle – between cities, towns, and rural areas; across different levels and functions of government (such as land-use planning, transport, and other infrastructure); and between economic, social, and environmental objectives. In practice, the economic arguments have been most prominent in recent UK policy, implying that the city region should be treated as a large, well-connected functional system that promotes growth through agglomeration economies. This approach is convenient in apparently endorsing house-building in places where there is less local resistance to new development, rather than where the housing constraints are greatest, as long as a case can be made that they are part of the same functional area. However, this is not necessarily in the best interests of the recipient communities, which may need a broader-based approach to regeneration, including economic and social development.

It is useful to look at the Thames Gateway initiative through a city region lens because it illustrates the contrast between local and regional agendas in concentrating a big increase in the supply of housing in order to meet growth pressures across the greater South East. It was chosen as a priority area mainly because brownfield sites were available and the local authorities were receptive to development. Depending on its success at attracting new households, the working population could increase substantially, many of whom will have to commute to London and elsewhere to work. Yet, the priority afforded to new housing does not correspond to the needs of existing residents for additional employment, skills, and community services. The emphasis on housing complicates the task of job creation in reducing

the supply of employment land. Medway has a porous economy and already functions as a dormitory area. This is not conducive to the overall health of the community and the integrity and quality of the city. More commuters will add to these concerns and put more pressure on stretched public services. If local regeneration was the top priority, there would be more focus on addressing economic and social weaknesses directly and less on using the location as a container for wider purposes and hoping for local benefits to permeate through.

It is not surprising that local decision-makers have grasped the opportunity to secure investment from the Thames Gateway initiative. Despite the discrepancy between regional and local priorities, there is scope to generate spin-offs for the area. Experience elsewhere suggests that close involvement in the redevelopment process by local authorities is important in this respect. Through their financial resources and planning controls they have power to negotiate improvements to the public realm by developers and employment and training opportunities for residents. They can also make the case for additional government support to absorb the impact of population growth on existing services and transport infrastructure. This will require a clear sense of purpose, an improved evidence base, and determination to maximize the Thames Gateway's contribution to Medway's future prosperity.

The Thames Gateway experience is not unique, but is relevant to other secondary cities and towns requiring revitalization in city regions elsewhere. Places with a legacy of deindustrialization or other locational disadvantages need forms of planning and investment that are responsive to local needs and circumstances, without neglecting the potential offered by the wider regional context for linking into external opportunities. While local planning policies devoid of a wider context risk being insular and inward-looking, a narrow city-region approach reflecting mainly regional interests can complicate the task such places face by reinforcing some of the weaknesses in the local economy and society, including the tendency to dormitory town status with weak local amenities, infrastructure and 'sense of place'.

Finally, this analysis has wider implications for the theory of city regions and its practical application in planning and development policy. It identifies a potential divergence between local and regional interests, and a risk that the needs of individual localities may get overlooked with the shift to a larger spatial scale of planning. Conventional city-region concepts tend to neglect this possibility in emphasizing the benefits of scale economies and intense flows of people, information, and resources between places. The analysis cautions against an oversimplified distinction between the core city and an undifferentiated hinterland, in which new housing for commuters can be located almost anywhere and connectivity is key. There are costs associated with a high degree of functional differentiation across very large city regions, particularly the concentration of housing in outlying areas with inadequate infrastructure and continued reinforcement of the core city as the only viable economic location. This may foster imbalanced and unsustainable development.

Places outside the core city have the potential to perform a variety of productive roles arising from their lower business costs, less congestion, distinct skill-sets, and availability of land and green space. These include light industry, logistics, shared business services, call centres, and development of new environmental technologies, renewable energy sources, and low-carbon goods and services. They can also serve as important consumption centres for the wider region, including leisure, recreation, entertainment, and education. A balanced city-region perspective can help such places to identify economic functions that complement those of neighbouring cities and towns, and thereby benefit from the prosperity of the wider regional economy. This is more consistent with the concept of a polycentric city region than a monocentric city region. To develop this kind of approach requires local and regional interests both to be represented in governance arrangements, with mutual respect shown for their different needs and constituencies.

Acknowledgements – The empirical work was originally undertaken as a city case study for the State of English Cities report. Considerable thanks are due to the twenty people working in senior positions in Medway who participated in lengthy interviews. Useful comments on an earlier draft of the paper were also received from John Parr, Mike Raco, and two anonymous referees.

APPENDIX 1: METHODS

The following people were interviewed during the course of the study in 2005. A draft report containing the main findings was submitted to the local authority and circulated among key respondents for factual corrections and comments.

Medway Council Leader
Director of Development and Environment
Director of Education and Leisure
Director of Public Health
Assistant Director of Economic Development
Assistant Director of Regeneration and Environment
Assistant Director of Leisure
Head of Urban Regeneration
Housing Strategy Manager
Research and Review Manager
Community Safety Manager
Local Strategic Partnership Coordinator
Senior Planning Official
Service Manager for Youth
Manager of JobCentre Plus
University of Greenwich Director of Regional Liaison
Racial Equality Council

Ethnic Minority Forum
Local Planning Consultant
Primary Care Trust Chairman

The following reports and documents were also consulted for background and supporting information.

AUDIT COMMISSION (2004) *Audit Commission Comprehensive Performance Assessment Improvement Report to Medway Council for Year Ending 31/3/ 2004.* Audit Commission, London.

DEAKIN H. and KINGSLEY SMITH B. (2005) *More of the Same? Response to Draft SE Regional Plan.*

Kent and Medway Health Overview Profile (n.d.) Kent and Medway NHS Trust, West Malling.

Kent and Medway NHS Annual Report 2002/03. Kent and Medway NHS Trust, West Malling.

MEDWAY COMMUNITY SAFETY PARTNERSHIP (2004) *Crime, Disorder and Drugs Audit.* Medway Community Safety Partnership, Chatham.

MEDWAY COUNCIL (2002a) *Economic Development Plan 2002–07.* Medway Council, Chatham.

MEDWAY COUNCIL (2002b) *Local Public Service Agreement.* Medway Council, Chatham.

MEDWAY COUNCIL (2002c) *Skills Framework.* Medway Council, Chatham.

MEDWAY COUNCIL (2003a) *2001 Census: Key Statistics and Update.* Medway Council, Chatham.

MEDWAY COUNCIL (2003b) *Employment and Employment Land in Medway.* Medway Council, Chatham.

MEDWAY COUNCIL (2003c) *Local Plan.* Medway Council, Chatham.

MEDWAY COUNCIL (2003d) *Property Price Report.* Medway Council, Chatham.

MEDWAY COUNCIL (2004a) *Community Report and Plan 2004–2007.* Medway Council, Chatham.

MEDWAY COUNCIL (2004b) *Comprehensive Performance Assessment: Qualitative Assessment Submission.* Medway Council, Chatham.

MEDWAY COUNCIL (2004c) *Creating a City of Culture 2004–2008.* Medway Council, Chatham.

MEDWAY COUNCIL (2004d) *Medway Waterfront Renaissance Strategy.* Medway Council, Chatham.

MEDWAY COUNCIL (2004e) *Performance Indicator Tables 2004–5.* Medway Council, Chatham.

MEDWAY COUNCIL (2004f) *Performance Plan 2004/ 05.* Medway Council, Chatham.

MEDWAY COUNCIL (2005a) *Area-wide Inspection Self Evaluation Report.* Medway Council, Chatham.

MEDWAY COUNCIL (2005b) *Economic Development Strategy Review.* Medway Council, Chatham.

MEDWAY PRIMARY CARE TRUST (2004) *Analysis of the Index of Multiple Deprivation.* Medway Primary Care Trust, Gillingham.

MEDWAY RACIAL EQUALITY COUNCIL (2004) *Annual Report.* Medway Council, Chatham.

West Kent NHS Local Delivery Plan 2003–06 (n.d.) Kent and Medway NHS Trust, West Malling.

Table A1. Employment by industrial sector, 2006

	Medway (*n*)	Medway (%)	South East (%)	Britain (%)
Total employee jobs	86 300	–	–	–
Full-time	57 400	66.5	69.3	68.9
Part-time	28 900	33.5	30.7	31.1
Manufacturing	8800	10.2	8.8	10.9
Construction	4300	5.0	4.5	4.8
Services	71 800	83.1	85.2	82.9
Distribution, hotels and restaurants	19 400	22.5	24.6	23.5
Transport and communications	4600	5.3	6.0	5.9
Finance, information technology, other business activities	16 600	19.2	24.1	21.2
Public administration, education and health	25 800	29.8	25.4	26.9
Other services	5400	6.2	5.2	5.3
Tourism-related	6200	7.2	7.9	8.3

Note: 'Percentage' is a proportion of total employee jobs.
Source: Office for National Statistics (ONS), Annual Business Inquiry Employee Analysis.

Table A2. Employment by occupation, 2006/2007

	Medway (*n*)	Medway (%)	South East (%)	Britain (%)
SOC 2000 major group 1–3	43 700	35.0	46.9	42.3
1. Managers and senior officials	14 000	11.2	17.5	15.1
2. Professional occupations	11 300	9.1	14.0	13.0
3. Associate professional and technical	18 400	14.8	15.4	14.3
SOC 2000 major group 4–5	32 600	26.2	22.4	22.9
4. Administrative and secretarial	16 700	13.4	12.4	12.0
5. Skilled trades occupations	15 900	12.8	10.0	10.9
SOC 2000 major group 6–7	22 500	18.1	15.2	15.7
6. Personal service occupations	11 400	9.1	8.0	8.1
7. Sales and customer service occupations	11 200	9.0	7.2	7.6
SOC 2000 major group 8–9	25 400	20.4	15.3	18.7
8. Process plant and machine operatives	11 000	8.8	5.2	7.2
9. Elementary occupations	14 400	11.5	10.2	11.5

Notes: 'Percentage' is a proportion of all persons in employment.
      SOC, Standard Occupational Classification.
Source: Office for National Statistics (ONS), Annual Population Survey (April 2006–March 2007).

Table A3. Jobs density for selected cities and large towns in the South East, 2006

	Jobs density
Medway	0.68
Hastings	0.71
Luton	0.84
Southampton	0.87
Brighton and Hove	0.90
Portsmouth	0.96
Maidstone	0.99
Guildford	1.00
Peterborough	1.00
Milton Keynes	1.00
Slough	1.06
Reading	1.17
South East England	0.88
Britain	0.84

Note: Jobs density is defined as the ratio of total employment to the working-age population.
Source: Office for National Statistics (ONS) via the National On-line Manpower Information System (NOMIS).

Table A4. *Workplace of Medway residents*

	Professionals, managers and employers (%)	Intermediate and technical occupations, and self-employed (%)	Routine and semi-routine occupations (%)	Total (n)
London	53.1	35.4	11.5	17 380
Kent	36.6	33.0	30.4	26 332
Medway	28.9	38.5	32.6	68 151
Elsewhere	50.7	30.1	19.2	3915
Total (%)	35	36.5	28.5	100
Total (n)	40 559	42 215	33 004	115 778

Source: Population Census (2001).

Table A5. *Origin of people who work in Medway*

	Professionals, managers and employers (%)	Intermediate and technical occupations, and self-employed (%)	Routine and semi-routine occupations (%)	Total (n)
Medway	28.9	38.5	32.6	68 151
Elsewhere	55.2	27.4	17.4	18 712
Total (%)	34.6	36.1	29.3	100
Total (numbers)	30 038	31 333	25 492	86 863

Source: Population Census (2001).

Table A6. *Qualifications, 2006*

	Medway (n)	Medway (%)	South East (%)	Britain (%)
NVQ4 and above	28 900	18.3	30.5	27.4
NVQ3 and above	62 300	39.4	49.4	45.3
NVQ2 and above	96 100	60.8	68.0	63.8
NVQl and above	127 300	80.5	82.7	77.8
Other qualifications	11 500	7.3	7.7	8.5
No qualifications	19 200	12.2	9.6	13.8

Notes: 'Percentage' is a proportion of total working-age population.
NVQ, National Vocational Qualification.
Source: Office for National Statistics (ONS), Annual Population Survey (January–December 2006).

REFERENCES

AUDIT COMMISSION (2004) *Audit Commission Comprehensive Performance Assessment Improvement Report to Medway Council for Year Ending 31/3/2004.* Audit Commission, London.

AUDRETSCH D. and FELDMAN M. (2004) Knowledge spillovers and the geography of innovation, in HENDERSON J. and THISSE J. (Eds) *Handbook of Urban and Regional Economics*, Vol. 4, pp. 2713–2739. North Holland, Amsterdam.

BARKER K. (2004) *Review of Housing Supply. Delivering Stability: Securing Our Future Housing Needs.* H. M. Treasury, London.

BENNETT J. and MORRIS J. (2006) *Gateway People: The Aspirations and Attitudes of Prospective and Existing Residents of the Thames Gateway.* Institute for Public Policy Research (IPPR), London.

BRACZYK H., COOKE P. and HEIDENREICH M. (Eds) (1998) *Regional Innovation Systems.* UCL Press, London.

BUCK N., GORDON I., HARDING A. and TUROK I. (2005) *Changing Cities: Rethinking Urban Competitiveness, Cohesion and Governance.* Palgrave, London.

CATNEY P., DIXON T. and HENNEBERRY J. (2008) Hyperactive governance in the Thames Gateway, *Journal of Urban Regeneration and Renewal* **2**, 124–145.

CHURCH A. and FROST M. (1995) The Thames Gateway – an analysis of the emergence of a sub-regional regeneration initiative, *Geographical Journal* **161**, 199–209.

COCHRANE A. (2007) *Understanding Urban Policy: A Critical Approach.* Blackwell, Oxford.

CROOKSTON M. (1994) East Thames Corridor. Lecture given to The Royal Institution of Chartered Surveyors (RICS) CPD course, University of Westminster, London.

DAVOUDI S. (2003) Polycentricity in European spatial planning: from an analytical tool to a normative agenda. *European Planning Studies* **11**, 979–999.

DAVOUDI S. (2008) Conceptions of the city-region: a critical review. *Urban Design and Planning* **161**, 51–60.

DEAKIN H. and KINGSLEY SMITH B. (2005) *More of the Same? Response to Draft SE Regional Plan.*

DEPARTMENT FOR COMMUNITIES AND LOCAL GOVERNMENT (DCLG) (2006a) *Strong and Prosperous Communities: The Local Government White Paper.* DCLG, London.

DEPARTMENT FOR COMMUNITIES AND LOCAL GOVERNMENT (DCLG) (2006b) *Thames Gateway Interim Plan Policy Framework.* DCLG, London.

DEPARTMENT FOR COMMUNITIES AND LOCAL GOVERNMENT (DCLG) (2007) *Thames Gateway: The Delivery Plan.* DCLG, London.

DEPARTMENT FOR COMMUNITIES AND LOCAL GOVERNMENT (DCLG) (2008) *Transforming Places, Changing Lives: A Framework for Regeneration.* DCLG, London.

EDDINGTON R. (2006) *The Eddington Transport Study.* H. M. Treasury, London.

FALUDI A. (2006) From European spatial development to territorial cohesion policy, *Regional Studies* **40**, 667–678.

FOTHERGILL S. (2005) A new regional policy for Britain, *Regional Studies* **39**, 659–667.

GONZALEZ S., TOMANEY J. and WARD N. (2006) Faith in the city-region?, *Town and Country Planning* **November**, 315–317.

GORDON I. (2006) Finding institutional leadership for regional networks: the case of London and the greater South East, in SALET W. (Ed.) *Synergy in Urban Networks*, pp. 136–160. Sdu, The Hague.

H. M. TREASURY (2006) *The Importance of Cities to Regional Growth. Devolving Decision Making: 3 – Meeting the Regional Economic Challenge.* H. M. Treasury, London.

H. M. TREASURY (2007) *Review of Sub-national Economic Development and Regeneration.* H. M. Treasury, London.

H. M. TREASURY (2008) *The UK Economy: Addressing Long-term Strategic Challenges.* H. M. Treasury, London.

HALL P. (2009) Looking backward, looking forward: The city region of the mid-21st century' *Regional Studies*, (this issue).

HALL P. and PAIN K. (2006) *The Polycentric Metropolis.* Earthscan, London.

HARDING A. (2006) Devolution in England: cause without a rebel?, in SALET W. (Ed.) *Synergy in Urban Networks*, pp. 27–48. Sdu, The Hague.

HARDING A., MARVIN S. and ROBSON B. (2006) *A Framework for City-Regions.* Office of the Deputy Prime Minister (ODPM), London.

HEALEY P. (2009) City-regions and place development, *Regional Studies* (this issue).

HOUSE OF COMMONS COMMITTEE OF PUBLIC ACCOUNTS (HCCPA) (2007) *The Thames Gateway: Laying the Foundations.* HC 693. The Stationery Office, London.

HOUSE OF COMMONS COMMUNITIES AND LOCAL GOVERNMENT COMMITTEE (HCCLGC) (2007) *Is There a Future for Regional Government?* HC 352-1. The Stationery Office, London.

HULL A. (1998) Spatial planning: the development plan as a vehicle to unlock development potential?, *Cities* **15**, 327–335.

JOHN P., TICKELL A. and MUSSON S. (2005) Governing the mega-regions: governance and networks across London and the South East of England, *New Political Economy* **10**, 91–106.

JONAS A. and WARD K. (2007) Introduction to a Debate on City-regions: New geographies of governance, democracy and social reproduction, *International Journal of Urban and Regional Research* **31**, 169–178.

JONES A., WILLIAMS L., LEE N., COATS D. and COWLING M. (2006) *Ideopolis: Knowledge City-Region.* The Work Foundation, London.

KEATING M. (1998) *The New Regionalism in Western Europe: Territorial Restructuring and Political Change.* Edward Elgar, Cheltenham.

KELLY R. (2006) Keynote Speech to the Thames Gateway Forum, November (available at: http://www.communities.gov.uk/thamesgateway/crossgatewaypriorities/).

Kent and Medway Health Overview Profile. (n.d.) Kent and Medway NHS Trust, West Malling.

Kent and Medway NHS Annual Report 2002/03. Kent and Medway NHS Trust, West Malling.

KINTREA K. (2007) Policies and programmes for disadvantaged neighbourhoods: recent English experience, *Housing Studies* **22**, 261–282.

LUCAS K. (1998) Upwardly mobile: regeneration and the quest for sustainable mobility in the Thames Gateway, *Journal of Transport Geography* **6**, 211–225.

LUPTON R. (2003) *Poverty Street: The Dynamics of Neighbourhood Decline and Renewal.* Policy Press, Bristol.

MARSHALL A. and FINCH D. (2006) *City Leadership: Giving City-Regions the Power to Grow.* Institute for Public Policy Research (IPPR), London.

MEDWAY COMMUNITY SAFETY PARTNERSHIP (2004) *Crime, Disorder and Drugs Audit.* Medway Community Safety Partnership, Chatham.

MEDWAY COUNCIL (2002a) *Economic Development Plan 2002–07.* Medway Council, Chatham.

MEDWAY COUNCIL (2002b) *Local Public Service Agreement.* Medway Council, Chatham.

MEDWAY COUNCIL (2002c) *Skills Framework.* Medway Council, Chatham.

MEDWAY COUNCIL (2003a) *2001 Census: Key Statistics and Update.* Medway Council, Chatham.

MEDWAY COUNCIL (2003b) *Employment and Employment Land in Medway.* Medway Council, Chatham.

MEDWAY COUNCIL (2003c) *Local Plan.* Medway Council, Chatham.

MEDWAY COUNCIL (2003d) *Property Price Report.* Medway Council, Chatham.

MEDWAY COUNCIL (2004a) *Community Report and Plan 2004–2007.* Medway Council, Chatham.

MEDWAY COUNCIL (2004b) *Comprehensive Performance Assessment: Qualitative Assessment Submission.* Medway Council, Chatham.

MEDWAY COUNCIL (2004c) *Creating a City of Culture 2004–2008.* Medway Council, Chatham.

MEDWAY COUNCIL (2004d) *Medway Waterfront Renaissance Strategy.* Medway Council, Chatham.

MEDWAY COUNCIL (2004e) *Performance Indicator Tables 2004–5.* Medway Council, Chatham.

MEDWAY COUNCIL (2004f) *Performance Plan 2004/05.* Medway Council, Chatham.

MEDWAY COUNCIL (2005a) *Area-wide Inspection Self Evaluation Report.* Medway Council, Chatham.

MEDWAY COUNCIL (2005b) *Economic Development Strategy Review.* Medway Council, Chatham.

MEDWAY COUNCIL (2006a) *Medway Regeneration Framework 2006–2016,* Medway: Medway Council.

MEDWAY COUNCIL (2006b) *Medway Renaissance 2006–2016: Technical Appendix,* Medway: Medway Council.

MEDWAY PRIMARY CARE TRUST (2004) *Analysis of the Index of Multiple Deprivation.* Medway Primary Care Trust, Gillingham.

MEDWAY RACIAL EQUALITY COUNCIL (2004) *Annual Report.* Medway Council, Chatham.

NATIONAL AUDIT OFFICE (NAO) (2007) *The Thames Gateway: Laying the Foundations.* HC 526. The Stationery Office, London.

NEUMAN M. and HULL A. (2009) The futures of the city region, *Regional Studies* (this issue).

NEW LOCAL GOVERNMENT NETWORK (NLGN) (2005) *Seeing the Light: Next Steps for City Regions.* NLGN, London.

OFFICE OF THE DEPUTY PRIME MINISTER (ODPM) (2003a) *Sustainable Communities: Building for the Future.* ODPM, London.

OFFICE OF THE DEPUTY PRIME MINISTER (ODPM) (2003b) *Creating Sustainable Communities: Making It Happen.* ODPM, London.

OFFICE OF THE DEPUTY PRIME MINISTER (ODPM) (2005) *Sustainable Communities: Homes for All. A Five-Year Plan from the ODPM.* ODPM, London.

ORGANISATION FOR ECONOMIC CO-OPERATION AND DEVELOPMENT (OECD) (2006) *Competitive Cities in the Global Economy.* OECD, Paris.

ORGANISATION FOR ECONOMIC CO-OPERATION AND DEVELOPMENT (OECD) (2007) *Higher Education and Regions.* OECD, Paris.

OXFORD BROOKES UNIVERSITY (2006) *Thames Gateway Evidence Review.* Department for Communities and Local Government (DCLG), London.

PARKINSON M., CHAMPION T., EVANS R., SIMMIE J. and TUROK I. (2006) *State of the English Cities.* Office of the Deputy Prime Minister (ODPM), London.

PARR J. B. (2005) Perspectives on the city-region, *Regional Studies* **39**, 555–566.

PIKE A., RODRIGUEZ-POSE A. and TOMANEY J. (2006) *Local and Regional Development.* Routledge, London.

PRIME MINISTER'S STRATEGY UNIT (PMSU) (2005) *Improving the Prospects of People Living in Areas of Multiple Deprivation in England.* PMSU, London.

RACO M. (2005) A step change or a step back? The Thames Gateway and the rebirth of the Urban Development Corporation, *Local Economy* **20**, 141–153.

RICE P., VENABLES A. and PATACCHINI E. (2006) Spatial determinants of productivity: analysis for the regions of Great Britain, *Regional Science and Urban Economics* **36**, 727–752.

RODRÍGUEZ-POSE A. (2008) The rise of the city-region concept and its development policy implications, *European Planning Studies* **16**, 1025–1046.

RYDIN Y. (1998) The enabling local state and urban development: resources, rhetoric and planning in East London, *Urban Studies* **35**, 175–191.

SALET W. (2006) How to cope with the metamorphosis of the city-region?, in SALET W. (Ed.) *Synergy in Urban Networks,* pp. 11–26. Sdu, The Hague.

SALET W., THORNLEY A. and KREUKELS A. (Eds) (2003) *Metropolitan Governance and Spatial Planning: Comparative Case Studies of European City Regions.* Spon, London.

SCOTT A. J. (Ed.) (2001) *Global City Regions: Trends, Theory, Policy.* Oxford University Press, Oxford.

SCOTT A. J. and STORPER M. (2003) Regions, globalisation, development, *Regional Studies* **37**, 579–593.

TITHERIDGE H. and HALL P. (2006) Changing travel to work patterns in South East England, *Journal of Transport Geography* **14**, 60–75.

TUROK I. (2004) Cities, regions and competitiveness, *Regional Studies* **38**, 1069–1083.

TUROK I. and BAILEY N. (2004) The theory of polynuclear urban regions and its application to Central Scotland, *European Planning Studies* **12**, 371–389.

TUROK I., KEARNS A., FLINT J., FITCH D., MCKENZIE C. and ABBOTTS J. (2006) *State of the English Cities: Social Cohesion Report.* Department of Communities and Local Government (DCLG), London.

URBAN TASK FORCE (UTF) (2005) *Towards a Stronger Urban Renaissance.* UTF, London.

West Kent NHS Local Delivery Plan 2003–06. (n.d.) Kent and Medway NHS Trust, West Malling.

WHEELER S. M. (2009) Regions, megaregions and sustainability, *Regional Studies* (this issue).

Regions, Megaregions, and Sustainability

STEPHEN WHEELER

WHEELER S. Regions, megaregions, and sustainability, *Regional Studies*. The rapid expansion of urbanized regions is problematic for sustainable development. Urbanization at large scales has inherent sustainability problems, and planning institutions and governance mechanisms have had limited success at the metropolitan scale, let alone at a megaregional one. A vision of more sustainable regional development includes an emphasis on balanced local communities to reduce regional mobility demands; the management of land, resources, and population to live within regional limits; efforts to improve equity and build social capital; and on economic development that strengthens the quality of the region's social and ecological systems rather than the quantity of production and consumption.

WHEELER S. 区域，巨型区域以及可持续性，区域研究。城市化地区的快速扩张是可持续发展所面临的挑战。大尺度的城市化进程本身存在内在的可持续性问题，同时规划机构以及政府机制都仅仅只在大都市区层面上取得了有限的成功，对于巨型区域却鲜有作为。一个更加可持续的区域发展（应当）包括，促进社区间平衡发展以减少区域性流动；加强土地、资源管理并限制某区域的人口居住数量；提升公平性，构建社会资本；经济发展重在提升区域社会、生态系统的质量而非增加生产、消费数量。

区域规划　区域　巨型城市区域　大都市可持续性　可持续发展

WHEELER S. Régions, mégarégions et durabilité, *Regional Studies*. L'expansion rapide des régions urbanisées est un problème pour le développement durable. L'urbanisation à grande échelle induit des problèmes inhérents de durabilité et les instances de planification ainsi que les mécanismes gouvernementaux ont connu un succès limité à l'échelle métropolitaine sans parler du niveau mégarégional. Une vision du développement régional plus durable nécessite de mettre l'accent sur l'équilibre des communautés locales afin de réduire les demandes en mobilité régionale, la gestion des terres, les ressources, le souhait des populations de vivre à l'intérieur des limites régionales, des efforts pour améliorer l'équité et construire un capital social; il faut mettre l'accent sur le développement économique qui renforce la qualité des systèmes sociaux et écologiques de la région plutôt que sur la quantité de la production et de la consommation.

WHEELER S. Regionen, Megaregionen und Nachhaltigkeit, *Regional Studies*. Die rasche Expansion urbanisierter Regionen ist für eine nachhaltige Entwicklung problematisch. Eine großflächige Urbanisierung ist mit inhärenten Nachhaltigkeitsproblemen verknüpft, wobei die Planungsbehörden und staatlichen Kontrollmechanismen aber auf metropolitaner Ebene bisher nur wenig Erfolg hatten – von der megaregionalen Ebene ganz zu schweigen. Eine Vision einer nachhaltigeren Regionalentwicklung ist verknüpft mit einer Betonung von ausgeglichenen lokalen Gemeinschaften zur Verringerung des regionalen Mobilitätsbedarfs, mit einer Steuerung von Land, Ressourcen und Bevölkerung für ein Leben innerhalb der regionalen Grenzen, mit Bemühungen zur Verbesserung der Gerechtigkeit und zum Aufbau von Sozialkapital sowie mit einer Betonung einer Wirtschaftsentwicklung, die die Qualität der sozialen und ökologischen Systeme der Region stärkt, statt die Quantität von Produktion und Konsum zu steigern.

WHEELER S. Regiones, megaregiones y sostenibilidad, *Regional Studies*. La rápida expansión de regiones urbanizadas es un problema para el desarrollo sostenible. La urbanización a gran escala presenta problemas inherentes de sostenibilidad y las instituciones de planificación y los mecanismos de gobierno tienen un éxito limitado a nivel metropolitano, no digamos ya a escala megaregional. Para obtener un desarrollo regional con una visión más sostenible se debería dar prioridad a las comunidades localmente equilibradas para reducir las demandas de movilidad regional, a la administración de las tierras, los recursos y la población que vive en límites regionales; a los esfuerzos para mejorar la igualdad y crear capital social y a un desarrollo económico que refuerza la calidad de los sistemas sociales y ecológicos de la región en vez de centrarnos en la cantidad de producción y consumo.

INTRODUCTION

The region is a vitally important scale to sustainability planning. It makes sense to consider many planning challenges at a regional scale since they are regional in nature and cross the boundaries of local jurisdictions. At the same time regional planning has lagged behind the need for such solutions. There are some success stories to be sure, but in terms of dealing with sustainability concerns such as greenhouse gas emissions, resource consumption, growing motor vehicle use, ecosystem health, metropolitan growth management, and disparities of wealth and social equity, regional governance has made relatively little headway, particularly in North America.

Part of the problem is institutional. Agencies often do not exist to plan for many types of regions, for example bioregions, watersheds, commutesheds, economic regions, or cultural regions. If they do exist, such institutions are frequently weak. But part of the problem, as will be shown, is that urbanization at ever-larger regional scales presents inherent difficulties in terms of sustainable development. This point has not been sufficiently appreciated to date.

Past regional planning initiatives have most often occurred at a metropolitan scale, a level at which many planning institutions exist with clearly defined boundaries. Urbanization processes are also frequently studied at a metropolitan scale. However, in recent years it has been proposed that urbanization is now occurring at an even larger scale: that of the megaregion or megapolitan region (CARBONELL and YARO, 2005; LANG and DHAVALE, 2005; DEWAR and EPSTEIN, 2006). Megaregions consist of a number of metropolitan areas linked by proximity and some shared characteristics. They are seen as the locus of much future development. For example, approximately three-quarters of the US population and employment growth by 2050 is expected to occur in eight to ten megaregions (DEWAR and EPSTEIN, 2006).

The following text explores the sustainability and governance difficulties of development at metropolitan and megaregional scales, considers the success of some regional sustainability planning initiatives to date, and reflects on the implications of sustainability theory for regional planning.[1] The aim is to help develop a vision of planning for sustainable regions, and to insert a note of caution into discussions of rapid regional development, since urbanization at these scales may be inherently more difficult to make sustainable than more locally oriented development. The primary focus of this analysis is North America, but regional planning in other parts of the world is considered as well.

SUSTAINABILITY IMPLICATIONS OF EXPANDING URBAN REGIONS

Rapid growth of urban regions, and coalescence of cities and towns into ever-larger regions, has been a fact of life worldwide for much of the past century. Much planning aims to accommodate or promote this trend. Regions can be a source of great dynamism and initiative; however, their growth is problematic for sustainable development in a number of ways that differ from similar growth contained within more localized communities.

The mobility issue

One basic problem is that integration of human activities over a regional scale assumes a high degree of mobility within the region. As labour and housing markets become regional in nature, travel distances lengthen, just as they lengthened at an urban scale within the growing 19th-century industrial city (CERVERO, 1998, 26ff.; US ENVIRONMENTAL PROTECTION AGENCY (US EPA), 2001, 19ff.). These distances increase not just for work trips, but for a great variety of household, social, and recreational trips as well (GRAVA, 1999). More transportation infrastructure is required, and extensive use of private motor vehicles for commuting within the metropolitan area or megaregion produces traffic congestion and high levels of resource consumption and greenhouse gas emissions. Although European nations might be able to meet much regional transportation need through integrated transit systems, and developing nations may meet it through a combination of public transit, ride sharing, and informal transit providers, in virtually every society the use of private motor vehicles is also growing, in part due to the dispersion of destinations throughout urbanized areas.

At the megaregional scale, air travel comes into play, as well as the long-distance regular motor vehicle use known as extreme commuting. Increasing numbers of workers routinely travel between cities several hundred miles apart, such as Los Angeles and San Francisco in California, Paris and Berlin, and Boston, New York and Washington on the eastern seaboard. Many individuals and families regularly travel similar distances to vacation homes or recreational amenities, as, for example, many British residents now travel to vacation homes in Spain. Although high-speed rail is frequently mentioned as the ideal form of megaregional transportation, the reality in most places is that much of this travel will be by either private motor vehicle or air. Air travel, especially for short-to-medium-range trips, has by far the largest impact on global warming per mile travelled of any transportation mode (INTERGOVERNMENTAL PANEL ON CLIMATE CHANGE (IPCC), 1999, p. 8), and the climate change impacts of regular air travel within or between megaregions will be severe.

Reducing mobility needs and the use of highly polluting transportation modes at either metropolitan or megaregional scales will not be easy. Three types of strategies will be needed: increasing mode choice, changing land use, and revising economic incentives. All are difficult to implement at large scales.

Making public transit a widely used mode choice at a metropolitan scale may be virtually impossible in areas with low densities and dispersed land-use patterns; at the least it would require massive investment in transit systems. At a megaregional scale, improving mode choice would require extensive networks of high-speed rail that only Europe and Japan have developed so far. Changing pricing is difficult politically at both levels, as shown by strong resistance to gas taxes many places. In terms of land use, compact, centred, balanced, and contiguous development of communities is usually seen to help reduce the use of motor vehicles (EWING *et al.*, 2002), though the debate is complex and nostalgic or simplistic views of the compact city are best avoided (BREHENY, 2003; NEUMAN, 2005; JENKS *et al.*, 1996; FREY, 1999). But changing land use is not easy in areas used to sprawl development, especially without strong regional governance to regulate land use.

The reality is that without major changes in planning, politics, and lifestyle it will be very difficult for urbanizing regions to avoid a high level of private motor vehicle use and air travel, with their attendant sustainability impacts.

Land and resource issues

A related set of problems in expanding urban regions worldwide concerns the use of land and resources (WANNOP, 1995; DANIELS, 1999; EWING and KOSTYACK, 2005). In the European Union, the amount of urbanized land is expected to double in this century, and suburban sprawl is seen according to a recent European Union report as an under-recognized challenge that 'threatens the very culture of Europe' and 'seriously undermines efforts to meet the global challenge of climate change' (EUROPEAN ENVIRONMENTAL AGENCY, 2006, p. 5). In the USA, the amount of urbanized area around metropolitan areas is expanding at an extraordinarily rapid rate. Other research has found that for six sample US metropolitan regions (Boston, Massachusetts; Atlanta, Georgia; Minneapolis-St Paul, Minnesota; Albuquerque, New Mexico; Las Vegas, Nevada; and Portland, Oregon), the amount of urbanized land area increased by 57% in the 1980–2005 period alone (WHEELER, 2008). This study also found that the most rapidly growing type of development within these regions, in terms of land area affected, is rural sprawl; that is, low-density subdivision with lot sizes of 1 acre or more. This form of development is difficult for local governments to service and often has disruptive ecological effects in that roads, fences, and developed lots interfere with wildlife corridors and habitat.

Such rapid development across regions is exacerbated by the current emphasis on mobility, and in turn requires high levels of motor vehicle travel from future residents, leading to increased fuel consumption and emissions. Resources such as water, forests, and high-quality farmland are also frequently overtaxed within rapidly growing regions. Water, for example, is one of the leading development challenges in urbanizing areas worldwide in terms of supply, quality, and control (UNESCO, 2006; BARLOW and CLARKE, 2003). Forests are frequently depleted near urban areas, especially in the developing world. Limits on consumption of many resources are avoided only by importing them from other places, but such imports have their own eventual limits.

Management of such resources at a megaregional scale often requires coordination over multiple states or countries as well as hundreds of local governments. Some state planning in the USA and national planning elsewhere aims at growth management objectives, but usually only for part of a megaregion. New Jersey, for example, has pursued statewide open space preservation planning, but only represents a portion of the US eastern seaboard conurbation.

Equity issues

Equity issues, both within and between regions, have been exacerbated in recent years by the increasing size and fragmentation of these areas. Of particularly concern are the concentration of poverty within parts of the region, growing disparities in tax base and opportunity (PASTOR *et al.*, 2000), and environment justice inequities (BULLARD *et al.*, 2000). Using geographic information systems (GIS), Myron Orfield has documented large and often increasing disparities in wealth, poverty, and tax base within US metropolitan areas (ORFIELD, 1997). Segregation by income grew substantially within these metro regions in the late 20th century, even as segregation by race declined slightly (ABRAMSON *et al.*, 1995). Interestingly, spatial concentration of the wealthy may be even higher than concentration of the poor and ethnic minorities (MASSEY, 1996), suggesting ongoing class segregation.

Within megaregions, disparities may be increasing between more dynamic and less dynamic sub-areas, for example between wages on California's coast and in its Central Valley (DRENNAN and MANVILLE, 2006). Meanwhile, to the extent that megaregions are serving as the economic engines of national development, an unfortunate by-product appears to be increasing disparities between these megaregions and other less fortunate areas within countries (DEWAR and EPSTEIN, 2006).

In the rush for economic competitiveness, equity concerns often take a back seat within regional planning. There is little organized constituency for them, as there is for economic development. RAST (2006, p. 249) criticizes recent regionalism as exhibiting 'a profound suburban, middle-class bias' because it does not sufficiently emphasize participation by low-income, minority, and central city constituencies, and because it often focuses on regional economic competitiveness that benefits elites while not necessarily improving the welfare of lower income groups.

Social and community issues

Having a metropolitan or megaregional scale as the dominant focus of 21st-century urbanization raises profound questions about local community, identity, and sense of place. In the past, small-scale development has often been equated with the human scale. Lewis Mumford railed against 'gigantism' and 'megalopolis' in publications such as *The Culture of Cities* (MUMFORD, 1938) and *The City in History: Its Origins, Its Transformations, and Its Prospects* (MUMFORD, 1961). Jane Jacobs celebrated the small-scale life of urban places in *The Death and Life of Great American Cities* (JACOBS, 1961). E. F. Schumacher's *Small is Beautiful: A Study of Economics as if People Mattered* (SCHUMACHER, 1973) articulated a philosophy of appropriate-scale development that is still seen today in new forms such as micro-lending and pedestrian planning. The older, small-scale places that such writers idealized are still some of the most popular communities to visit or live.

Emphasis on 'sense of place' throws into question the move towards ever-larger scales of regional development, which are frequently less tied to local place and tradition. Sense of place in fact is undermined by the particular urban form patterns that regional urbanization is currently taking. The relatively connected 19th-century metropolis has morphed into the physically fragmented 21st-century post-modern region. Recent forms of development such as subdivisions, office parks, and shopping malls are inwardly focused with few physical connections to surrounding land uses (SOUTHWORTH and OWENS, 1993; WHEELER, 2003). Although journalist Joel Garreau hypothesized the emergence of relatively compact 'edge cities' within the spread-out metropolis (GARREAU, 1991), the reality in many cases is low-density non-centred spread (LANG, 2003; LANG et al., 2006). This fragmentation of form and land use in suburbia may well be tied to the decline of social capital; Robert Putnam identifies a 'sprawl civic penalty' of 20% on most measures of community involvement (PUTNAM, 2000, p. 215).

It is certainly possible that local identity can thrive within a world dominated by global forces, as advocates of 'glocal' approaches argue (e.g. FEATHERSTONE et al., 1995; BORJA and CASTELLS, 1997; BAUMAN, 1998). But the balance is not an easy one, and the risk is that global forces will be dominant within large urbanized regions, while the local context is given little attention. Development of regional malls, for example, provides a locus for global networks of supply and consumption within the metropolitan area and is made possible by the creation of regional infrastructure such as freeways that opens up broad markets to retailers. Regional 'power centres' with their 'category killer' stores drive

more locally based retailers out of business, promote standardized products and lifestyles, and contribute little to the locality in terms of character, wealth, and identity.

The economic development issue

The type of economic development promoted by ever-larger urbanized regions is yet another sustainability concern. Sprawling metropolitan areas often consist largely of low-density and discontiguous communities, with few prominent downtown areas or neighbourhood centres – what LANG (2003) has termed the edgeless city. This land-use pattern works against small-scale local businesses and in favour of strip development or big box retail along arterial roads or freeways (SCHLOSSER, 2001). The chain retailers that dominate such landscapes are problematic in terms of sustainability, as seen by recent controversies surrounding Wal-Mart and McDonald's. Boosterish regional development policies are problematic in that they focus on multinational industrial employers who often demand exorbitant subsidies, pay low wages, relocate jobs elsewhere over time, contribute little to civic life, and damage the environment (SHUMAN, 2000). Historically, many urbanists and sustainability advocates have viewed smaller, locally or regionally based businesses within more traditional urban contexts as advantageous in terms of their effects on local communities (JACOBS, 1961, 1969; MORRIS, 1982; BEATLEY and MANNING, 1997).

THE ONGOING STRUGGLE OF REGIONALISM

Although metropolitan and megaregional sustainability planning will be very much needed in the future, especially if these regions continue to grow, the track record of action at such scales is not promising. Regional planners historically have had great difficulty in seeing their proposals implemented. Nineteenth-century predecessors of regional planning such as Ildefons Cerda (in both his larger philosophical proposals and elements of his plan for the extension of Barcelona, Spain) and Frederick Law Olmsted and his two sons (in their large-scale proposals for metropolitan greenspaces systems) had limited success in persuading authorities to implement their visions. Portland in Oregon, for example, has only in the past few decades developed a greenspaces system inspired in part by the 40-mile loop of parks and parkways first proposed for it more than a century ago by the OLMSTED BROTHERS (1904).

SIMMONS and HACK (2000) identify Burnham and Bennett's Plan of Chicago of 1909 as the first comprehensive plan for a modern city region, but implementation of this celebrated proposal was only partial as well, consisting mainly of the lakefront portion of the park system. In Britain, Ebenezer Howard's garden city vision was never carried out in a way that included his concerns for collective land ownership and local employment, although it did help inspire the Abercrombie Plan for London of 1944 and the creation of transit-oriented New Towns. Patrick Geddes's holistic approach to regionalism was admired in theory, but largely ignored in practice by later practitioners, as was the closely related ecological regionalism promoted in the USA by Mumford and the Regional Plan Association of America (SUSSMAN, 1976; LUCCARELLI, 1995).

The pragmatic metropolitan regionalism exemplified by Thomas Adams and the *Regional Plan for New York and Its Environs* (REGIONAL PLAN ASSOCIATION, 1929) has had somewhat greater success than more visionary regional philosophies, particularly within regional transportation planning. However, in practice such plans have often degenerated into lists of infrastructure improvements that are undertaken piecemeal. In many places traffic congestion and housing difficulties have persisted or worsened following such initiatives. Extensive freeway building around the world's metropolitan areas, for example, has often fuelled suburban sprawl, increased congestion, and worsened air quality. Even while regional planning theory in the USA aimed for ever-more-comprehensive strategies during the 20th century, few regional agencies had significant statutory authority to plan, and in practice the field has often characterized by 'pervasive ineffectuality' according to urban historian Robert Fishman (FISHMAN, 2000, p. 108).

Since the 1980s there has been an upsurge of interest in metropolitan regionalism in the USA as well as in other countries (DOWNS, 1994; WEITZ and SELTZER, 1998), and greater incorporation of environmental, quality of life, and equity issues into a regional agenda often dominated by economic development. This resurgence has sometimes been referred to as the 'new regionalism' (WHEELER, 2002). In ways reminiscent of early 20th-century regionalism, late 20th-century writers often took holistic views of the region and emphasized the role of spatial planning (BANAI, 1993). New understandings of the importance of regional design have also taken hold, integrating neo-traditional and humanistic urban design approaches at site, neighbourhood, district, city, and regional scales (NEUMAN, 2000; CONGRESS FOR THE NEW URBANISM (CNU), 2000; DUANY *et al.*, 2000). The vision of the transit-oriented metropolitan area promoted by Peter Calthorpe in *The Next American Metropolis: Ecology, Community, and the American Dream* (CALTHORPE, 1993), Calthorpe and William Fulton in *The Regional City: Planning for the End of Sprawl* (CALTHORPE and FULTON, 2001), and in a different way by Robert Cervero in *The Transit Metropolis: A Global Inquiry* (CERVERO, 1998) stem in part from this more urban-design-oriented perspective. Although economic development goals remain a central theme of

regionalism, especially in Europe (DANSON, 2000), the agenda of regional planning in North America has shifted towards what SAVITCH and VOGEL (2000) describe as a 'new metropolitan agenda' focusing on:

> tax sharing among localities, limiting sprawl, building affordable housing in the suburbs, revitalizing the core central city, and fostering sustainable economic growth and development.
>
> (p. 198)

Yet although metropolitan regionalism appears to be on the upswing, it is still a weak level of government in most places, and it is far easier to analyse city regions than to plan for them. In his review of global cities, Mark Abrahamson concludes:

> Although metropolitan areas are now the economically most important subunits within nation-states, and contain a large percentage of the total population, it may be difficult to envision them becoming more significant political entities any time soon because metropolitan governance is so poorly developed. In most of the world's largest metropolitan areas, city-suburban integration is limited to a few functional areas, such as coordinated transportation.
>
> (ABRAHAMSON, 2004, p. 169)

STRUCTURAL OBSTACLES TO REGIONAL PLANNING

To a large extent the problems with regional governance are institutional and political in nature and stem from the position of regions in the hierarchy of governmental institutions, the fragmentation of jurisdictions and communities within the region, and fierce political resistance to many forms of planning, especially those involving land use, within capitalist economies.

The metropolitan region is generally seen as an in-between level of government, without strong support from above or below (SELF, 1982; SHARPE, 1995; ALTSHULER *et al.*, 1999). Regional agencies often serve at the whim of higher-level government, which tends to be reluctant to part with power and can capriciously dissolve or reorganize them, as Margaret Thatcher's Conservative government dissolved the Greater London Council in 1986, and the Province of Ontario amalgamated Metro Toronto out of existence in 1998. Meanwhile, local governments may bitterly resent metropolitan agencies, especially in nations with a strong tradition of local control over land use such as the USA. Local elected officials have little political incentive to collaborate regionally, and tend to resist any loss of local power. Many citizens also do not think regionally or have a cognitive sense of what the region consists of (LYNCH, 1976).

Fragmentation of the metropolis into often-competing jurisdictions and communities undermines attempts at unified planning, and is exacerbated by large regional size and population. Such fragmentation of governance is one of the dominant features of the post-modern metropolitan landscape in North America (DANIELSON and DOIG, 1982; BARLOW, 1991; KLING *et al.*, 1991; RUSK, 1993; LEWIS 1996; DEAR, 2000; ORFIELD, 2002). The number of local governments in US metropolitan areas has proliferated as suburban jurisdictions have resisted annexation and incorporated to preserve their identity, protect the tax base, or keep out urban constituencies. In the absence of strong regional government, it becomes very difficult to coordinate action across hundreds of local government bodies. Such problems are even more severe at the megaregional scale, as megaregions may overlap states and nations. Within fragmented regions, competition for economic development and the tax base also frequently set local governments against one another and undercut environmental, land use, or social equity regulation. This problem is particularly acute in places such as California where state limitations on local use of property taxes have led to competition for sales tax revenue and a resulting fiscalization of land use in order to lure sales tax-generating businesses such as auto malls and big box stores.

The sheer size of contemporary metropolitan areas makes political organizing and coalition building, particularly along the lines of traditional grassroots politics increasingly difficult. Much political discourse must of necessity be conducted through the media, which requires different tactics and is often difficult for non-governmental organizations to access. Participatory planning, consensus building, and social learning become problematic as well.

Resistance to planning of any sort tends to be expressed particularly vigorously at the regional level, particularly when growth management initiatives threaten to interfere with capitalist land development. To many elites and members of the public, regional planning has less clear justification than local government (which provides basic services) or state and national governments (which have a deeply rooted historic basis). Growth coalitions often channel this public resistance to planning through sympathetic local officials to undermine regional initiatives.

A further set of difficulties has to do with deeply rooted institutional and social capital deficits within particular regions. As Putnam argues in his study of social capital in Italy, those differences may go back many hundreds of years and be extremely difficult to change (PUTNAM, 1993). In this way, the current difficulty in rebuilding New Orleans in Louisiana may be partly due to the long-term dysfunction of politics and institutions in that metropolitan area, not to mention broader biases in US society against low-income groups and communities of colour (DAVIS, 2006).

The history of regional planning itself may be an impediment to more successful regionalism in some places. Many single-purpose metropolitan agencies

have been created with specific, limited mandates and little incentive to think holistically. This 'silo-based' regionalism may work to administer single-issue functional planning, for example to develop transportation systems, but works less well at developing broader regional sustainability agendas or addressing concerns such as equity that present no pressing functional demands on the region. At a more philosophical level, there is also a tension between the detached, scientific approach of the past regional studies field, within which many current regionalists were trained, and the need for more politically engaged regionalism in order to bring about sustainable development (COUNSELL and HAUGHTON, 2006).

REGIONAL SUSTAINABILITY PLANNING TO DATE

Although sustainability language has been present within many regional planning documents for some time (GIBBS, 1998), and there is evidence that many regional plans are making an effort to integrate environmental, economic, and social objectives as called for by much sustainable development philosophy (e.g. DÜHR, 2005), effective implementation of metropolitan or megaregional sustainable development policies has been limited in most parts of the world and faces substantial challenges.

Within the USA, regionalism of any sort remains an uphill battle. Portland in Oregon remains the best-known US metropolitan regional planning jurisdiction on the strength of its directly elected Metro Council, its urban growth boundary (UGB), and successful downtown revitalization, green spaces, and transit initiatives. Planning institutions in the Portland area have been refined for more than 40 years (ABBOTT, 1983; SELTZER, 2004), and a culture of planning created (ABBOTT, 1997). The region even appears to be making some progress on global warming; per capita emissions declined by 7% between 1990 and 2000 (PROGRESSIVE POLICY INSTITUTE, 2003). But even the Portland area has had its share of problems. The UGB was established quite far distant from the central city initially, allowing a great deal of suburban sprawl to take place inside the boundary. Somewhat belatedly, in the 1990s, Metro and local governments developed more detailed urban design regulation to try to correct this problem. While the UGB has successfully preserved agricultural land outside the boundary, leap-frog growth now threatens to escape the jurisdiction of Metro and spread to outlying towns. Vehicle miles travelled has risen faster than the rate of population (as is the case almost everywhere in the USA), and persistent questions of housing affordability and social equity remain.

Although planning initiatives have been undertaken in many other US metropolitan areas, regional governance to manage growth has usually been spectacularly unsuccessful. California, for example, has seen at least 60 years of failed attempts to manage growth regionally (PINCETL, 1994). DOWNS (2005) finds that smart growth has had little success in terms of implementation in the USA because of long-established traditions of local home rule and low-density land development. Planning methods such as the natural factors overlay analysis pioneered by Ian McHarg (MCHARG, 1969) have been useful at the site scale and in subregional applications such as habitat conservation planning, but are rarely applied in a more comprehensive way to guide regional development.

American metropolitan governance since the 1960s has been dominated by the Councils of Governments (COGs), voluntary associations of local governments that have little or no statutory authority over metropolitan growth and development. Many of these COGs do channel federal and state transportation funds toward local projects, and under liberalized federal transportation policy since 1991 has handled these funds somewhat more flexibly to encourage alternative transit modes. But generally the COGs do not seek to challenge prevailing patterns of land development, economic development, or motor vehicle-dependent infrastructure.

Consolidation of governments within the metropolitan area has had some success in helping US city regions provide services more effectively, but has not led to stronger leadership on topics related to sustainable development. The Indianapolis-area UniGov, for example, formed through three institutional consolidations in the 1960s and 1970s, appears to have helped with downtown revitalization. However, it has not necessarily done so through progressive and equitable financing means, and has not played a substantial role in managing the region's growth, which is now well beyond the consolidated government's borders (ROSENTRAUB, 2000). Similar city–county consolidation in Jacksonville, Florida, met the agenda of area elites in terms of improving services, but has not necessarily increased government efficiency or addressed sustainability issues (SWANSON, 2000).

Single-issue regional planning has had some success in the USA, in part because the institutions involved have had more definite mandates and authority to plan. The South Coast Air Quality Management District's plans for improving air quality in the Los Angeles basin, the Tahoe Regional Commission's efforts to protect environmental quality around Lake Tahoe in the Sierra Nevada mountains, and efforts to protect environmental quality in New Jersey's Pine Barrens are examples. However, these initiatives occurred in contexts where a strong public motivation was present, and do not extend to managing overall growth and quality of life in these regions. Single-purpose regional agencies may also compartmentalize

planning and work against broader development of a regional public interest (BOLLENS, 1997).

Sustainability planning at the megaregional scale has been even more difficult. The campaign across parts of the USA and Canada for environmental protection in the Great Lakes area, for example, has achieved some notable successes, such as establishment of a multi-institutional framework for collaboration and substantial cleanup of point-source pollution. However, the regional governance framework remains vulnerable to changing local, state, and national politics, and has yet to make headway on other problems such as non-point-source pollutants and the introduction of exotic species (RABE, 1999).

In Canada, despite a somewhat stronger tradition of metropolitan governance, planning and development patterns appear to be converging with those in the USA (ROTHBLATT, 1994; ROTHBLATT and SANCTON, 1998). Canadian regional agencies often fail to integrate different subfields of planning, and also suffer from their nature as creatures of the province (CHURCH, 1996, p. 100). The former Metro Toronto, poster child of 1950s regionalism, served in large part as a construction agency providing roads and other infrastructure for the region, and was not able to implement broader planning initiatives such as the 1970 Toronto-Centred Region policy successfully (WHEELER, 2003). The bioregional vision for the Toronto area developed in the early 1990s by the Crombie Commission (ROYAL COMMISSION ON THE FUTURE OF THE TORONTO WATERFRONT, 1992) was thwarted in part by provincial antipathy and continuing political fragmentation of the region. Over vigorous opposition the province of Ontario reorganized local governments in the Toronto region in 1998, but left it without any overall regional authority. As a result, that metro area is still struggling to find institutional foundations with which to coordinate its development.

Vancouver is a more successful example of Canadian regionalism, in large part due to the 1996 Greater Vancouver Regional District's Livable Region Strategic Plan. This plan has sought many sustainability objectives such as to solidify a Green Zone of protected agricultural areas and parks, ensure compact and balanced development, develop a regional network of urban centres supported by public transit, and build institutional partnerships to implement such objectives (GREATER VANCOUVER REGIONAL DISTRICT (GVRD) 1996). A detailed set of indicators has been established to monitor progress. Through 2004, implementation had achieved a number of successes. Some 53 700 hectares of land had been protected in an Agricultural Land Reserve, 762 km of greenway had been established, transit ridership was rising, the proportion of short commute trips was increasing, and 67% of new housing development was in the form of apartments or rowhouses, helping to achieve compact city goals (GVRD, 2004). However, other indicators were less favourable. Vehicle-kilometres driven continued to rise, the percentage of growth that occurred in the Growth Concentration Area was below target, and housing affordability and equity concerns remained.

In Australia, a review of sustainability initiatives at several levels of government by SMITH and SCOTT (2006, p. 15) finds 'legislative failure' at Commonwealth and state levels, a lack of action at the local level, and a strong 'silo effect' among functional public agencies. Recent sustainability oriented metropolitan strategies for Sydney, Melbourne and Brisbane offer some hope, but most implementation of such policies remains for the future.

In the UK, regional institutions have waxed and waned several times over the past century (HOUGHTON and COUNSELL, 2004). In the 1990s, the national government adopted sustainability as an integrating theme for planning guidance. However, its regional planning directives have provided rather general guidance and housing targets with the aim of managing growth and improving human quality of life (following the viewpoint often termed 'weak sustainability') rather than more ecocentric approaches emphasizing fundamental acknowledgement of limits to economic growth and consumption (HOUGHTON and COUNSELL, 2004; GLASSON, 1995). Regional planning guidance does appear to have strengthened environmental management as well as stakeholder involvement in some areas (COUNSELL and BRUFF, 2001), and the early 2000s saw an increased focus on spatial initiatives and greater attention to environmental justice (AGYEMAN and EVANS, 2004). Many sustainable development initiatives are underway nationally and within large metropolitan areas, especially London. However, many difficulties of implementation remain.

Across Europe, there has been a resurgence of interest in large-scale regional spatial planning in recent years (FALUDI, 2002; ALBRECHTS et al., 2003; HEALEY, 2004), embodied particularly by the European Spatial Development Perspective (ESDP) formulated by the European Union in 1999 (COMMISSION OF THE EUROPEAN COMMUNITIES (CEC), 1999). Sustainability is a stated goal of this and other plans, but linkages to implementation are often unclear. There seems, for example, to be agreement on the somewhat vague concept of polycentricity, which would nudge the physical structure of Europe away from a centralized constellation of cities between London, Germany, and Northern Italy, designated as the 'blue banana' on spatial diagrams, toward a 'bunch of grapes' model in which clustered development is spread across the continent (WATERHOUT, 2002). But how this shift would be accomplished and how it would specifically promote sustainable development remain to be spelled out.

Since the 1990s, 'regional development' within European Union policy has been broadened to 'regional sustainable development' (RAVETZ, 2004). Regional policies within a number of member countries have

followed suit, often focusing on particular portions of a country rather than metropolitan regions or urbanized megaregions. For instance, since 1998 sustainable regional development has been the principal goal of German spatial planning (DÜHR, 2005). In France, sustainable development has likewise become a goal of regional development planning. However, French regions view sustainability largely in environmental terms, definitions and evaluation mechanisms vary between regions, public participation in developing sustainability policies is limited, and linkages to political levels are still highly uneven (BERTRAND and LARRUE, 2004).

There appears to be a basic tension in European countries between desires to allow regional constituencies to participate actively and develop their own sustainability agendas, and the need for national governments to establish broad policy and ensure a reasonable degree of coordination. However, in Britain the establishment of regional chambers to create sustainable development frameworks is seen by some as a valuable exercise, even though these have created divergent conceptions of sustainable regional development (BENNEWORTH et al., 2002).

Although planning mechanisms tend to be stronger in European countries than in North America, their capacity to bring about sustainable regional development is open to question. Even in the Netherlands, regional collaboration is not as strong as might be expected. A study by KANTOR (2006, p. 812) concludes that within that country competitive pressures of the global economy 'powerfully segment and divide business, labor, and government within the region'. He points out that plans for consolidated metropolitan governments around Dutch cities have failed, and that local collaboration with the designated steering committee for the celebrated Randstad region has been sporadic. The new economy is also leading to the centrifugal spread of Dutch cities. However, at a national level – a scale that might be considered regional in many other nations – the Netherlands appears to be doing relatively well in terms of sustainability planning due in part to continual refinement of national environmental policy over several decades.

ROBERTS (1997) has noted that historically European regional planning has not always helped improve sustainability:

> much of regional planning in the past was hijacked and forced to help deliver the products of tonnage ideology – more growth, excessive consumption, less equity and increased environmental degradation.
>
> (p. 881)

Given the tendency of concerns about economic competitiveness to outweigh environmental and equity agendas, whether the new wave of European regionalism will be different remains to be seen. A meta-analysis of European sustainability evaluation programmes found that there is still little consensus on definitions of sustainability or means of evaluating it (MARTINUZZI, 2004). More specific linkages between sustainability theory and practical application appear to be needed.

In the developing world regional expansion appears to be creating a great many sustainability problems, although a detailed analysis of these cannot be attempted here. In a study of Sao Paulo in Brazil and Beijing in China, MELCHERT (2005) emphasizes the extent to which large developing-world metropolitan areas are sacrificing environmental quality to gain a toehold in the global economy, and sees globalization as directly linked to the deterioration of the regional environment. In South Africa, some regional plans appear to be taking a more integrated and multi-sectoral approach with a specific emphasis on sustainability, but not necessarily with sufficiently strong environmental policies (TODES, 2004). There is some evidence that recent strengthening of metropolitan governance in a number of Asian countries is resulting in improved regional service provision, as it did in past decades in North America (LAQUIAN, 2005). However, it is not clear that broader sustainability objectives are being achieved, and without careful mediation environmental and social objectives often conflict, for example with open spaces in or near cities being seized for informal housing (HSIAO and LIU, 2002).

All in all, we seem still far from the type of ecological planning, at either metropolitan or megaregional scales, promoted by Geddes, Mumford, and the Regional Planning Association of America (RPAA) in the early 20th century and optimistically foreseen nearly 30 years ago by FRIEDMANN and WEAVER (1979).

IMPLICATIONS OF SUSTAINABILITY THEORY FOR REGIONALISM

Sustainability planning can be seen as having a strong theoretical foundation rooted in ecological ways of viewing the world as opposed to the Cartesian mindset of modernist science (WHEELER, 2004, 27ff.). These theoretical dimensions have a number of implications for efforts towards regionalism.

The first main consideration is a long-term time horizon, implicit in the term 'sustain'. Currently regional planning frameworks in North America are often twenty years; expanding these to 50 or 100 would be good. It would also be desirable for regional planners to develop and use more actively indicators showing whether the region's development is headed in sustainable directions or not in the long-term. Bureaucratic, political, and economic structures should be modified to the extent possible to encourage such longer-term thinking.

A second main implication of ecological thought is to emphasize holistic approaches, in particular inter-relationships between goals (for example, the oft-cited

'three E's' of environment, economy, and equity), disciplines, research methodologies, analytic perspectives, scales of planning, and time horizons. Integration of regional planning topics such as transportation and land use is common in rhetoric but less followed in practice, especially in locations with single-purpose functional regional agencies. Integration of perspectives such as design and policy is difficult as well. Integration of scales is yet another challenge, one that may require the formation of new patterns of incentives, assistance, or reinforcement between institutions at different levels. SAVITCH (1997, p. 1) and others have termed this quality 'institutional thickness', defined as:

> horizontal, vertical, and coalitional relationships among the private sector, mass organizations, and nonprofit and governmental bodies
>
> (AMIN and THRIFT, 1994, p. 14)

identify four determinants of institutional thickness: (1) a strong institutional presence in the region (and a multitude of institutions); (2) high levels of interactions between them; (3) development of 'patterns of coalition' that serve to normalize constructive action, and (4) development of mutual awareness and a sense of common enterprise among participants. Many of these relationships can be facilitated or incentivized by higher levels of government. Political organizing and coalition building, both within and outside government, will also often be necessary to support effective regional action, as COUNSELL and HAUGHTON (2006), WEIR (2000), and others suggest.

Another consideration of sustainability theory has to do with the concept of limits. The catalytic work *The Limits to Growth* (MEADOWS et al., 1972), in which the term 'sustainable development' seems to have been used in print for the first time, championed this theme on a global scale. The acknowledgement of limits to regional growth might mean more vigorously managing or ending physical expansion, stabilizing population, reducing or ending non-renewable resource use, and adopting economic development policies that aim for qualitative improvement in the region rather than quantitative expansion of its output.

The importance of local and regional sense of place is a further implication of ecological thought, since sustainable solutions to problems must take context into account. Bioregional thinkers have stressed this point extensively (SALE, 1985; HOUGH, 1990; THAYER, 2003), emphasizing long-term relationships between human communities and their ecological contexts. Rather than continue on the current path toward a 'geography of nowhere' (KUNSTLER, 1993), regional planners and designers can highlight those ecological settings, materials, architectural styles, technologies, cultural practices, and traditions that reflect the uniqueness of the place. KELBAUGH (1997) proposes that a critical regionalism form the basis for ecological design, while KEIL (1996) emphasizes the role that place-oriented politics can play in helping communities pursue sustainability planning in the face of globalization.

A final implication of sustainability planning theory is that regional planners should become more actively engaged in helping to bring about regional sustainability. Within an ecological worldview knowledge and action are part of a seamless whole. The era of the regional scientist studying the region abstractly and leaving practical action up to policy-makers is over; moral responsibility for the future of the region extends to all, especially to those with the knowledge or power to affect its development. In practice, this means a number of things. Regional scholars can proactively develop options for a sustainable future. Civic officials can take more proactive leadership to build regional vision and institutions. Planners can call attention to long-term trends, expand the range of policy options under consideration, help educate the public, and ensure that underrepresented perspectives are heard in debates.

A VISION OF SUSTAINABLE REGIONALISM

Regional sustainability planning is a tough challenge, and the trend towards ever-larger urbanized regions should be viewed with caution. Promoting the physical expansion of regions should not be a goal of national or regional planning unless steps can be taken to address sustainability problems related to mobility, growth management, equity, economic development, and governance. It is important to plan at these scales, but to promote sustainability rather than regional growth.

Despite the challenges, the preceding analysis points towards a vision of how more sustainable urbanized regions might be planned for. This model would include the following:

- A focus on smaller-scale community development within the region, with attempts to maintain separation between local communities in terms of labour markets, housing markets, road systems, and land development. Even if the region is linked as a whole, much of life can still be local, and this approach seems the only way to deal with the inherent mobility problems of the large region. Particular incentives, such as carbon taxes or road-pricing reforms, could help discourage the public from viewing long-distance travel within metropolitan areas or megaregions as a routine part of life. More balanced land development – carefully integrating homes, jobs, and community facilities within each local place – will be essential as well.
- Management of land, resources, and the population to live within regional limits. The current rapid physical, economic, and population expansion of urbanized areas cannot go on indefinitely, and leads to

large environmental and social costs. Public discussion of long-term impacts of such trends is needed. Agencies need to develop a range of policy alternatives that can really meet goals such as managing urban growth, improving environmental quality, lowering motor vehicle use, reducing greenhouse gas emissions, stabilizing population, and ensuring affordable and resource-efficient housing. A sustainable region will be one that is in balance with its land and resources – not necessarily a static balance, but a dynamic relationship aimed at improving the quality of human and ecological systems.

- Development of a stronger sense of regional identity and bioregional stewardship. Within a sustainable region planners and public officials would seek to enhance public knowledge about the ecology, culture, history, and identity of the region, and to awaken a deeper sense of stewardship. Ecological restoration would be an important rallying point. Preservation of cultural, architectural, and ecological landmarks would be a focus as well. Commitment to businesses that use local resources and draw upon the region's culture and traditions could be part of this effort. Fledgling efforts at megaregional identity in the Pacific Northwest are an example of some of these themes.
- Steps to improve regional equity and social welfare. A region moving towards sustainability would take action to reduce disparities between communities in terms of income, wealth, tax base, education, health-care, and environmental quality. Metropolitan tax sharing might well be involved, as well as changes to tax structures and strong investment in social services and education at metropolitan, state, or multi-state levels. Such steps might have to be mandated and incentivized by higher level governments.
- Revised approaches toward economic development. A sustainable region would focus on forms of economic development that improve social and ecological welfare rather than increasing quantities of material production and consumption. Needless to say, this is easier said than done. Practical steps toward this end might include prohibitions on large-scale retail; preferential economic development incentives for smaller, green businesses; strong governmental efforts to promote reuse and recycling of products; and tougher regulation of industries and products.
- An intergovernmental framework supporting regionalism. A more sustainable region would most likely exist within a framework in which higher levels of government require that particular sustainability goals be met and provide resources to enable this. National governments or international agencies would play an active role to overcome local or regional inertia. Ideally, local governments would learn to support regional initiatives as well, since they would presumably benefit from regional

coordination and incentives. Existing single-purpose regional agencies would link up their work to create more holistic frameworks for planning within the region.

- Regional organizing and coalition building. Robust relationships would exist between non-governmental organizations, business groups, public agencies, and other players in the sustainable region. These relationships would build social capital (FOSTER, 2000) and provide political support for regional sustainability planning. Particularly essential is that the business community participate in a way that addresses overall regional interests rather than a particular economic agenda.

- New themes and leadership to galvanize the public. Appropriate themes and leadership would emerge to focus public attention on regional needs. A variety of environmental threats could be used in this way; for example, the decline of the Chesapeake Bay has led to regional watershed planning in the mid-Atlantic states. Though it must be approached cautiously, the megaregion concept is itself such a potentially useful theme to stimulate regionalism. It appears (at the moment at least) as new and newsworthy, and is being used within several US megaregions to generate support for high-speed rail. It may also be useful within regions such as Cascadia (the Pacific Northwest) for developing regional identity around ecological planning (e.g. SELTZER *et al.*, 2005). The global warming crises may also help galvanize the public into supporting stronger planning at regional scales if it can be shown that this is a useful level at which to plan to reduce emissions or adapt to climate change.

Such motivation might be the trump card that overcomes the inherent difficulties of planning for regions and megaregions. If a perceived regional, national, or global crisis exists that can be communicated to the mass of the public and decision-makers through new leadership, then regional political and institutional gridlock can potentially be broken. Potentially, at least, regional planning can then join other levels of activity to address the threats that the current global juggernaut of unsustainable development is creating.

NOTE

1. The term 'region' is used here to refer to both metropolitan areas and megaregions.

REFERENCES

ABBOTT C. (1983) *Portland: Planning, Politics, and Growth in a Twentieth-Century City*. University of Nebraska Press, Lincoln, NE.

ABBOTT C. (1997) The Portland Region: where cities and suburbs talk to each other – and often agree. *Housing Policy Debate* 8, 11–51.

ABRAHAMSON M. (2004) *Global Cities*. Oxford University Press, New York, NY.

ABRAMSON A. J., TOBIN M. S. and VANDERGOOT M. R. (1995) The changing geography of metropolitan opportunity: the segregation of the poor in U. S. Metropolitan Areas, 1970 to 1990. *Housing Policy Debate* 6, 45–72.

AGYEMAN J. and EVANS B. (2004) 'Just sustainability': the emerging discourse of environmental justice in Britain? *Geographical Journal* 170, 155–174.

ALBRECHTS L., HEALEY P. and KUNZMANN K. R. (2003) Strategic spatial planning and governance in Europe. *Journal of the American Planning Association* 99, 113–129.

ALTSHULER A., MORRILL W., WOLMAN H. and MITCHELL F. (Eds) (1999) *Governance and Opportunity in Metropolitan America*. National Academy Press, Washington, DC.

AMIN A. and THRIFT N. (Eds) (1994) *Globalization, Institutions, and Regional Development in Europe*. Oxford University Press, New York, NY.

BANAI R. (1993) Social theory and the region: from the Regional Planning Association of America to the restructuring of socio-spatial theory, with policy implications. *Environment and Planning C* 11, 447–464.

BARLOW I. M. (1991) *Metropolitan Government*. Routledge, New York, NY.

BARLOW M. and CLARKE T. (2003) *Blue Gold: The Battle Against Corporate Theft of the World's Water*. Earthscan, London.

BAUMAN Z. (1998) *Globalization: The Human Consequences*. Columbia University Press, New York, NY.

BEATLEY T. and MANNING K. (1997) *The Ecology of Place: Planning for Environment, Economy, and Community*. Island Press, Washington, DC.

BENNEWORTH P., CONROY L. and ROBERTS P. (2002) Strategic connectivity, sustainable development, and the new English regional governance. *Journal of Environmental Planning and Management* 45, 199–217.

BERTRAND F. and LARRUE C. (2004) Integration of the sustainable development evaluation process in regional planning: promises and problems in the case of France. *Journal of Environmental Assessment Policy and Management* 6, 443–463.

BOLLENS S. A. (1997) Fragments of regionalism: the limits of Southern California governance. *Journal of Urban Affairs* 19, 105–122.

BORJA J. and CASTELLS M. (1997) *Local and Global: The Management of Cities in the Information Age*. Earthscan, London.

BREHENY M. (2003) Planning the sustainable city region. *Town and Country Planning Review* 62, 71–76.

BULLARD R. D., JOHNSON G. S. and TORRES A. T. (Eds) (2000) *Sprawl City: Race, Politics, and Planning in Atlanta*. Island Press, Washington, DC.

CALTHORPE P. (1993) *The Next American Metropolis: Ecology, Community, and the American Dream*. Princeton Architectural Press, Princeton, NJ.

CALTHORPE P. and FULTON W. (2001) *The Regional City: Planning for the End of Sprawl*. Island Press, Washington, DC.

CARBONELL A. and YARO R. (2005) American spatial development and the new megalopolis. *Land Lines* **17**, 1–4.

COMMISSION OF THE EUROPEAN COMMUNITIES (CEC) (1999) *European Spatial Development Perspective: Towards Balanced and Sustainable Development of the Territory of the EU*. Office for Official Publications of the European Communities, Luxembourg.

CERVERO R. (1998) *The Transit Metropolis: A Global Inquiry*. Island Press, Washington, DC.

CHURCH G. (1996) The North American failure: the governance of regional cities, in KEIL, R., WEKERLE G. R. and BELL D. V. J (Eds) *Local Places in the Age of the Global City*. Black Rose, Montreal.

CONGRESS FOR THE NEW URBANISM (CNU) (2000) *Charter of the New Urbanism*. McGraw-Hill, New York, NY.

COUNSELL D. and BRUFF G. (2001) Treatment of the environment in regional planning: a stronger line for sustainable development? *Regional Studies* **35**, 486–492.

COUNSELL D. and HAUGHTON G. (2006) Sustainable development in regional planning: the search for new tools and renewed legitimacy. *Geoforum* **37**, 921–931.

DANIELS T. (1999) *When City and Country Collide: Managing Growth in the Metropolitan Fringe*. Island Press, Washington, DC.

DANIELSON M. N. and DOIG J. W. (1982) *New York: The Politics of Urban Regional Development*. University of California Press, Berkeley, CA.

DANSON M. W., HALKIER H. and CAMERON G. (2000) Regional governance, institutional change, and regional development, in DANSON M., HALKIER H. and CAMERON G. (Eds) *Governance, Institutional Change, and Regional Development*, pp. 37–44. Ashgate, Aldershot.

DAVIS M. (2006) Who is killing New Orleans? *The Nation* **10 April** (available at: http://www.thenation.com/doc/20060410/davis).

DEAR M. J. (2000) *The Postmodern Urban Condition*. Blackwell, Malden, MA.

DEWAR M. and EPSTEIN D. (2006) Planning for 'Megaregions' in the United States. Paper presented at the Association of Collegiate Schools of Planning conference, November 2006, Fort Worth, TX, USA.

DOWNS A. (1994) *New Visions for Metropolitan America*. The Brookings Institution, Washington, DC, and the Lincoln Institute of Land Policy, Cambridge, MA.

DOWNS A. (2005) Smart growth: why we discuss it more than we do it. *Journal of the American Planning Association* **71**, 367–380.

DRENNAN M. P. and MANVILLE M. (2006) Falling behind: California's interior metropolitan areas. Paper presented at the Association of Collegiate Schools of Planning Conference, Fort Worth, TX, USA.

DUANY A., PLATER-ZYBERK E. and SPECK J. (2000) *Suburban Nation: The Rise of Sprawl and the Decline of the American Dream*. North Point, New York, NY.

DÜHR S. (2005) Spatial policies for regional sustainable development: a comparison of graphic and textual representations in regional plans in England and Germany. *Regional Studies* **39**, 1167–1182.

EUROPEAN ENVIRONMENTAL AGENCY (2006) *Urban Sprawl in Europe: The Ignored Challenge*. Office for Official Publications of the European Communities, Luxembourg.

EWING R. and KOSTYACK J. (2005) *Endangered by Sprawl: How Runaway Development Threatens America's Wildlife*. National Wildlife Federation, Smart Growth America, and Nature Serve, Washington, DC.

EWING R., PENDALL R. and CHEN D. (2002) *Measuring Sprawl and Its Impact*. Smart Growth America, Washington, DC.

FALUDI A. (2002) *European Spatial Planning*. Lincoln Institute of Land Policy, Cambridge, MA.

FEATHERSTONE M., LASH S. and ROBERTSON R. (Eds) (1995) *Global Modernities*. Sage, London.

FISHMAN R. (2000) The death and life of American regional planning, in KATZ B. (Ed.) *Reflections on Regionalism*. Brookings Institution Press, Washington, DC.

FOSTER K. A. (2000) Regional capital, in GREENSTEIN R. and WIEWEL W. (Eds) *Urban–Suburban Interdependencies*. Lincoln Institute of Land Policy, Cambridge, MA.

FREY H. (1999) *Designing the City: Towards a More Sustainable Urban Form*. E&FN Spon, London.

FRIEDMANN J. and WEAVER C. (1979) *Territory and Function: The Evolution of Regional Planning*. Edward Arnold, London.

GARREAU J. (1991) *Edge City: Life on the New Frontier*. Doubleday, New York, NY.

GIBBS D. (1998) Regional Development Agencies and sustainable development. *Regional Studies* **32**, 365–381.

GLASSON J. (1995) Regional planning and the environment: time for a SEA change. *Urban Studies* **32**, 713–731.

GRAVA S. (1999) Mobility demands of urban fields. *Transportation Quarterly* **53**, 109–120.

GREATER VANCOUVER REGIONAL DISTRICT (GVRD) (1996) *Livable Region Strategic Plan*. GVRD, Vancouver, BC.

GREATER VANCOUVER REGIONAL DISTRICT (GVRD) (2004) *2004 Annual Report: Livable Region Strategic Plan*. GVRD, Vancouver, BC.

HEALEY P. (2004) The treatment of space and place in the new strategic planning in Europe. *International Journal of Urban and Regional Research* **28**, 45–67.

HOUGH M. (1990) *Out of Place: Restoring Identity to the Regional Landscape*. Yale University Press, New Haven, CT.

HOUGHTON G. and COUNSELL D. (2004) Regions and sustainable development: regional planning matters. *Geographical Journal* **170**, 135–145.

HSIAO H.-H. M. and LIU H. J. (2002) Collective action toward a sustainable city: citizens' movements and environmental politics in Taipei, in EVANS P. (Ed.) *Livable Cities: Urban Struggles for Livelihood and Sustainability*, pp. 67–94. University of California Press, Berkeley, CA.

INTERGOVERNMENTAL PANEL ON CLIMATE CHANGE (IPCC) (1999) *Aviation and the Global Atmosphere.* Cambridge University Press, Cambridge.

JACOBS J. (1961) *The Death and Life of Great American Cities.* Random House, New York, NY.

JACOBS J. (1969) *The Economy of Cities.* Random House, New York, NY.

JENKS M., BURTON E. and WILLIAMS K. (1996) *The Compact City: A Sustainable Urban Form?* E&FN Spon, London.

KANTOR P. (2006) Regionalism and reform: a comparative perspective on Dutch urban politics. *Urban Affairs Review* **41**, 800−829.

KEIL R. (1996) World city formation, local politics, and sustainability, in KEIL R., WEKERLE G. R. and BELL D. V. J (Eds) *Local Places in the Age of the Global City.* Black Rose, Montreal.

KELBAUGH D. (1997) *Common Place: Toward Neighborhood and Regional Design.* University of Washington Press, Seattle, WA.

KLING R., OLIN S. and POSTER M. (Eds) (1991) *Postsuburban California: The Transformation of Orange County Since World War II.* University of California Press, Los Angeles, CA.

KUNSTLER J. H. (1993) *The Geography of Nowhere: The Rise and Decline of America's Man-Made Landscape.* Simon & Schuster, New York, NY.

LANG R. E. (2003) *Edgeless Cities: Exploring the Elusive Metropolis.* Brookings Institution Press, Washington, DC.

LANG R. E. and DHAVALE D. (2005) *Beyond Megalopolis: Exploring America's New 'Megapolitan' Geography.* Metropolitan Institute at Virginia Tech, Alexandria VA.

LANG R. E., SANCHEZ T. and LEFURGY J. (2006) Beyond edgeless cities: office geography in the new metropolis. Paper presented at the Association of Collegiate Schools of Planning Conference, Fort Worth, TX, USA.

LAQUIAN A. A. (2005) Metropolitan governance reform in Asia. *Public Administration and Development* **25**, 307−315.

LEWIS P. (1996) *Shaping Suburbia: How Political Institutions Organize Urban Development.* University of Pittsburgh Press, Pittsburgh, PA.

LUCCARELLI M. (1995) *Lewis Mumford and the Ecological Region: The Politics of Planning.* Guilford, New York, NY.

LYNCH K. (1976) *Managing the Sense of a Region.* MIT Press, Cambridge, MA.

MARTINUZZI A. (2004) Sustainable development evaluations in Europe − market analysis, meta evaluation, and future challenges. *Journal of Environmental Assessment Policy and Management* **6**, 411−442.

MASSEY D. S. (1996) The age of extremes: concentrated affluence and poverty in the twenty-first century. *Demography* **33**, 395−341.

MCHARG I. L. (1969) *Design With Nature.* Natural History Press, Garden City, NY.

MEADOWS D., MEADOWS D. L., RANDERS J. and BEHRENS III W. W. (1972) *The Limits to Growth.* Universe Books, New York, NY.

MELCHERT L. (2005) The age of environmental impasse? Globalization and environmental transformation of metropolitan cities. *Development and Change* **36**, 803−823.

MORRIS D. J. (1982) *Self-Reliant Cities: Energy and the Transformation of Urban America.* Sierra Club Books, San Francisco, CA.

MUMFORD L. (1938) *The Culture of Cities.* Harcourt, Brace, New York, NY.

MUMFORD L. (1961) *The City in History: Its Origins, Its Transformations, and Its Prospects.* Harcourt, Brace & World, New York, NY.

NEUMAN M. (2000) Regional design: recovering a great landscape architecture and urban planning tradition. *Landscape and Urban Planning* **47**, 115−128.

NEUMAN M. (2005) The compact city fallacy. *Journal of Planning Education and Research* **25**, 11−26.

OLMSTED BROTHERS (1904) Report of the Olmsted Brothers, Landscape Architects. In *Report of the Park Board.* City of Portland, Portland, OR.

ORFIELD M. (1997) *Metropolitics: A Regional Agenda for Community and Stability.* Brookings Institution Press, Washington, DC, and Lincoln Institute of Land Policy, Cambridge, MA.

ORFIELD M. (2002) *American Metropolics: The New Suburban Reality.* Brookings Institution Press, Washington, DC.

PASTOR M. JR, DREIER P., GRIGSBY III J. E. and LÓPEZ-GARZA M. (2000) *Regions That Work: How Cities and Suburbs Can Grow Together.* University of Minnesota Press, Minneapolis, MN.

PINCETL S. (1994) The regional management of growth in California: a history of failure. *International Journal of Urban and Regional Research* **18**, 256−274.

PROGRESSIVE POLICY INSTITUTE (2003) Driving down carbon dioxide, 24 November [online] (available at: http://www.ppionline.org/ppi_ci.cfm?knlgAreaID=116&subsecID=900039&contentID=252224) (accessed on 12 August 2006).

PUTNAM R. B. (1993) *Making Democracy Work: Civic Traditions in Modern Italy.* Princeton University Press, Princeton, NJ.

PUTNAM R. B. (2000) *Bowling Alone: The Collapse and Revival of American Community.* Simon & Schuster, New York, NY.

RABE B. G. (1999) Sustainability in a regional context: the case of the Great Lakes Basin, in MAZMANIAN D. A. and KRAFT M. E. (Eds) *Toward Sustainable Communities: Transition and Transformations in Environmental Policy*, pp. 247−282. MIT Press, Cambridge, MA.

RAST J. (2006) Environmental justice and the new regionalism. *Journal of Planning Education and Research* **25**, 249−263.

RAVETZ J. (2004) Evaluation of regional sustainable development − mapping the landscape. *Journal of Environmental Assessment Policy and Management* **6**, v−xxi.

ROBERTS P. (1997) Strategies for the stateless nation: sustainable policies for the regions in Europe. *Regional Studies* **31**, 875−882.

ROSENTRAUB M. S. (2000) City-county consolidation and the rebuilding of image: the fiscal lessons from Indianapolis's UniGov Program. *State and Local Government Review* **32**, 180−191.

ROTHBLATT D. (1994) North American metropolitan planning: Canadian and U.S. perspectives. *Journal of the American Planning Association* **60**, 501−520.

ROTHBLATT D. and SANCTON A. (Eds) (1998) *Metropolitan Governance Revisited: American/Canadian Intergovernmental Perspectives.* Institute of Governmental Studies Press, Berkeley, CA.

ROYAL COMMISSION ON THE FUTURE OF THE TORONTO WATERFRONT (1992) *Regeneration: Toronto's Waterfront and the Sustainable City: Final Report.* Queen's Printer of Ontario, Toronto, Ont.

RUSK D. (1993) *Cities Without Suburbs.* Johns Hopkins University Press, Baltimore, MD.

REGIONAL PLAN ASSOCIATION (1929) *Regional Plan of New York and Its Environs.* Regional Plan Association, New York, NY.

SALE K. (1985) *Dwellers in the Land: The Bioregional Vision.* Sierra Club Books, San Francisco, CA.

SAVITCH H. V. (1997) *Small Ships on a Global Sea: Local Democracy in a Turbulent Age.* Occasional Paper No. 18. Woodrow Wilson International Center for Scholars, Washington, DC.

SAVITCH H. V. and VOGEL R. K. (2000) Metropolitan consolidation versus metropolitan governance in Louisville. *State and Local Government Review* **32**, 198–212.

SCHLOSSER E. (2001) *Fast Food Nation: The Dark Side of the All-American Meal.* Houghton-Mifflin, Boston, MA.

SCHUMACHER E. F. (1973) *Small is Beautiful: A Study of Economics as if People Mattered.* Blond & Briggs, London.

SELF P. (1982) *Planning the Urban Region: A Comparative Study of Policies and Organizations.* University of Alabama Press, Tuscaloosa, AL.

SELTZER E. (2004) It's not an experiment: regional planning at metro, 1990 to the present, in OZAWA C. (Ed.) *The Portland Edge: Challenges and Successes in Growing Communities,* pp. 35–60. Island Press, Washington, DC.

SELTZER E. (Ed.) (2005) *Ecolopolis: Making the Case for a Cascadian Supercity.* Draft, 15 August. Portland State University, Portland, OR (available at: http://www.america2050.org/pdf/ecolopoliscascadia.pdf) (accessed on 2 December 2006).

SHARPE L. J. (Ed.) (1995) *The Government of World Cities: The Future of the Metro Model.* Wiley, New York, NY.

SHUMAN M. (2000) *Going Local: Creating Self-Reliant Communities in a Global Age.* Routledge, New York, NY.

SIMMONS R. and HACK G. (Eds) (2000) *Global City Regions: Their Emerging Forms.* E&FN Spon, London.

SMITH G. and SCOTT J. (2006) *Living Cities: An Urban Myth? Government and Sustainability in Australia.* Dural Delivery Centre, Rosenberg, NSW.

SOUTHWORTH M. and OWENS P. M. (1993) The evolving metropolis: studies of community, neighborhood, and street form at the urban edge. *Journal of the American Planning Association* **59**, 271–287.

SUSSMAN C. (Ed.) (1976) *Planning the Fourth Migration: The Neglected Vision of the Regional Planning Association of America.* MIT Press, Cambridge, MA.

SWANSON B. E. (2000) Quandaries of pragmatic reform: a reassessment of the Jacksonville experience. *State and Local Government Review* **32**, 227–238.

THAYER R. (2003) *LifePlace: Bioregional Thought and Practice.* University of California Press, Berkeley, CA.

TODES A. (2004) Regional planning and sustainability: limits and potentials of South Africa's integrated development plans. *Journal of Environmental Planning and Management* **47**, 843–861.

US ENVIRONMENTAL PROTECTION AGENCY (US EPA) (2001) *Our Built and Natural Environments: A Technical Review of the Interactions between Land Use, Transportation, and Environmental Quality.* US EPA, Washington, DC.

UNITED NATIONS EDUCATIONAL, SCIENTIFIC, AND CULTURAL ORGANIZATION (UNESCO) (2006) *Water, A Shared Responsibility.* UNESCO, Paris.

WANNOP U. A. (1995) *The Regional Imperative: Regional Planning and Governance in Britain, Europe, and the United States.* Jessica Kingsley, London.

WATERHOUT B. (2002) Polycentric development: what is behind it?, in FALUDI A. (Ed.) *European Spatial Planning.* Lincoln Institute of Land Policy, Cambridge, MA.

WEIR M. (2000) Coalition building for regionalism, in KATZ B. (Ed.) *Reflections on Regionalism.* Brookings Institution Press, Washington, DC.

WEITZ J. and SELTZER E. (1998) Regional planning and regional governance in the United States 1979–1996. *Journal of Planning Literature* **12**, 361–392.

WHEELER S. M. (2000) Planning for metropolitan sustainability. *Journal of Planning Education and Research* **20**, 133–145.

WHEELER S. M. (2003) The evolution of urban form in Portland and Toronto: implications for sustainability planning. *Local Environment* **8**, 317–336.

WHEELER S. M. (2004) *Planning for Sustainability: Creating Livable, Equitable, and Ecological Communities.* Routledge, London.

WHEELER S. M. (2008) The Evolving Metropolitan Region: Historic and Current Built Landscapes, *Journal of Planning Education and Research* (forthcoming).

Index

Page numbers in *Italics* represent tables.
Page numbers in **Bold** represent figures.